Rift
Valley
Rambles

Wendy Maitland

Published by Dolman Scott in 2018

ISBN: 978-1-911412-65-6
iBooks: 978-1-911412-66-3
Kindle: 978-1-911412-67-0

Printed by Dolman Scott Ltd
www.dolmanscott.co.uk

INTRODUCTION

This memoir started when I was asked to write an account of my wartime experiences for an archive in Leeds, and then the story continued to unfold as people began reading it and wanting to know what happened next. The first part of the story is told in *Rambles with my Family* where the people closest to me during those early adventures come in and out, accompanied by others who reappear in this second book.

First there is Adam who, as the story begins, is waiting to meet me at Nairobi airport and from there events take hold. Family friends, the McCubbins and Hemsteds rally round while remote support is provided by my father Dr Alfred Craddock (Fa) and mother, Fay Craddock (Muz). Elaine and Ros are my sisters and we have one brother, Andrew, called Spindle on account of his long spindly legs. Babs is Fa's inamorata, the subject of much conflict and heartache among the rest of us. My own inamorato Lanner, another heart-breaker, never entirely disappears.

Nakuru, at the time of this account, in the sixties, was a small town in the Kenya highlands where I grew up. Fa was a partner in a GP practice with Dr Arthur Griffiths, known as Bunny, who was a much-loved though sometimes erratic doctor.

My daughter Louise has drawn a map to show places mentioned and has been a great support in assisting the telling of this story, as have my sister Ros and husband Charles, together with all those many friends and readers who have encouraged me to carry on. Sue Daly, writer, photographer and film-maker extraordinaire, has once again helped me to assemble photos and text. And what would I do without the invaluable assistance of Vivien Lipski who I am so lucky and grateful to have as editor. Thank you all.

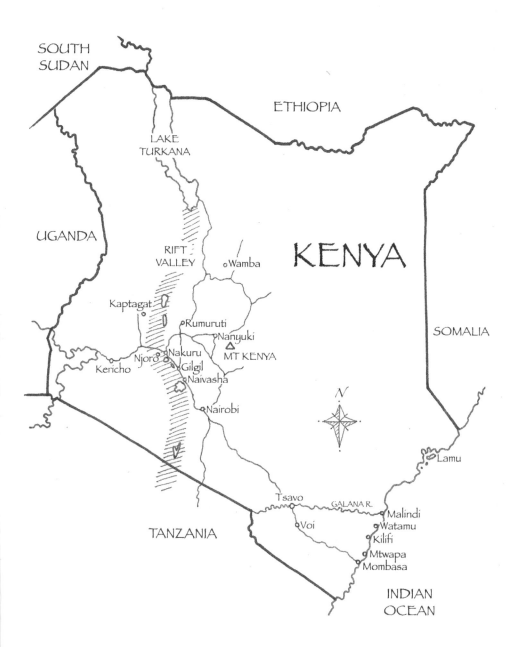

CONTENTS

CHAPTER 1

The flight to Nairobi with Hunting Clan, the budget airline of its time in 1962, was once again three days of long, hot, slow and tedious low-altitude hops between refuelling outposts. This time there was no return ticket. I was on my way to a very different life in a country on the verge of independence, with someone I wanted more than anything to be with, sharing a new identity and purpose together as a married couple. He was waiting for me. The farm was waiting for me. Africa with all its promise and challenge, dreaming its bold and mysterious dreams across the widest of continents, was there, and my children would be born there.

Abstracted by these thoughts, slumped in my seat, staring out of the window at nothing much outside, the woman sitting next to me interrupted. 'Have you looked under your seat?'

'No. Why?'

'There's a parachute underneath it. We've all got one.' Looking uneasy, she added, 'No one said anything about parachutes. You don't really think we might have to jump out if anything happens, do you?'

I had a look and pulled the package out far enough to see printed instructions. I laughed. 'Well, you'll have to go first. I'm stuck here by the window!' She fidgeted, as if my flippant remark made the prospect more real. 'I wish I'd put slacks on,' she said, 'just in case.'

We fell silent then, stifled by the heat in the cabin, with no emergencies or other diversions to occupy us during the interminable hours and days of monotonous flying, lulled by the drone of the Viking's twin engines while a seemingly endless series of harsh empty landscapes passed inchingly slowly underneath. The contrast in climate after leaving Europe and entering the coastal regions of north Africa as we turned south, was sudden and extreme. Every few hours the plane nosed down from a cruising attitude of 9,000 feet, to re-fuel at depots where clusters of 40 gallon drums with hand pumps stood incongruously in limitless wastes of desert sand. For budget passengers this form of air travel was normal and offered elements of adventure, but the effects could be enervating. The last proper wash for anyone had been in Malta where we stayed overnight, before setting course to Benghazi in Libya for our first re-fuelling stop in Africa. The next stop was at Marsa Matruh in Egypt where the only shelter from a merciless sun once we landed, was the meagre shade offered by a tin shed where we stood drooping beside it while clutching mugs of lukewarm water to drink. Onwards then to meet the Nile further south in Sudan, with a night stop at Wadi Halfa. This was a miasmic oasis on the great river with accommodation in a houseboat half-submerged among dense swamps of papyrus. Night sounds of creaking and croaking were accompanied by swarms of insects, so that next morning we were glad to see ground staff with flit-guns pumping insecticide around the plane cabin where we could escape the buzzing hordes. Our route followed the wide green ribbon of the Nile to Khartoum for our first stop that day, and then continued south to Malakal and Juba for further stops before, at last, reaching the Sudan/Kenya border with Mount Kenya soon rising up splendidly in front showing us the way to Nairobi and home. As we approached Nairobi, those iconic sentinels of the city, the Ngong Hills, came into view and the plane dipped, flying low over the Masai plains and game park where grass was parched at this time of year and river beds snaked with cracks. The same acrid smell of dust and smoke rose from the burnt earth, the most evocative smell in the world to me and, as we landed, there was Adam waiting and waving. I was home.

Kissing in public was not favoured by men of his upbringing but our hugs made up for it, and when luggage from the plane had been unloaded into a dusty pile, Adam picked up my one suitcase to take outside to his Land Rover. Parked beside the airport building, it looked battered, its fading green paintwork dented and scratched, its canvas roof sagging and torn in places. Adam grinned with pride at this evidence of energetic safaris, while brushing a drift of gritty dust from the passenger seat as I climbed in. From the driving seat he leaned over, putting an arm out to pull me towards him. 'Nothing but a gear stick between us now,' he said happily. 'We'll go to the club for a wash and breakfast.'

He told me about a recent lucky escape when he was very nearly banned from Muthaiga Club. After a drunken party he had driven his Land Rover up the steps and into the foyer of another club, causing some older members of the Country Clubs Association to object and call for his membership to be suspended. Outlandish escapades like this were habitual and indulged to a certain extent by clubs, but damage to club property was not. In this case, as it was only minor: Adam got off with a warning. I was relieved about this as Muthaiga Club provided a much-loved second home and hub of social gatherings for us and other members in the welcoming embrace of its long, low, rose-coloured building. Most of the members were upcountry farmers and ranchers, while the business community in Nairobi had their own club that, in our view, had none of the character and whimsical charm of Muthaiga.

After breakfast in the reassuringly familiar surroundings of Muthaiga's dining room with its panelled walls and hunting prints, we went for a walk in the garden before setting off for Nakuru. Stopping beside some giant stands of bamboo that threw long patterns of shade across the path, Adam turned me towards him. Putting his hands on my shoulders, looking intently at me, he said, 'I keep thinking you're a mirage, and if I look away you'll be gone.'

Laughing at this remark and touched by it, I said, 'Hold me tighter then. Make sure I'm really here.'

He moved his hands down to my waist, stretching both hands wide as I breathed in, to see if he could get his thumbs and middle fingers to meet in the middle. There was a gap and we both laughed. 'I can get thinner, so your hands can reach all the way round if you want,' I offered.

'No, I don't want you any different from the way you are,' he said. 'Not an inch more, and not an inch less.'

'I'd like to put on a few pounds so I can look good in a bikini for our honeymoon,' I suggested, expecting a smile and quip in return. Instead, a shadow passed across his face and there was an awkward pause. It's the expense of a honeymoon embarrassing him, I thought. The honeymoon can be postponed. As long as the wedding goes ahead without delay, that's all that matters. 'We can announce our engagement in the paper and make it official now I'm here ... and set a date for the wedding,' I continued in a rush. 'You know I've brought my wedding dress with me. I told you I was bringing it. Hardly anything else would fit in the suitcase.' I wanted to make him laugh again, and feeling excited now about having arrived safely with the dress, went on: 'You can't see it until the actual day of course, otherwise it would be bad luck.' Getting no response, I stopped, feeling uncertain, while he stood looking at me with a fixed stare as if suddenly incapable of speech.

When he spoke, it was almost casual. 'I don't think we should rush into getting married. You've only just arrived. We need time to get to know one another again.' He waited for me to say something, but it was my turn now to stand and stare, as he went on, 'I've only just started as manager on the farm and I'm not earning much yet. The parents feel I should be concentrating on my new responsibilities before taking on any extra ones.'

Oh, so it's the parents, I thought. I might have guessed. But I wasn't going to let it rest like that. 'We always agreed the main reason for waiting all this time was for me to finish nurse training in England and get a qualification, to provide extra income if we needed it. You've got a house now, a steady job, we love each other, what more do we need?'

He put his arms around me, saying softly close to my ear, 'Please be patient, it will all work out. You've only just arrived. We've got plenty of time.'

Such a bland statement was more alarming than reassuring. I felt my face turn hot and said sharply, 'We've waited three years already. That ought to be enough.' But to myself I was thinking: I'm back now. I'm here. I'm home. Today is too good to spoil. Adam is not Lanner. We'll find a way.

Driving from Nairobi to Nakuru, a ninety-mile journey through some of the most varied and dramatic scenery in the world, was always exhilarating. After leaving the city, the road climbed and meandered through Kikuyu highlands of rich red soil, with dairy farms and luxuriant forest among clusters of huts and maize crops. It was green and fertile at this higher altitude where forest trees attracted steady rainfall and mornings were damp with mist. Along the roadside Kikuyu women trudged, bent double under monstrous bundles of firewood held in place by leather straps stretched across their foreheads. Pressure from these straps, over time, dug grooves so that older women of the tribe had almost a deformity of the skull. This, along with the hardship of their lives, showed in their thin bones and wizened faces as they bore these punishing loads, hands grasping the leather strap on either side to ease the strain.

Leaving the burdened women and uplands behind, for several miles the vegetation became drier and sparser, until at the edge of the Great Rift Valley a scene of immense wonder opened up with an escarpment in front plunging more than a thousand feet. Stopping at the side of the road, gazing into that limitless space, there was a sense of being weightless like a bird drifting on currents of air high above the plains below where volcanoes and lakes were hazy in eddies of heat. All who come to pause at this same view-point, spellbound, carry with them these sensations in their minds for ever. Something made me shiver as I stood there silently beside Adam.

Driving down the escarpment is to this day an experience of strong nerves on steep bends, needing good brakes and concentration while distracted by profusions of colour from Cape Chestnut trees spreading their pink blossoms on slopes above, and stupendous views in front. From the passenger side, peering over the edge of the road, the rusted wrecks of lorries and other vehicles could be seen hundreds of feet below, crumpled on rocks.

Once safely down on flat land again at the foot of the great drop, the road then levelled out to run straight as a ribbon across plains where roving herds of gazelle, antelope and zebra grazed as they had done for millennia. Giraffe browsing near the road were prone to galvanise themselves and lope along the verge at the sight of a car, as if provoked by its speed to keep pace. Their impossibly elongated legs stretched out in slow motion seemed hardly to touch the ground as they galloped alongside, no longer ungainly but graceful. This was not a moment for any car to accelerate in a mad race to out distance the giraffe as they could turn abruptly and try to cross the road in front, oblivious to any danger.

Adam's father, Cen, returning from Nairobi one afternoon, was driving along this road with accompanying giraffes when one of them decided to cross. Misjudging the distance it jinked and tried to jump over the car, but failed to make the leap cleanly and a front leg smashed through the windscreen, hooking itself under the dashboard. Kicking furiously in its attempts to break free, it demolished the interior front part of the car while Cen crouched under what was left of the dashboard, trying to keep out of range of the wildly hammering hoof. Once the giraffe had freed itself and given its leg a good shake, releasing showers of glass and debris, it sauntered off, leaving the car wrecked and Cen unfolding himself from the foot well, relieved to find that he was still intact.

The road at this point continued through ancient flattened lava plains with outcrops of rock where only coarse bleached grass and grey-green leleshwa bushes grew, but this was good ranch land sustaining herds of Boran cattle that wandered in loose knots across the plain. Dominating this pastoral scene was Mount Longonot rising from the wide plain to a peak of nine thousand feet, and a little further on a welcome sight – the Bell Inn – a regular watering hole on the main road passing through Naivasha. This was a convenient place to stop for a coke or cold beer, and while sitting at one of the tables on the dusty veranda, invariably there would be other people we knew passing through on their way to or from Nairobi, glad to have a chat and catch up on news. Naivasha was a small petrol-stop of a town, its one glory lying to the west of the road. This was (and still is) an immense shimmering lake of flat blue water reaching into the far distance, edged with yellow fever trees and reed beds full of hippo, where fish eagles fly overhead calling to one another in that eerie shriek that is for ever evocative of African waterways.

Some miles further on from Naivasha the road passed through an even smaller town, Gilgil, where there was at that time just one row of *dukas* (shops) beside a railway station, with trains hissing and clanking as they shunted on the single line that ran all the way south from Gilgil to Mombasa, and north to Kisumu on Lake Victoria. The trains were loading goods, fuel and passengers, as they prepared for the many laborious climbs up and down escarpments and mountainous regions along the challenging route, which the Indian drivers were expert at negotiating.

Every mile of the way, driving along that road with all its familiar sensations, was a mile nearer home, and even Adam's sudden reticence about the wedding could not spoil my anticipation. The plan, as we had discussed many times in letters during the past few months, was for me to stay with family friends in Nakuru, Pat and Hugh McCubbin, while arrangements for the wedding were made, expecting that this would go ahead without any hold-ups once I was safely back in Kenya.

The McCubbins had laid on a welcome as exuberant, noisy and generous as ever. Their affection for us as a soon-to-be-married couple was almost embarrassing in its presumption that all was well. Other close friends, Joan and Stephen Hemsted, had expected that I would go to them, but it was easier at this stage to be based in Nakuru rather than miles out at their Subukia coffee farm. It was only after Adam left in the evening to go back to his parents' farm, Glanjoro, and my suitcase was pulled out in a clamour to see the dress, that I had to explain the wedding was temporarily on hold.

'*What!* What do you mean … he hasn't got cold feet has he?' Pat cried in alarm.

'I don't think it's him. It's the parents. You know what they're like.'

'That's outrageous! You mustn't let them stop you. They can't be allowed to behave like Victorian parents. It's beyond reason.' Pat was incensed.

'We're supposed to be having the reception in their garden, so the wedding can't go ahead without their agreement,' I explained, trying to sound calm and rational.

Hugh, a clear-thinking Scot, said, 'Why don't we have the reception in our garden? It's big enough, and the church is just down the road.'

I felt a rush of relief and gratitude. These dear people genuinely cared about my happiness, and Adam's.

'That's settled then,' said Hugh. 'Now we can all go to bed.'

Pat helped me hang the gauzy white cloud of my wedding dress in one of her cupboards, with the box containing a crystal coronet and veil on a shelf above. All that was left in my suitcase now was a thin assortment of clothes with a few other pieces rattling about. 'Your trousseau looks like a typical Craddock one, minimal and mainly threadbare,' Pat laughed. But she knew how difficult it would have been for me to assemble anything like a normal bride's collection of items, which traditionally included linen and baby clothes, put aside in a bottom drawer ready for marriage.

Lying in bed later, glad to close my eyes and sink into the luxury of a clean bed and cool sheets, I listened to the hum of cicadas outside and briefly composed in my head a note I would send to Adam the next day, telling him about the new plan for the reception. There was no phone at his house, so we had devised a system of communication with notes left at the Sports Club, which he could pick up when doing farm errands in the town. Evenings for him were working times, supervising the milk-cooling process that went on until late, and days off were infrequent.

I didn't have enough money to buy a car, and needed a job urgently, so I presented myself to the matron of Nakuru War Memorial Hospital with my new certificates. Nurses usually had to be recruited from England with fares paid by the government, so Matron was glad to be able to avoid this process and take me on straight away. Accommodation was provided at the nurses' home on site which meant I no longer needed to take advantage of the McCubbin's hospitality, and moved into a room at the home, leaving my wedding dress hanging in Pat's cupboard.

Adam came to see me whenever he could, and if we both had a day off we enjoyed more than anything the togetherness and seclusion of a day's fishing for trout at the farm, or alternatively the excitement of a day out hunting buffalo with Adam's close friend, Tony Seth Smith. Tony was an honorary game warden responsible for controlling the numbers of buffalo roaming areas where they were a menace, destroying crops. I loved the hunts, which started well before dawn when Tony's Land Rover was filled with chattering Nderobo trackers and their panting buffalo dogs, held in check on lengths of string. These were a motley pack of scraggy animals trained to chase buffalo once located, while their handlers ran close behind. The dogs would be flying like darts through the bush yelping with excitement on the heels of the buffalo, until one or more of these turned to face and engage the dogs, who would hold them at bay, barking hysterically while Tony and Adam ran to catch up and try to get a clear shot. The rest of us would be following at a more leisurely pace, and this could go on for hours. Buffalo are aggressive and wily and, turning to face the dogs on a first stand-off, there might be some tossing and goring with a lot of commotion. If the men had not caught up in time for a shot, the buffalo would storm off for another long chase.

At the start of the hunt and all the way up to the point where buffalo tracks were picked up, the Nderobo with their keen eyes would be looking out for any sign of an augur buzzard, flying or sitting on a tree branch, with its chestnut tail facing towards them. If seen, it was a bad omen (the word 'augur' having precisely that definition, meaning a sign) and the hunt would be called off. As it turned out, I remember only one hunt ending this way. Most of them were successful in the finding and chasing stage, but not always successful in the final stage: stopping the buffalo long enough to get a shot and bring it down. When this happened there was rejoicing and satisfaction both for a successful hunt and the prospect of feasting on buffalo meat for the Nderobo trackers. Wasting no time once the animal was dead, one of them would produce from the folds of his rawhide cloak the fire sticks he always carried together with a handful of dry grass (as anyone else might carry matches), and in minutes by energetic manipulation of these sticks the grass would be smouldering and showing flickers of flame that could be built into a cooking fire. The first prized portion cut from the buffalo was the tongue, if the beast was young enough to be decently edible, and this I was glad to let Tony have while Adam carved out rump steaks, leaving the trackers to seize the liver which they sliced and ate raw on the spot.

Tony had by this time married a very young, charming and unworldly German girl, Renate, known as Renny. They had met when she was still a teenager and he was instantly smitten, scooping her up and taking her back to Kenya after marrying her in Germany. Renny then became chatelaine of Tony's rather grand family home with its many rooms and servants on the family farm at Njoro. The house had been built by Italian prisoners of war, who were put to work on construction projects all around the country after it was discovered how proficient they were in these skills. They presented no threat and many became close friends with the people they were sent to work for. Other Italian POWs were employed building roads and bridges, all accomplished with such expertise that these have lasted for generations and provided valuable infrastructure for the country.

Renny came on many of the buffalo hunts and so did Kathleen, Tony's mother, who had her own house on the farm where she lived in the manner of a dowager after Tony's father Donald died. He had been one of the legendary White Hunters, as had Kathleen, unusually for a woman at that time. She had a chilling story of an incident on safari many years before when she had been charged by an infuriated rhino after a client missed his shot. Its horn became hooked into her scalp, tearing the top portion right off with her hair still attached. The rhino then ran off with this trophy stuck on its horn until the piece of scalp was brushed off on a thorn bush. Kathleen's gun bearer, with commendable presence of mind, retrieved the gory piece and rinsing it in clean water from a drinking bottle, clapped it back on her head where it reattached itself in due course and no lasting damage was done. Stories like this were legion among hunters, and Tony himself later wrote a book recounting his own graphic experiences.

His clients included members of European royalty and Hollywood film stars whom it was interesting to meet when he and Renny entertained them as guests at the farm, relaxing after the drama and exertion of tented safaris. We were often invited for dinner along with other friends and neighbours, providing a chance for the clients to meet different people and see how we lived in this (to them) exotic country. Renny was a consummate hostess despite her very young age. At dinner parties she would radiate confidence as multiple courses of excellent food were served, full of the flavours of German cooking, the African cooks trained by her and everything beautifully presented.

Renny was a stunning girl, slender with rosy cheeks and a thick sheen of dark hair that fell to her shoulders. She dressed plainly but well, always looking svelte, and spoke perfect English with the most gentle of accents and a beguiling lisp. While giving an appearance of sophistication, she had also a naïve and ingenuous quality that was part of her quiet charm.

Among Tony and Renny's friends were English aristocrats who had settled in Kenya to farm and open up the land. I noticed that they, and people like Kathleen who had been born into privileged families and might have been expected to lead indulgent lives, conversely did nothing of the sort, never parading their financial or social status as a kind of entitlement earning any special place among the rest of us. They seemed to have ingrained in them a culture with its own distinctive characteristics. They didn't complain or make a fuss about anything, however difficult or unpleasant. Mentally robust and stoical, nothing seemed to faze them. Above all, good manners were seen as paramount, so with these and personal grit they faced life's hurdles, remaining cheerful in all circumstances and never, ever, being lazy. Laziness or failing to make an effort was considered a sign of moral degeneration, while the behaviour of those notorious hedonists who had tainted Kenya's colonial history with their antics, was not admired by anyone outside their own small closed circle.

On my first buffalo hunt with Kathleen and the others, while we were resting at one point for a drink, she raised the subject of the delayed wedding and said firmly that nothing should stand in the way of Adam and me getting married. I was surprised that she felt strongly enough to say so in forthright terms, and was grateful and touched to be given her blessing, which was immensely reassuring just then. I think she saw my friendship with Renny as an important factor in helping her to feel secure in Kenya which was still a very foreign country to her in many ways, so it would cement an even closer bond if I married Adam and came to live nearer to Njoro,

When I told Adam about the McCubbins' offer to have the reception in their garden, he dismissed it as not even worthy of discussion, saying that his parents would be mortally offended if it was not held in their garden at the farm and, as a sign they were coming round to accepting the idea, I was invited to spend Christmas with them. This was certainly a happy surprise and he added that his sister Elisabeth, with her husband Peter, would be there too. Adam's brothers, Johnny and Andy, were away: Johnny at Massey Agricultural College in New Zealand and Andy still at Cheltenham College in England. I told Adam I would have to see about getting time off on Christmas Day; as the latest arrival at the hospital I was expected to pick up any extra shifts, and these were often the least popular ones.

I had been looking forward to working at the hospital which was as familiar to our family as our own home territory, with Fa having worked there for so many years. Many of the nurses were long-standing colleagues of his and there was much affection between them, so I had expected a friendly reception. It was quite a surprise then to find some of them distinctly frosty, and the sister whose ward I was allocated to was more suspicious of me than even fearsome Sister Kerrigan during my training at the Royal Free. I think the Nakuru nurses saw me as an upstart who might try to upstage them through my connection to Fa. I imagined them saying: '*She's coming here, Dr Craddock's daughter, all fresh and full of herself with certificates from a London hospital, thinking she knows it all.*'

My ward sister set increasingly tricky tasks for me, waiting for me to trip up, so that I began to feel isolated and unsure of my own competence. The doctors however had no such alternative agenda and were intent only on dealing with the many routine or challenging cases that came in all the time. Bunny Griffiths was still there, and was still one of the most capable and skilled practitioners that we had, when he was sober. There were times when calling him from home on an emergency he might be unsteady on his feet, and I would have to sit him in the nurses' office with strong cups of coffee until his hands stopped shaking enough to put up a drip. Nurses were not allowed to put up drips and this was very frustrating as it was a simple life-saving procedure that could have been done easily by any of us.

Dr Gerald Anderson was another of the attending GPs at that time, immensely popular with patients and staff. I was working with him one morning when a farmer from Naivasha was brought in. Earlier that morning while walking on his farm, he had jumped over a log lying across the path, unaware that a swarm of bees had fallen from a tree and landed on the other side. The impact of the farmer landing on top of the swarm caused it to disintegrate into a ferocious mass, covering him in stings. By chance he was found soon after by a farm worker and driven to hospital, but by the time he arrived he was unconscious and barely breathing. Getting the man, who was very large, hairy and heavy, into a clinic room, Dr Anderson put me to scraping off the stings one by one as fast as I could, while he administered life-saving injections, putting up a drip and putting in an airway.

'Every single one of those stings has to come out,' he said, 'without squeezing any of the sacs.' It was a slow laborious process, not assisted by dense body hair caught up in the scores of stings and squashed bees. 'He's an ox of a man,' remarked Dr Anderson. 'With that sort of constitution he's not going to take things lying down for long.' Gerald Anderson had been a doctor and surgeon in Africa for so many years he was expert in knowing what to do and what the outcome was likely to be. The Naivasha farmer came round slowly, and by teatime was sitting up in bed most disgruntled to find himself in hospital, asking why the farm truck had not waited to take him back as soon as he'd had the injections.

In a country where disease and accidents were frequent and hospitals few, we had to be ready for emergencies arriving at any time of the day or night. There were no ambulances so that sick or injured people were transported in any vehicle that was to hand. The sight of one arriving at speed in front of the hospital prompted the nearest person to grab a trolley and collect the casualty. When one of these was wheeled into a single room on the ward where I was working one afternoon, I recognised Ryan, a young farmer I knew, being hastily transferred from the trolley onto the bed. He was bleeding from a stomach ulcer and looked very pale, but was making light of this and joking in his usual offhand way as we waited for Bunny Griffiths to come and put up a drip. I stayed with Ryan, keeping a check on his blood pressure. He was thirsty and showing signs of shock, which worried me. Then, without warning, he started vomiting blood, so much blood that it spilt over onto the floor and the bed had to be moved to another room to make a clean space to stand in. He was slipping into unconsciousness and Bunny was needed urgently. Sending for bottles of blood from the donor bank and setting up for a transfusion, my hands were shaking and there was no time to wash blood off them. When Bunny at last put his head round the door it was an immense relief, especially as he was clear-headed, but as soon as he felt for a pulse and listened for a heartbeat, he shook his head. 'It's too late,' he said. 'He's gone. No one can survive this kind of event.'

I was stricken. 'Look, the bottles are here. Let's try.'

'It's hopeless,' Bunny said, 'He's already anoxic. Look at his colour.'

'Please,' I said.

Good man that he was, Bunny relented and got the blood up within seconds. We ran it through at full bore and Bunny kept checking for a heartbeat, his stethoscope pressed to Ryan's chest. I was sure that he was still breathing, or was it my imagination? Willing him to hold on I rubbed his arms and chest, hoping to stimulate any circulation that might respond to encouragement as we put up a second bottle of blood. He was tall and muscular, and young. The bleeding had stopped as far as we could tell. His body could fight back.

Bunny, leaning over, checking again for any sign of life, looked up and raised his eyebrows. His face registered both doubt and surprise as he said, almost in a whisper, 'Come and listen for yourself. It's just a murmur, no volume … but there's something.'

He handed the stethoscope to me and I listened. It wasn't quite a heartbeat, it was more like a very faint ripple. We sent for more blood and I kept up the rubbing, moving to his legs now, hoping to see some colour come back into his skin that had taken on a deathly tinge. We barely noticed the sun begin to sink outside as we worked, when, as the air grew lighter and a slight breeze sprang up, Ryan's eyelids flickered and he stirred as if waking from sleep. He attempted to smile when he saw us standing there, looking anxiously at him. 'Were you saying something?' he asked. 'I'm sorry. I fell asleep.'

We had been trying to contact his wife, and when she arrived she asked to speak to me privately in another room before going to see her husband. She was a striking girl, model-thin, dressed more for the city than upcountry, standing there looking at her watch. 'I can't stop,' she said. 'I can't let anyone see me like this.' I thought she meant that she was afraid of losing her composure in the face of this crisis. I put out a hand to steady and reassure her.

'No, you don't understand' she said. 'I'm pregnant. I have to wear this awful corset, you see, to hide my stomach.'

'Why?' was all I could think of saying.

Her eyes filled with tears. 'I can't bear to look like this. I can't bear to be seen … in this state.'

There was no sign of any enlargement around her waist. 'You look wonderfully slim, and beautiful,' I told her.

'It's only because I'm wearing this corset,' she wailed, as if that was the only thing on her mind, while her husband was fighting for his life in another room. Trying to get her to tear herself away from the triviality of how she looked, and focus on her husband's situation, I faced her: 'Your husband Ryan very nearly died this afternoon, and he's still very seriously ill. We don't know if his ulcer is still bleeding, and he's too weak to be operated on.'

Her face crumpled, 'I just don't know what to do. What can I do?'

'Go and sit with him, hold his hand, be loving to him. But don't try to make him talk. He needs all his energy to survive.'

I didn't see her again after this encounter, and years later meeting Ryan at a party, completely recovered now, I asked if he remembered anything of that day at the hospital.

'Yes, I remember everything,' he said. 'Every word that passed between you and the doctor when he thought I was dead. I remember you twisting his arm to give me the transfusion. I was desperately trying to tell you that I was still alive, not to give up. But no words would come out.'

'It's wonderful seeing you back to normal, looking so well,' I said, feeling quite emotional about it. 'I hope something got done about the ulcer.'

'Yes,' he said. 'I got sent to Nairobi for someone to look at it. That's why I didn't see you again.' He reached out to touch my hand. 'Thank you. I've been wanting to say that.'

'Let's drink to good fortune then,' I said, raising my glass to his as we clinked and smiled at each other. I wanted to ask him about his wife and the baby, but was afraid of the answer, and didn't want to spoil the moment.

Life, for me, had settled into a steady rhythm of working and occasional free days with Adam who seemed content with this arrangement, even suggesting that until we were officially engaged we should not feel tied down. This was far from reassuring and raised questions, making me feel uneasy, but the invitation to lunch on Christmas Day with his family I felt had to be a landmark. I was looking forward to it, intrigued to meet his parents Cen and Alison again, and see how the family functioned on a feast day after my previous lunchtime experience with them, when ravenous cats stole the roast joint and Spam was served instead.

'Don't worry,' Adam said when I teased him about it. 'The cats have all been shot. All except Tiger, the house cat.'

Tiger was a grey Persian, tormented by burrs stuck in his long fur, which became matted so it was difficult to remove ticks embedded in the knots.

Poor Tiger, instead of luxuriating in his status as an aristocrat of the cat species wearing a silky silver coat, he looked more like a dishevelled muff, but he bore this indignity with a grace that defined his Persian character. He was much loved and even the dogs respected him.

When I arrived on Christmas Day, Elizabeth and Peter were already there. Elizabeth gave a shriek when she saw me, running down the veranda steps surrounded by leaping dogs. Vigorously shaking my hand in exaggerated welcome she shrilled, 'How *nice* to meet you. Do get down, dogs. *Down, down*, blast you,' while their toes scrabbled at the front of my dress leaving brown streaks.

Peter stood stiff and formal in his Christmas suit, having been to Mass at the Catholic church, and peered at me through heavy horn-rimmed glasses. A sherry glass was pressed into my hand as we went in for presents to be given out from under the tree. This was a branch cut from a thorn tree, with blobs of cotton wool impaled on the thorns for snow, and strips of coloured tissue paper draped around the spiky twigs. The effect, though sparse, looked just right for a hot dry African Christmas. While presents were being unwrapped, provoking more shrieks from Elizabeth, the dogs, now slumped on the wooden floor, fell to licking themselves with loud slurping noises and when bellowed at to shut up, thumped their tails on the floor in apology. Left to myself, I could look around, unobserved.

Elizabeth was thin and angular like her mother and had inherited from Alison's family the glossy dark hair of the appropriately named Black family. Alison's mother, Elizabeth Wrigley, had married Reginald Black (a grandson of the redoubtable Adam Black of Edinburgh publishing fame who lived to the grand age of 89), and on her marriage had commissioned furniture to be made for her new home – all of it in ebony with ivory inlay – the ebony symbolic of her entry into the Black family. This furniture was in due course passed down through the family and when I was told the story of how it came to be made, I found it touchingly romantic. A few of these family treasures had succeeded in making their way to Glanjoro, and one of these was a glowing French armoire that now stood at the dining end of the sitting room.

Peter had taken up position beside the armoire, waiting for lunch to arrive, opening a bottle of wine ready to pour into glasses. He was a large round-faced man, pink and perspiring, with American and Irish ancestry. 'Irish gentry' he explained later, sitting next to me at the table, wiping his big shiny face with a starched napkin.

No commotion erupted this time at the window when the turkey was brought in, Cen sharpening the carving knife to produce thin slivers which were placed in front of each of us by Pedro the houseboy. Vegetables in silver entrée dishes were brought round in strict order: ladies first, then the men. Each man got two potatoes and four Brussel sprouts, while women were allowed one potato and three sprouts. If anyone was unwary enough to take more than their share, Pedro would stage-whisper, '*Rudisha moja* (put back one)'. This rationing suited my Craddock appetite, but Peter looked pained, though he must have been used to it by then.

When the Christmas pudding came, Elizabeth leapt up in a fuss to serve the portions herself, wanting to make sure everyone got a silver sixpence or other token in their piece. Adam was the last to be served, with the rest of us sitting there waiting to start as Elizabeth fished for something that I saw her poke into Adam's slice before it was passed down the table to him. I wondered what it was, and when he bit on a small hard object and took it from his mouth, I saw it was a khaki trouser button. Elizabeth clapped her hands. 'Look everyone, Adam's got the bachelor button! That means no marriage prospects for at least another year. Bad luck Wendy, you're going to have a very long wait.' She was jubilant at the success of this sleight of hand, while Adam looked embarrassed, and for me it was a warning of another kind as I realised that I might not be able to rely on her as an ally.

Elizabeth, Adam told me later, had endured her own battles when she got engaged to Peter. Despite his unquestioned advantages: having a private income and belonging to the right social class, he was Roman Catholic, while the Hills were robustly Protestant. Adam said that Granny Hill (Cen's mother) on being told of Elizabeth's engagement, was horrified that Elizabeth was marrying what she called a 'Papist', bringing Catholic blood into the family, making it sound like some kind of disease. Granny was still going on about it years later, to me, making sure I understood how important family values were.

My friend Judy, the one who didn't notice when the wheels fell off her car, was a convert to Catholicism and an ardent follower of the faith. It was unthinkable for her to marry anyone other than a fellow Catholic, so I thought it might be helpful to introduce her to a friend of mine, Charles Forbes, a practising Catholic. He was an estate manager with African Highlands Tea Company in Kericho where I had met him some years before during visits with Fa to patients there. Charles was a little older than I was and had taken me out a few times during those weekends at Kericho. He was an earnest, tweedy sort of man, small and wiry, not my type (apart from which I was unsuitable as any future prospect due to being Protestant), but kind and courteous and, with a few whiskies, could become quite animated and flirtatious.

My introduction of Judy to Charles had dramatic results as they were married very quickly, and then went on to produce a baby each year for four years. This had been gratifying at first, but the strain involved in such a rapid output began to affect Judy's health so an application to the Pope for a special dispensation was made, which was granted, and they were allowed to stop.

In the New Year of 1963, after my Christmas with the Hills, Judy invited me to go and spend a weekend with them at Kericho. 'If Adam can't make up his mind about marrying you, he's no good for you. You're better off finding someone with a mind of their own, not already married to their parents. Your match-making when you brought Charles and me together was such a good deed, we want to do the same for you, and we've got a perfect match already lined up.' I didn't want anyone else, but I was getting nowhere with Adam, just drifting, and Elizabeth's charade with the bachelor button had cautioned me, especially as Adam's reaction had been merely to smile in a feeble way instead of throwing the button back at her for such cattiness.

Now that I had a steady wage coming in, I had been able to borrow enough from the bank to buy a car, which meant I was not reliant on Adam for transport and could drive up to Kericho or anywhere else, happily on my own. The splendour of a journey to the tea estates always excited me with the long drive through majestic landscapes, passing through Londiani and miles of indigenous forest with the chance of seeing leopard or other shy animals like bush buck, before reaching the high tea gardens rolling out across the hills in a lush green coverlet.

Judy had organised the weekend very precisely with a dinner party on Saturday night where I was seated next to Kericho's most eligible bachelor, Jon Low, who in her eyes was an ideal match for me. He was a few years older at thirty, which seemed quite old, but this seniority meant he was already an estate manager with a good house and salary. 'All he needs now is a good wife, Judy observed. 'Every available girl for miles around has been after him for years but he is very independent and self-contained. You'll have to see if you can get through that.'

Whatever the attraction of these assets and attributes in a new man, I didn't want them. I wanted Adam. But I was getting impatient and could see myself choosing Kericho if the door closed on life at Glanjoro. Jon didn't kiss my hand on being introduced, as Adam had the first time we met. Jon was a very different kind of person; he would not be comfortable with extravagant mannerisms. Though tall and well-spoken like Adam, Jon was reserved, sandy-haired and thick-set with craggy good looks. He was sure of himself in a natural unselfconscious way, seeming to me the classic image of a tea planter. I liked him straightaway, and it was mutual, much to Judy's gratification. After the other guests had gone, Judy and Charles tactfully left us talking until early morning when Jon finally said goodbye, inviting me to his house for lunch the next day.

When I arrived in time for pre-lunch drinks, there was the usual collection of over-excited dogs bounding out to bark at the car, and the usual attempts to quell them as Jon opened the car door for me, apologising for the scrum, but failing to keep them under control. His house was double storied, built of local stone, plain but spacious. After taking me on a tour of the garden, which like all Kericho gardens was luxuriant in that region of high rainfall, we went indoors for a drink and I sat holding mine, sinking into a sofa that sagged almost to the floor. Bachelor furniture, I thought to myself grimly, trying not to let my skirt end up around my waist. Jon didn't seem to notice and was chatting amiably as he sat in an armchair which was evidently his accustomed place.

After a few minutes I began to feel itchy, but with a glass in one hand and my knees pointing towards the ceiling, it was difficult to change position or have a scratch. The itching got worse until I noticed that the sofa was jumping with fleas, which were now jumping onto me, and biting me all over.

Embarrassed and furious I sprang up, not caring about spilling my drink as I ran upstairs to find a bathroom and get my clothes off, shaking them into the bath. But not before locking the door to make sure Jon didn't follow and offer to help. Getting dressed again I went downstairs, expecting to find Jon abject with apologies. Instead his response was casually offhand. Explaining that it was impossible to keep the dogs off the sofa, he hoped I hadn't got bitten too badly.

The Hills for all their idiosyncrasies did not allow dogs to occupy the furniture. I was readjusting my opinion of Jon when he surprised me by suggesting a weekend in Nairobi to watch rugby, knowing that I was a fan. There was a big match coming up and we could stay with friends of his whom he would like me to meet, he said. When I told Judy she was ecstatic that things were going so well he wanted to take me away for the weekend – a very promising sign she thought – and that if all continued to go well I might be joining her at Kericho.

The following week when I told Adam that I couldn't go fishing with him on the Sunday because I was spending the weekend in Nairobi with Jon Low, he was shocked. 'You can't go to Nairobi with someone else,' he objected, outraged at the audacity. 'We're engaged.'

'No we're not,' I reminded him. 'Nothing has been announced. Nothing has been decided. No wedding plans have been discussed. You're still waiting for your parents to give their approval. I don't want to be just a girlfriend. Jon looks as if he needs a wife, and I like him. I like rugby too. And I haven't been to Nairobi for ages.'

These revelations seemed to have a galvanising effect on Adam. He grabbed my hand and said urgently, 'We can announce our engagement right away. And next weekend we can go to Nairobi and buy a ring. You can tell Jon that.'

I told Jon, and then it was he who registered shock, and dismay. Protesting, legitimately, that he had been misled into believing that I was free.

CHAPTER 2

The Thorn Tree café at the New Stanley Hotel in Nairobi was a social hub, habitually populated by numerous people we knew, most of them on shopping trips from upcountry. The café's centre piece was a tall slender Acacia tree, spreading its yellow-green branches and feathery leaves over our heads as we sat having coffee or lunch. On this occasion it was a celebratory lunch after that most extreme of shopping experiences – buying an engagement ring. This had been found at one of the Indian jewellers along the road from Queensway and was the classic design I had imagined and hoped for: a square emerald set with a diamond on either side; the emerald a luminous deep green and flawless. When I tried it on in the shop and it fitted exactly, there could be no doubt that it was a perfect choice. The price was £125 which Adam was able to pay out of savings, and walking out of the shop with it safely on my finger was a delirious feeling.

After lunch we went to the office of the *East African Standard* to put an announcement in the paper, and then to Muthaiga Club where Stephen and Joan Hemsted had asked us to join them for champagne and more celebrations. Proposing the toast Stephen also proposed that, as Fa's best friend, he was entitled to give me away. So it was agreed, and choosing a wedding date was the next pressing topic. Adam was in a twitch about discussing dates before consulting his parents and telling them that he and I were now officially engaged, but he would see them next day at the farm.

At last, when this final hurdle had been cleared, he seemed more relaxed and liberated. We were both in a state of euphoria, carried along on wafts of what felt like pure oxygen, thinking nothing bad could ever happen again. Always tender and expressive in his feelings towards me and generous with compliments, Adam was a passionate and lyrical fiancé, extravagant in his attentions. If I had crawled through a thorn bush, emerging tattered and tangled, Adam would still have told me I looked wonderful. I used to tease him that he said the same thing to all the girls he met, as a chat-up line, but he always denied it. Couples in love drift into a strange state of illusion, believing they are unique in what they are experiencing, so that this rarity gives them a matchless grasp of the world around them and now, we too, were floating in this high-octane atmosphere. Along with the elation came a new confidence, brushing aside the nervousness I previously felt when invited to visit Adam's parents. We were due to have drinks with them to discuss wedding plans, and they would change their view of me now that I was officially a prospective daughter-in-law, I told myself.

After champagne had been poured and handed round, the toast to our marriage was proposed by Cen as formally as if he were announcing a new appointment to one of his boards of directors, and was greeted with more excitement by the dogs than anyone else. Sensing that some kind of event was planned they lifted their heads, ears and noses alert, then realising this did not include shooting (no talk of guns entering the conversation), their tails sagged and they lay down again, bored. After the toast, Cen handed me a book to read. The title was: *Shipshape and Bristol Fashion*, which he explained was a history of the Hills' ship-building company founded in the nineteenth century that had become an extremely prosperous business, and was still trading. In his view it was important that I should understand what sort of family I was marrying into.

Later Adam laughed about this as he demolished the illustrious image, saying the ships were slave ships and the piles of money stashed away by the family were dishonourable gains. But none of that was true. Cen's grandfather, Sir Edward Hill, had indeed been rather grand as member of parliament for Bristol South, and had married a suitably well-connected girl, Fanny Tickell, from another 'good' family. It was a love match and the marriage was happy and long. Eight children were born, and in due course when Edward and Fanny died, the main part of their fortune passed to their eldest son, Eustace. The youngest son, Percy (Cen's father), inherited what was considered a modest portion, but was in reality a considerable sum. This enabled him to live in style in a mansion, Rookwood, built by his father in Llandaff, Wales, where Percy installed his bride when he in turn got married. His wife was Zelia David, related to Elizabeth David, the Delia Smith of her day. Zelia held herself in high regard due to her connections and social status, conscientiously pasting into an album (which she later showed to me) photographs and invitation cards from the many glittering events she and Percy attended, including royal balls at Buckingham Palace. Splendidly matriarchal, Zelia was the Hill grandmother who had so disapproved of Elizabeth's marriage to Catholic Peter.

Within fifteen years of her own marriage, Zelia faced a catastrophe that must have tested all her resources, and brought out the steel in her character. Percy lost his fortune in some kind of financial disaster, the details of which were never discussed among the family apart from whispers that his partner in a business venture had made off with all the money, leaving him and Zelia with barely a guinea to their names. In these reduced circumstances, Rookwood was sold, and Percy, Zelia, with their only son Cen and daughters Katharine, Monica and Diana, moved to a small hamlet near Taunton in Somerset where a modest former hunting lodge became their new home. Years later Monica remarked how mortifying it had been, when they no longer had a butler to open the door to visitors, to have to open the door themselves to anyone who called.

It occurred to me that in my own parents' families, one of them was much more likely to have been a butler than to have had one. Muz used to tell us about an aunt of hers who was housekeeper to a wealthy family living in a large house like Rookwood. The aunt was involved in a 'Servants' Rights' movement, campaigning for better pay and conditions as well as proper recognition for their services, as these armies of loyal people working below stairs had no entitlements, the benevolence of the master and mistress of the house being entirely a matter of good or bad luck.

My own status as a nurse I saw was not rated very highly by the Hills, in comparison with Elizabeth who, Alison explained, had been a debutante and then went on to become secretary to the governor's wife in Government House in Nairobi. This was seen as prestigious, and meant that Elizabeth met the right kind of people. These snippets of (for them) important information about the family, were supplied in between the more urgent (for Adam and me) discussion of wedding dates. Eventually it was decided that the first day of June would be suitable, and plans went ahead to book the church and vicar, catering services and a marquee, which would be set up on the lawn in front of Glanjoro House.

A gift shop offering wedding present lists had just opened in Nakuru, in a side street opposite Ismail Abdi the Somali butcher where we bought our meat. The new gift shop had modern marvels like Scandinavian glass and fine china dinner sets, with pottery from Denby and Wedgwood. The contrast between this stylish shop and Abdi's rather primitive premises across the street was incongruous, but we all liked Abdi who was large and loud and cheerful. His prices were the best in town, but his blackboard display was a disgrace, stating: 'Boys & Dogs = 50 cents per lb,' bracketing meat for Africans and dogs together. When I objected to Abdi about this, he thought I was trying to make a joke, which made it worse.

Since buying the wedding dress I had lost weight due to the worry about Adam changing his mind, and despite his insistence that he liked me being thin and had a phobia about big breasts (caused by daily contact with dairy udders, he said), I was not convinced. Trying on the wedding dress to check if it still fitted was even more disconcerting as it now hung from my shoulders like a long white tube, with the skirt mushrooming out at hip level. This was a disaster and I went to Bunny Griffiths for advice on how to gain the necessary pounds quickly. He prescribed an anabolic steroid, a fashionable drug for body builders, and predicted that the effects would become evident quite soon. He was right. Within a remarkably short time I had developed a thick neck, broad shoulders, extra body hair, and my waist disappeared completely. Adam was appalled and Bunny was rueful, but pleased to emphasise that I had put on several pounds. 'In all the wrong places,' I pointed out.

'If you stop the pills now, your normal shape will return, but the weight will stay on,' Bunny assured me, adding as consolation, 'and when you get pregnant, your metabolism will change and give you a new weight configuration.'

During the time that I was developing the new square shape, Elizabeth and Peter invited me for a weekend at their farm, graciously accepting that I was going to be a sister-in-law and they would like to get to know me better. They lived at Dundori, a rather bleak mountainous district involving a long drive up the eastern side of the Rift Valley through dark forest, getting colder and wetter, while mud under the wheels of my car grew deeper and stickier. The farm was quite small, clinging to the side of a hill where sheep and dairy cows huddled on the steep slopes shrouded in mist. Farm buildings were mostly of timber from the forest and their house was the same wooden construction, plain and weathered, with roof tiles cut from tree bark. Steps led up to a veranda where rain dripped from the eaves in watery filaments like a curtain.

Peter came down the steps holding an umbrella, beaming at me: 'Do come in out of the wet and get warm,' he said affably. 'We've shut the dogs in the kitchen so they won't jump on you with muddy paws.' Thank God for that, I thought, trying to duck under the umbrella and avoid a minor waterfall overhead as I ran up the steps. A glass-panelled door led into the sitting room, where a minefield of pots and pans was spread around the room to catch rain pattering from holes in the roof. Peter smiled apologetically. 'Sorry about the orchestra,' he said, waving a hand to indicate the medley of utensils with rain drops plinking into them. 'I'll find you a dry spot to sit down,' he added as Elizabeth hurried in from the kitchen. She looked flushed but much calmer than on previous occasions. 'I'm so glad you made it through the mud,' she said. 'It's at its worst just now. Rainy season and all that.' More like the monsoon, I thought – how can people actually choose to live in a place like this.

Elizabeth continued, 'Come and see my kitchen, I'm making rice pilau.' It sounded exotic after Glanjoro catering, and wafts of fragrance coming from the kitchen smelt promising too. 'What have you put in the pilau that smells so good?' I asked. 'Lots of garlic and a few spices,' she told me. 'Benson the cook is roasting a chicken to go with it.'

After a couple of stiff gins followed by this satisfying dinner, we returned to the sitting room with its raindrop orchestra, sitting hunched in stiff armchairs around a morose fire where small sodden logs smouldered and flickered. Tiny cups of coffee were handed round as Peter and Elizabeth took turns in giving me lyrical accounts of life on the farm, eagerly scanning my face for signs of enthusiasm as they exclaimed on the delights waiting the next day when I was due to be shown round, hoping the rain would have eased by then.

That night, trying to sleep in the damp chill of the spare room, the cold was so penetrating that I had to pull rugs off the floor and pile them on top of the bedclothes to keep warm. The rugs were heavy with dog hairs and doggy smell but the insulation was superb, so that in the morning when asked if I had slept well, I was able to answer truthfully that I had. Not mentioning the rugs.

I couldn't face spending another night there, so decided to make apologies and leave after the obligatory tour of the farm. Its centrepiece was the dairy and milking shed where a small herd stood patiently up to their hocks in a bog of mud and liquid manure, under steely skies heavy with more rain. This was a world away from Glanjoro milking bails standing on fresh grass under sunny skies, but these two farmers were inordinately proud of their herd and the round metal churns lined up ready for collection by the milk lorry.

Later, driving back to Nakuru, leaving the clouds and mud behind as the road spiralled downwards to the wide mellow sun-baked plains that were home for me now, the sense of relief was overwhelming. I had never been so glad to see dust again.

Calling in at the Sports Club I found a note from Adam suggesting dinner at his house the next evening as his 'housekeeper' was making a Kikuyu speciality called *mutura* that he was very keen I should try. The housekeeper, Mungai, whom Adam referred to as his 'Gentleman's Gentleman', had been his personal servant during army service and ran the household in the style of a military bunker with very few concessions to comfort. Mungai himself was a small, dark, glowering presence with bloodshot eyes, who looked more like a fugitive from Mau Mau than one of its opponents. He combined the duties of cook and butler with a devotion to Adam that was both admirable and sinister.

I thought *mutura* might be some kind of vegetable dish as the Kikuyu are inventive with vegetables, even producing something tasting like spinach from a nondescript roadside weed they called *mchicha*. *Mutura* however was quite different. It was a ball-shaped sausage, like a haggis, made from blood and guts. I didn't know this beforehand so was not put off in advance, and found it surprisingly edible with a good rich flavour. Both Adam and Mungai were gratified to see me pass the *mutura* test.

The house had no inside kitchen, only a soot-filled cooking hut enclosing the standard wood-burning stove and chopping table. The hut stood some distance from the back door to avoid the whole house burning down if the kitchen caught fire. Other essential services were provided by a 'long-drop' halfway down the garden. I told Adam that a proper bathroom needed to be put in before the wedding, and also a gas cooker somewhere inside the house accessible to the dining room, with a working area for myself, to supplement Mungai's efforts in the black hole outside. This was agreed, but the only space suitable for my cooker was a small passageway linking the dining room with the back door where it would have to be squeezed in, allowing barely room to turn around while producing dishes for the numerous guests ready to arrive as soon as a woman's touch made the house inviting.

When Alison heard about the *mutura* dinner, via the servants' grapevine, she sent for me in some agitation about the impropriety of dining alone together in Adam's house when we were not yet married. Lunch apparently was allowed (daylight, in her view, precluding intimacy), but we must not spend time alone after dark unchaperoned, in case anyone got to hear of it. She may also have felt a duty of care towards my reputation in the absence of my parents, but whatever it was, she insisted I must go and live in the main house with her and Cen until after the wedding. I was still working at the hospital but that was not a problem as it was little more than twenty minutes' drive from the farm. I didn't like to tell her that Fa had proclaimed enthusiastically to the assembled family during a mealtime discussion before I left, expounding on the subject of love: 'All of you must understand that sexual love is one of life's principle pleasures, which no man or woman should deny themselves, and moreover it is universally free.' This startling statement was received by the rest of us in resigned silence as just another of Fa's embarrassing *bon mots,* while Muz sat looking pained.

It was agreed that I would go to the Hemsteds a couple of days before the wedding since I would be leaving for the church from their farm. The wedding cars had already been organised by Stephen, who was a vintage car enthusiast and had a Bentley that was to be festooned with white ribbons for the drive to the church. Edmund, their son, would be driving us, with Stephen by my side in the back as he was giving me away. Later, for our going-away car, he was lending us his 1925 Rolls Royce Silver Ghost.

Meanwhile, moving to Glanjoro with my suitcase ready to be unpacked in what Alison called her 'best spare' (room), was momentous for me, as my address now officially became Glanjoro Farms Ltd. The plural in the title reflected the way that Uncle Jack David's original small farm which Cen inherited, had been added to over the years as he bought up neighbouring farms. The 'best spare' was one of three bedrooms in a separate building connected to the main house by a covered passageway, designed to provide privacy for Cen and Alison as well as for guests, so it was ideal for Adam coming to visit me whenever he liked, unnoticed by the parents. We were able to spend more time together in the 'best spare' than ever could have been possible at his house.

Cen had lunch at the club most days, very sensibly as Alison's lunches at home were painfully abstemious, consisting each day of one thin slice of cold meat, one lettuce leaf, half a boiled potato and a piece of bread. Even for Craddocks like me this was beyond frugal, and as I was trying urgently to develop some rounded curves in time for the wedding and honeymoon, it was not desirable to end up with a whippet figure like Alison's, so I contrived to have lunch at the hospital whenever possible.

Evening dinner at Glanjoro was slightly different as certain concessions were made when Cen was present, and three courses were provided. This started with something called 'first toastie'. Served by Pedro with pre-dinner drinks, these were fingers of toast spread with Gentlemen's Relish or fish paste. The next course, taken at the table, was always a clear soup made from broth into which was sprinkled drops of a concoction known as 'Piri-Piri-Ho-Ho'. This was an invention of Cen's, intended to give the soup a fiery bite as otherwise it was flavourless. The Ho-Ho brew was made by him, very precisely, putting three or four red chillies into a glass decanter which was then filled with sherry and shaken vigorously to distribute the chilli infusion. If this failed to energise the soup, a bottle of Maggi flavouring was handed round. Maggi was a salty brown liquid guaranteed to mobilise any sluggish taste buds. Once the soup had been fortified to Cen's satisfaction, the meal began.

Invariably the main course would be something that had been shot by Cen, Adam or a guest. It might be reedbuck steaks, or more usually roast guinea fowl or partridge, hung by its neck in the larder until it dropped off the hook, signalling that it was ready to eat. By the time it came to the table, carved into wedges by Cen, the putrid fumes were sometimes so noxious that those of us of a more fragile disposition than the robust Hills, had been known to feel overcome, departing suddenly clutching a handkerchief. Cen would be mystified by this behaviour, exclaiming loudly: 'What the hell's got into them, missing the best part of the meal,' as he mopped up puddles of rancid blood on his plate with swabs of very dead meat. 'There's enough left for second helpings,' he would call out encouragingly.

Second toasties came after pudding, or sometimes replaced pudding. These were similar to first toasties, except that the bread was not toasted but fried and crispy, and instead of paste there was a topping of curried scrambled egg. I particularly enjoyed this and would have been quite content if dinner had been just one large plate of curried eggs with fried bread.

On occasions when a pudding was produced it would be something steamed like spotted dick, or better still, syrup sponge. After all day working at the hospital I was often famished by dinnertime and one evening when a pudding was brought in, steamed with lots of currants, I took a big helping and Pedro poured custard over it. After a few mouthfuls I noticed there was something strange about the currants. Looking more closely, needing to peer at my pudding in the dim light of the dining room, I saw that what I had thought were currants were in fact large black flies, baked into the sponge. Neither Alison nor Cen had noticed, so I remarked on this rather pointedly, and Alison sighed, 'Poor Benjie (the cook). He's half-blind and the kitchen is in a terrible state. Anyway flies are impossible to deal with at this time of year.'

Ignoring the risk of enteritis, guests flocked to the house. They called in during shopping trips to Nakuru, and others who arrived from further away like Mr and Mrs Mars of chocolate bar fame, came all the way from America to talk about gun dogs. Visitors from England, Scotland or Wales, came for guinea fowl shoots, and the Hordern family from Sydney, Australia, came for the polo. Cen and Adam both played polo and kept a string of ponies in stables at Glanjoro.

Shooting was a major sport and formal drives took place on the farm each year during the season, with a gamekeeper employed to feed and protect the wild guinea fowl and other game birds from predators. Labradors and Pointers were kept by the Hills, not just as pets but trained to retrieve. So alert were these dogs that any talk of shooting, casually mentioned in conversation, would register immediately even if they seemed flat-out asleep. Their heads would lift, ears prick, noses wiffle, and tails start thrashing at the slightest remark or indication of shooting. If something was said such as, 'Let's take the dogs and see if we can flush some quail,' they would be up almost before the sentence was finished. On a formal day with driven birds they would be quivering with excitement hours before anyone else was ready, waiting beside the gun safe, rapt with anticipation.

One frequent guest at Glanjoro was a young District Officer, David Jukes, who came on breaks from Wamba, a remote administrative post in Northern Kenya. David was a very correct public-school Englishman recruited to this solitary life with its few outlets and I tried to liven his visits with little escapades, such as sneaking out of the house at night (picking up Adam on the way) to go game-watching by torchlight down at Lake Nakuru. This skulking about around the lake shore caused the flamingos in their great dozing flotillas to set up a collective squawking, an arresting sound coming from those hundreds of bird throats, our torches spooking them so they flapped about in the shallow water. This disturbed other creatures around the shore, and various commotions would be trapped in our torch beams as we padded about.

We had to be careful when returning to our beds later at Glanjoro as Cen kept a revolver beside his bed against intruders and there was an occasion when, hearing someone creeping across the lawn in the dark, he sprang out and delivered a warning shot into the rose bed before the terrified guest identified himself.

One night during David's visit I heard him sounding rather ill in the next room. I went to knock on his door, opening it a crack and calling out to him. He replied in a weak voice that he was all right, but in the morning when I went to see if he was still alive, he pointed to a glass carafe on the bedside table from which, half-asleep during the previous night, he had poured himself a drink of water. Strands of green slime floated in the stagnant liquid and poor David had drunk a full glass of this pond-water before being violently sick. The carafe must have stood there for months with water that was never changed, breeding algae and assorted organisms. No one inspected the spare rooms; they were not on Alison's housekeeping radar.

Cen was gregarious, loving a good party and vigorous socialising, while Alison detested any form of mingling that might involve having to go around pretending that she was enjoying herself. Despite this, once the wedding became an inevitability she rallied to the occasion and undertook all the arrangements with surprising efficiency and pleasure, organising armies of helpers and drawing up lists of guests that ran into more than three hundred, as no one could be left out. There were dozens of people on the list that I had never heard of, but it didn't matter because I was thrilled to be having a big wedding. If it had been a Craddock one, numbers would have been pared down to as many as could fit into a waiting room, which was the only room with any space at the doctors' surgery in Redhill where my family now lived. None of them were coming to the wedding since Fa had decided that fares could not be afforded. Such concerns did not deter members of the Hill family and Johnny was summoned from New Zealand to come and be best man, while flower girls and ushers were chosen from among Adam's cousins and mutual friends. Two choirs were booked for the service at St Christopher's Church to ensure strong singing, with George Swannell the vicar officiating. Everything possible was thought of and organised down to the smallest detail, such as having a mechanic standing by in case any of the cars broke down. Most surprising of all, Fa offered to pay for the champagne, which was accepted with amazement in view of his own aversion to alcohol.

Adam's house at this stage was furnished with the barest of essentials: just two camp chairs with a small table for meals, and a camp bed. These were easily folded up and packed into the Land Rover for safari trips, so from a bachelor point of view they met most requirements. Alison, coming to inspect the household arrangements, felt they were not suitable for a new wife setting up home, and generously suggested the farm would give us £100 to buy furniture from the local auction rooms. Adam's cousins, Cyrus and Joan Morrall, gave us their old double bed as a wedding present, saying it would bring us luck since they had conceived four children in it. They themselves were now getting a new one, having worn out the other one they told us cheerfully. The bed certainly looked well used, with a sagging mattress and springs, but we were glad to have any sort of double bed, the alternative being twin camp beds.

I waited impatiently for a day off when I could go to the auction rooms to find essentials like a dining table and chairs, with maybe the luxury of a sideboard so we would have somewhere to put our wedding-present china. Arriving at Dalgety's rooms full of anticipation on a viewing day, I was greeted warmly by Harry Mortlock, the auctioneer, who had been one of our neighbours when we first arrived in Nakuru in 1951 and was a good friend. He was a bluff New Zealander with arms and hands like a prize fighter, and a permanently red face from sunburn, lit up by the biggest smile and biggest foghorn voice. 'By crikey, Wendy, you're a bit late if you were wanting anything from last week's sale,' he said genially.

'No, I was hoping to look at things for the next one,' and I started telling him about Alison's offer, when he stopped me. 'I think you've got it wrong,' he said. 'Mrs Hill was here last week buying stuff for Adam's house. It was collected by the farm lorry next day. I expect you'll find it all set out in his house by now.' He laughed heartily and winked as if it was a secret surprise waiting for me. I was speechless, staring at Harry in disbelief. Adam hadn't said anything about this. I managed to mumble thanks for letting me know as I turned to get into the car and drive out to see for myself what had been bought.

Adam was not at home when I arrived at the house and Mungai ambled out with the insolent look he seemed to reserve especially for me, as he muttered, '*Jambo Memsahib, Bwana si hapa.*'

'Yes, I know,' I replied (in Swahili). 'I've come to see the new furniture.'

Mungai scowled, not wanting to let me into the house. His resentment of me was becoming more blatant as realisation set in that his command of the household would be ended as soon as I moved in. I smiled, hoping to defuse the standoff. 'Bwana told me to come,' I said. He would not be able to stop me going into the house now.

He followed me inside, pointing out with a proprietorial gesture the newly arrived furniture, stacked in a pile in the dining room. Plainly a job lot, every piece was damaged or faulty in some way. A crudely made wardrobe had doors so warped they hung open like broken wings, and when Mungai trying to be helpful attempted to close them, one of the hinges fell off. There must be a mistake I thought, asking Mungai if perhaps the pile was being stored in the house to keep it dry, ready for chopping into firewood.

'No,' he said with a smirk, 'these are new things from the mother of Bwana Adam. She came to see them herself after the lorry brought them. To make sure everything was good.'

'Has the Bwana seen them?' I asked.

'Yes. He was pleased.'

That was enough to send me driving around the farm until I found Adam. He was sewing up the leg of a cow that had ripped itself on a barbed-wire fence. It was not a moment to talk about furniture so I waited, and when he was washing his hands in a bucket, I mentioned the job lot as casually as I could. Adam stood up quickly, drying his hands on a clean piece of towel his assistant held out to him (he was fastidious about hygiene when treating animals).

'I know, sweetheart,' he said. 'It's a bugger about the furniture. Mum promised we could choose our own bits and the farm would pay. But she can't resist auctions. Harry will tell you she's there at every sale, bidding for anything going cheaply. She doesn't really want any of it. Everything goes back into the next sale. She knew we were supposed to be choosing things for ourselves, but she couldn't resist going and getting them herself. It's a sort of addiction.' I understood now why Harry had winked at me. I had no idea that Alison was a regular at the auction rooms with this strange compulsion to buy useless rubbish.

Adam continued, 'Don't worry darling, I'll get the farm *fundi* to patch up the worst of it, and we can buy anything else we need out of wedding-present money.' He gave me a hug, and said to cheer me up, 'I can take the rest of the day off. What would you like to do?' Any time alone together was precious so I felt instantly better and couldn't go on being cross. By this stage wedding invitations had gone out and presents were beginning to arrive, so the prospect of opening presents together was the most obvious and best pleasure. There were piles of parcels and envelopes containing cheques waiting in my room at the main house, and we were always glad to have any excuse to go and shut ourselves in there.

The Hemsteds had sent a present which came in the form of a letter enclosing a map. This was a map of Avondale, their old farm at Londiani, that had been rented out when they moved to Subukia. The letter with the map said, astonishingly, that the farm was their wedding present to us, if we would accept it. The implications of such a stunning offer took some moments to sink in and we kept re-reading the letter, and looking at the map, trying to believe what was in front of our eyes. There was just one condition. We needed £2000 of our own money to provide working capital and pay the land transfer fee that had to be paid by any new owner.

We already had near enough the sum required in wedding-present cheques alone, with more coming in daily. The offer was so extraordinary I went a bit crazy, jumping around waving the letter, literally dancing for joy, hugging Adam until he got annoyed and told me to calm down. I couldn't calm down and was so overwhelmed with excitement it made my voice go squeaky. 'What do you think?' I managed to say. He seemed overcome and was silent for such a long time that I took this to be amazement at the Hemsteds' generosity. It was completely unexpected when he said, evenly and rather reproachfully, 'You know we can't accept. You do know that, don't you?'

'Why ever not?' I exclaimed. 'We've got enough money from all the cheques. It's the chance of a lifetime. It's manna from heaven. We *have* to accept.'

'It's out of the question. You have to understand that I can't let my parents down by leaving so soon. They gave me this job trusting that I would stick at it, and take over from Dad in due course. Anyway, Glanjoro is my home, and soon will be yours too.'

I knew him well enough by now to realise that it was pointless arguing. Nothing was going to move him or make him change his mind. I would have to explain to the Hemsteds and, just as painfully, I would have to swallow my own ambitions in order to allow him to follow his.

Stricken with disappointment I went to see the McCubbins for consolation. They were soothing and sympathetic, but not surprised. 'You have to remember,' Hugh said, 'you are not just marrying Adam, you're marrying into a family, a dynasty. Avondale doesn't fit into that set-up.'

'I don't think I fit into it either,' I replied, 'but in order to be a Hill wife I'll have to do my best, fittingly or unfittingly.

It was already the end of May and a few days later I was back at the McCubbins' house to collect my wedding dress on the way to the Hemsteds, preparing for the wedding itself on Saturday, 1st June, 1963. Pat had packed the dress with tissue paper in a long cardboard box, and my going-away outfit was in a new Revelation suitcase, a wedding present, replacing my shabby old one. The outfit had been made by Indian tailors at Choitram's in Nakuru, and was a pencil-line dress in peach linen, with matching jacket and matching picture hat covered in silk peach-coloured petals, bought at Madame de Haff in Nairobi. The hat by itself had cost almost as much as the wedding dress, but I could afford it now with my job at the hospital.

After prolonged farewells on leaving the McCubbins, when I arrived at the Hemsteds' house, there were Stephen and Joan with Edmund their son and Marc (Joan's father), jostling an entourage of giant St Bernards and small fat pugs, all swarming down the steps to engulf me in tail whacks from the dogs and big hugs from everyone else. When the hubbub subsided, Joan stood back and looked at me: 'Dammit, you're looking peaky. What you need is a good hot bath and a large whisky.' She was right. But first, what I needed more than anything else was a strong cup of tea before breaking the news about Avondale.

CHAPTER 3

When things were calmer after the madness of the St Bernards lumbering about like small ponies and they were slumped outside on the veranda, we sat down with cups of tea and got onto the subject of Avondale. Joan's cup almost flew off its saucer when I broke the news about Adam's rejection of their offer, and I tried to explain why he felt unable to accept it.

'Do you really mean he is so blinded by duty to his parents he can't see the necessity for you to start off married life with your own place?' Joan was incredulous. I didn't want them to think badly of Adam and could see that she and Stephen were trying to avoid seeming too critical, doing their best to remain tactful so close to the wedding. 'Adam's a splendid chap, already running that farm very competently and you're going to be such an asset to him,' Stephen put in, 'but we worry about you coping with those two, Cen and Alison, as parents-in-law. Living on the same farm with them – they won't give you an easy time – you'll have to be prepared for that.'

'Adam says the secret to getting along with them is kow-towing, but I don't think I'm going to be very good at that. I'll just have to do my best. They don't approve of me, so whatever I do is never going to please them. I can't change Alison's complaint that I'm not out of the right drawer.'

'She hasn't said that to you, has she?' Joan asked sharply.

'No, not directly to me. Susie Dunlop (one of the Morrall cousins) was mimicking Alison complaining to her twin sister Consie about the unsuitability of the marriage. Because of the wrong drawer and marrying above my station – that kind of stuff. Susie was laughing, putting on Alison's voice and the way she sniffs, imitating her saying like someone out of a Jane Austen novel: "It's so tiresome. Wendy has no connections … and no money either."

'It isn't really funny,' Joan interrupted as I was about to go on with more gems from the reported conversation. 'It just proves how resilient you'll have to be, to survive that kind of unpleasantness. It's totally mad clinging onto such rubbish these days. You could be an heiress with a title but only half a brain and a face like one of the pugs, and that would be all right as far as they are concerned. It's too absurd. That's why we worry about you.'

'Well, they have been very kind and generous over the wedding, and I think they've accepted me now, sort of. Anyway our house is a mile away from theirs so we won't be bumping into each other that much.'

'You wouldn't be bumping into them at all if you went to Avondale,' Stephen reminded me. 'That was the whole idea, getting you away from Glanjoro. Getting away from those parents, enjoying running your own farm together, like Joan and me.' But we all knew the subject was not up for negotiation. Adam would not be persuaded.

On the morning of the wedding, when we sat down for breakfast, I found two small blue triangular pills on my side plate, which Joan told me I must take. She always had a pile of pills on her plate every morning as armaments in the battle she waged against all kinds of imaginary ailments. While surrounding herself with these batteries of pills and tales of chronic infirmity, no evidence of such indisposition was apparent in any physical manifestation as she boomed about the place, a model of robust good health. Large, round and muscular, she possessed a spectacular frontage firmly buttoned into a navy safari jacket, her short legs in matching navy trousers, ready for any task related to home or farm. She was an immensely jovial and capable woman, looking after all the livestock on the farm as well as running a market garden which grew a range of vegetables and flowers for export to British supermarkets, while Stephen ran the coffee plantations.

I asked Joan what the blue pills on my plate were for. 'You have to take them,' she said. 'You'll never get through the day without them. They're Purple Hearts. American Marines take them. You can get through anything with a couple of those inside you.'

I asked for the packet to see what was in them, not wanting to take any unidentified substance. The principle ingredients were amphetamine and phenobarbitone. The former, also known as 'speed', was a stimulant, while the latter was a tranquilliser, so the two chemicals had opposing effects and looked likely to cancel each other out. 'Oh no,' said Joan, 'they act independently, keeping you on top form all day, never having to worry about a thing. I take them all the time,' she added. 'That's why I have so much energy, keeping me going and getting things done.'

If I could be like Joan, I thought, I'll go through the day completely unfazed, which was a very attractive idea as my nerves were already jangled before I'd even started to get dressed or ready for what lay ahead. I swallowed the pills and Joan cheered.

After that everything went blank and my only memory is of Joan steering me towards a bath full of bubbles and steam, next being given a scrub by her and my hair washed, while the St Bernards dipped their great heads over the side of the bath, not to be left out, and the pugs kept jumping up to see what was going on. One of them jumped too high and plunged in, disappearing under the foam, which caused a great deal of thrashing about. Joan shouted for Stephen to come and get the dogs out, and I sat with wet hair and garlands of soup suds feeling rather exposed while Stephen scooped up the dogs.

The Purple Hearts continued to kick in so that I floated through the rest of the day in a trance, drifting on the white cloud of my dress supremely unbothered about anything, knowing that Adam was there to hold my hand while the wedding unrolled like a film, with hundreds of extras crowding around as we played our leading roles.

Some scenes remain like stills. One was when I walked over a patch of grass where a swarm of flies had settled (probably on something nasty) and the swarm flew up my skirt between the layers of organza, buzzing about repulsively. Getting them out was an unscripted sequence with guests helping and diving under the crinoline. Another unscripted moment was a surprise phone call from Fa and Muz, on a radio telephone. They had found a local radio 'ham' in Redhill, able to connect us from a garden shed where he monitored the world's airwaves on his amateur radio. The wavering sounds of different family voices made them seem further away than ever; poor Ros during the few seconds she was allowed on the echoing line, fretting that she wasn't there with us, as she felt all of them should have been.

Johnny had answered the phone after retreating to the house with a serious hangover from the previous night's stag party, and was using a wall to prop himself up, looking deathly pale and sick. Ted Berridge, one of Adam's many bachelor friends, stepped in to take over as best man, while Johnny endeavoured to stay vertical long enough to appear in the photo line-ups. Adam, whose fragile state was only slightly less debilitating, kept himself sustained during the reception with packets of Sportsman cigarettes and hairs of the dog. Under his morning suit, his skin was plastered with dried white paint from waist to knees (a stag party ritual for bridegrooms) which, despite strenuous efforts with turpentine, took weeks to peel and flake off.

At Kenya weddings the real drama is saved for those final moments when bride and groom depart on honeymoon. As soon as they have changed into going-away clothes, emerging for a dash to their car, the assembled crowd of guests surges forward to try and prevent their escape by surrounding and disabling the getaway vehicle. Precautions had been taken by Stephen to avoid damage to his vintage Rolls, and guards had been employed to prevent anyone tampering with it beforehand, while Edmund was to be our driver. My new Revelation suitcase felt symbolic of new adventures as it was loaded together with Adam's old one into the Rolls when we made a dash for it, pursued by the throng.

Either the guards had been bribed, or tricked, as instead of the powerful engine idling ready for us to jump into the car, Edmund was still trying to get it started when we took our seats behind him. Something appeared to have gone wrong, which was a mystery until it was discovered that saboteurs had removed all the spark plugs on one side. But the laugh was on them failing to be aware that the Rolls had two sets of spark plugs, and soon roared into life with a little encouragement from Edmund, and the farm staff giving it a push. We were off at last, with the customary thunder flashes hurled around at this stage providing no more than a distant rumbling as we rode away, waving graciously until everyone was out of sight.

Adam's Land Rover had been parked at a secret location in Nakuru where no one would find it for further sabotage, and Edmund dropped us there to change vehicles and set off by ourselves for the drive of seventy miles to Limuru and the Farm Hotel where we were to spend the night. This was a very small hotel, hardly more than a farmhouse with spare bedrooms and a bar serving meals; its seclusion in the cool misty uplands of Limuru making it a favourite hideaway. The main bedroom had a luxurious bed and huge fireplace where a log fire added romance and kept out the cold. There is something extraordinarily sensual about going to bed in the flickering glow of firelight dancing with shadows when the lamps are turned off. Not that we needed any extra arousing and were in that state of sleepy euphoria that all post-wedding couples feel when they are finally alone, lingering over dinner, looking back on the day together, relieved that it's over and the best part of being married lies ahead. The Purple Heart effect was wearing off, and I was glad to feel normal again.

There had been no hint that Limuru was hosting a rugby match that Saturday with teams planning to meet at the Farm Hotel later in the evening, and we hadn't noticed that our room was next door to the bar. As we sank into the rapturous softness of our big bed, replete from a candlelit dinner, a sudden violent uproar shook the room as the teams arrived next door with loud stamping of boots and raucous shouting. The decibel level rose as drinks were poured down eager throats and when these had been wetted, singing started with more banging and thumping which shook the walls of the room. 'They'll wear themselves out soon,' I murmured hopefully as we lay side by side stunned by the noise, but then an ominous creaking started when some of the drinkers leaned against the wall from the other side. At this point we noticed that the wall was not solid as we had thought, but was made of hardboard and quite flimsy. In the firelight we watched nervously as the wall bulged inwards, looking as if it might give way for a bunch of rugby players to tumble through on top of us. Just then someone must have suggested a game of *bok-bok,* as the leaners abruptly left the wall and reassembled themselves elsewhere for this notorious game, played only when the participants are so drunk that no feeling is left in any limb or body part and brains are entirely disengaged. The game begins when several members of a team have bent down one behind the other in a line, heads pushed against bottoms scrum-style, with the front man's head and hands braced against the wall. In this case, not our wall, luckily, as they needed a solid one, and we heard everyone veering towards the other end of the bar, which however did not reduce the volume of noise. In this game, members of the opposing team vault one by one across the top of the crouching line, leap-frog style, attempting to collapse the line. Roars go up as a vaulter lands on top and the line holds. Ultimately everyone ends up on the floor in a tangle like a collapsed scrum, and more drinks are required.

This carried on until the early hours and very little sleep was had by anyone. As a wedding night experience it was memorable, for all the wrong sorts of reasons. We were more than ready for breakfast the next morning and this was done with exemplary Farm Hotel composure as if nothing unusual had taken place the night before. Fortified with Limuru's best Uplands sausages and bacon we climbed back into the Land Rover for the next stage of our honeymoon safari: connecting with the overnight train to Mombasa at Nairobi station. After supervising the loading of the car onto a flatbed truck, we sank gratefully into one of the elegant old-fashioned compartments with its bunk beds and superb valet service, able to relax completely at last.

The overnight train journey from Nairobi to Mombasa was legendary for the comfort and ease of that leisurely way of travelling. Everyone looked forward to the silver service dinner served with charm and style in the dining car while the African night passed in slow motion beyond the windows, all its shadowy features lit by moonlight. During dinner, unseen while we were eating, bunks were made up in carriages ready for our return. Sleeping in a bunk on a train is one of life's exquisite pleasures, while on this train there is the added ecstasy of easy travel through an African wilderness with frequent stops along the way. At one of these stops I climbed down from the top bunk (which I had chosen for preference) and opened the window to look out. A rush of warm air heavy with the scents of dry bush touched my face as I breathed deeply and was filled by the moment. Adam woke and called out softly, 'What are you doing?

'Looking out of the window, sniffing the air and feeling it on my skin,'

'How about coming over here and feeling me on your skin?' he suggested.

The privacy of the small compartment with nothing outside but the immense plains of Tsavo was a perfect honeymoon bolt-hole.

Another one was waiting for us after the train journey. Robin Wainwright, Provincial Commissioner for the Coast Province, had given us as a wedding present sole use of the guest cottage in the grounds of his large Moorish-style residence fronting the beach at Malindi, for as long as we wanted. The cottage was simple, thatched with *makuti* (dried palm leaves), close to the beach and the boundary of Robin's compound. There was a mosque next door, its slender minaret rising high above us as we explored our surroundings. Robin was away and his chief of staff, resplendent in a white turban and robe with gold-braided waistcoat, came to receive us and make sure everything was in order for our stay. The guest cottage was staffed with workers to cook and clean and tend the hot-water boiler that needed to be fed with pieces of wood all day. Members of staff were introduced and each one greeted us in the traditional Swahili coastal way that is so charming, saying:

'*Shikamo*' (I hold your feet).
To which the reply is: '*Marahaba*' (You are welcome).

There is a poignancy in this greeting since it originates from those times when slavery was an accepted way of life along the coast, and slaves approached their masters in an attitude of subjugation, literally kneeling to touch their feet as an act of servitude.

We were asked if there were any particular instructions to be carried out, and what time we would like meals to be served and baths to be run. Adam replied in Swahili in its most correct form, known at the coast as *Kiswahili Kisafi*, which translated literally means 'clean' or 'pure' Swahili as distinct from the less grammatical up-country version spoken then by most Europeans and those Africans whose mother-tongue was their tribal language, but Adam always spoke the correct form as a matter of principle and respect.

There was a small parade ground behind the cottage that we had thought might be used for occasional ceremonial purposes, until the next morning at six o'clock when we found out rather abruptly that its purpose required us to be in attendance. We had already been woken earlier, before dawn, by the muezzin calling the faithful to prayer at the mosque, and were startled when this further interruption came with loud knocking at the door. When Adam went to investigate he found a large African policeman standing to attention outside.

Adam, wearing only a *kikoi* (loincloth), felt more than a little discomposed as the policeman snapped a salute and announced, 'Prisoners ready for inspection, sir.' Robin had not warned us that a work gang from the local prison was paraded each morning at this time, to be allocated tasks around the compound for the 'hard labour' part of their sentence. In Robin's absence, it was assumed that Adam would deputise and issue orders for the day. Before any orders were given however, the prisoners had to be marched up and down the parade ground, military style, in preparation for being lined up waiting for instructions. Whatever they thought about Robin's substitute standing there rumpled and half-naked, no one would have been impolite enough to indicate by even the flicker of an eye that they had noticed anything unusual. The 'hard labour,' we discovered, entailed short bursts of desultory wood chopping or water carrying, in between long sessions of sitting propped against the outside wall of our cottage chatting. This became intrusive whenever we wanted to retire for a quiet siesta, but not as intrusive as the dawn calls to prayer next door, or the six o'clock parades.

The cottage was not luxurious but it was comfortable, and hotels along the beach were within strolling distance for a change of scene and diet. There was Lawfords, still low-key with thatched cottages; the more elegant Arabian-Nights-style Sindbad which was popular with honeymooners, and the slightly *demi-monde* Eden Roc further along at the north end of the beach. All of these became regular haunts for us as time went on and we looked for new people to talk to instead of just each other. Malindi had never been a hub for holiday activities, offering water sports no more adventurous than gentle surfing or snorkelling, neither of which had great appeal for us, but riding horses along the beach did appeal, and we had local friends with horses they could lend us.

These friends were Rose and Will Powys whose dairy farm Kisima was just outside the town. They were doyens of Kenya settler society, having arrived among the first pioneers when Will left England to work for Lord Delamere as a shepherd on his Soysambu estate spread across thousands of acres of good grazing land in the Rift Valley. They were elderly now and had retreated to the coast as many people did when ready to retire. Keeping horses at the coast was problematic due to disease carried by Tsetse fly and the only survivors were those who had developed immunity, so it was lucky that the Powys's had some survivors. After the morning parade, while it was still cool, we went to the farm where Will and Rose had a couple of horses waiting for us, as well as breakfast with mangoes from their own trees and porridge with cream from the dairy. They were glad to have news from up-country and I was glad to meet two people who had become legendary in the story of Kenya's early settlers. After breakfast we rode from the farm down to the beach where we let go with a short exhilarating canter, before a long walk on firm sand at the edge of the water, and then back again to the farm. This was a highlight for us; much more exciting and satisfying than dips in the sea, as we were discovering that beach holidays could become surprisingly monotonous.

There were surf boards at the cottage and we had taken these out soon after arriving, when I made another discovery: Adam couldn't swim. The 'swimming party' several years ago at Glanjoro that had been our first 'date', had been a sham. He admitted that he had in fact never let go of the sides of the water tank that doubled as a swimming pool, and had simply splashed around pretending to swim. I was shocked to hear this, especially as we regularly fished in fast rivers. Swimming lessons now became almost as compelling as other honeymoon activities, absorbing hours each day, staving off lassitude as we started getting bored with life at the beach, and I started getting queasy. There was a possible explanation for this, but it surprised me as I had not planned a pregnancy and had been carefully following precise instructions from the Stoke Newington family planning clinic that I visited before leaving London. Alternatively, it could be that our rather basic kitchen arrangements at the cottage had resulted in some kind of gastric sensitivity, so I decided on a wait and see approach.

A few hours' drive inland from Malindi the Game Department had a base for one of their projects at Galana on the river. Tony Seth Smith, who was now working for the department, was stationed there with Renny and their new baby, Nettie. Another friend, Ian Parker, was also employed on the project, with Chris his wife and their small child. Conditions at the base were primitive but idyllic in that wild setting and we could not miss visiting them on our way home, this time by road instead of rail. A final parade of prisoners and house staff was staged for us by Robin's major domo and Adam made a little speech, thanking them. Then, touchingly, they all stood lined up waving to us as we climbed into the Land Rover and set off for Galana.

This time the bumpy road caused waves of sickness for me and there seemed no doubt what could be causing it. I had been slightly apprehensive about Adam's reaction to this premature news but was happily surprised when, instead of thinking it rather careless, he took it as triumphant proof of virility, scoring a bullseye on the first round. He was so pleased, he could not stop talking about it, and teasing me.

'Now you've got a passenger on board, you'll have to give up your vices,' he said.

'What vices?' I was indignant.

'Wild dancing. Fast driving. Climbing trees. Flirting with strange men. For a start.'

'You're the big flirt, not me.'

'In a man, it's a skill. In a woman, it's a vice,' he said provokingly.

'In this case,' I replied, 'if I've got it, I got it from you. As well as something else I've got from you. Making me feel sick, and not just in the mornings either. When I tell you to stop the car, you'll have to stop fast for me to get out.'

'Not too fast. Might shake up the passenger. We'll stop for a break anyway at the next comfort station.'

The reference to comfort stations came from a book, *The Nylon Safari*, written by an American woman, Rehna 'Tiny' Cloete. After she married the

South African writer Stuart Cloete, he took her on safari to show her the wonders of Africa, but failed to warn her about some of its drawbacks. Tiny was dismayed to find that the wonders of Africa did not include roadside washrooms, and found herself frequently on alert looking out for patches of bush that might be leafy enough to be accommodating.

It was reassuring to find Adam so solicitous and accepting of this unexpected diversion to our plans as he mused on the sudden additional presence now accompanying us, and watched for a shady place to stop. It gave us the opportunity for a drink as we sat with tin mugs filled from the four-gallon clean water supply always carried on long drives. Radiator water was kept in separate cans, and spare petrol in jerry cans well away from other supplies. As we sat balancing the mugs on our knees while gazing far into the distance where grey-green scrub reached to the horizon on every side, Adam raised his mug: 'Here's to my darling beautiful wife, Mrs Hill, and our precious new passenger who couldn't wait to join us,' he said with a big smile and an arm around me. No amount of incipient nausea could quell the sense of calm and synergy of that moment, as if I had now become an intrinsic part of him, and of the land my feet were touching, belonging in a way I had not felt before. Later, staying overnight at the Galana camp where the Seth Smith and Parker families gave us an enthusiastic welcome, it reinforced the sense of consummation, that so many previously disparate pieces of my life had come together and made it complete at last.

The low altitude of Galana with almost no breeze to lift the heat made it a challenging place to live, especially with young children. The houses were very basic with mud walls and tin roofs to catch any rain that might fall. Doors were left open all day and Renny was constantly on watch for snakes using their house as a cool and shady place to escape the worst temperatures of the day. The camp seemed to be a magnet for animals and had become an orphanage for small ones whose mothers had abandoned them, or been killed by poachers. Renny was trying to develop a milk formula for one very small baby elephant that was failing to thrive on a mixture made with powdered cow's milk. It took several years and much experimentation before Daphne Sheldrick at her animal orphanage in Tsavo, perfected the technique. A larger orphaned elephant living at the

Galana camp was a feisty female no longer needing milk from a bottle, but not yet foraging for herself. She had become a problem due to her size as she blundered about the place looking for food to steal or smaller animals to chase and tease.

Another orphan the Parkers had adopted and raised was a warthog. Imaginatively called Pig, he had arrived as a small piglet and joined the dogs in the house where he grew up thinking he was one of them, as there were no other warthogs in the camp on which he could model himself. Pigs are intelligent and this one, like a naughty child, had become increasingly delinquent as he learnt how to avoid being caught and punished when he misbehaved, causing general mayhem around the camp with his antics and unruly behaviour. When he grew out of being mothered by the dogs, he attached himself to the young female elephant, who took him under her protection and a close bond developed between them. Whenever Pig went on the rampage, knocking things over and being a menace, causing camp staff to shout and throw things at him, all he had to do was squeal and the elephant would come pounding to his aid, so he could hide between her legs safe from being caught. One day Pig was discovered in the process of some particularly destructive act and ran squealing towards the Parkers' house with the elephant following. As Pig ran inside, the elephant tried to follow him through the front door, which was too narrow for her size and she got stuck. This made her frantic and she began heaving at the door frame so vigorously that the house started to shudder and threatened to fall apart. All hands were summoned to the scene, pulling and pushing, while Pig smirked and rubbed his backside against the wall inside, quite safe while all attention was diverted to saving the house.

'It's bloody worse than *Animal Farm*,' Adam remarked after the elephant had been freed and sauntered off with Pig trotting after her. 'Bloody animals causing chaos. Too many running around the camp out of control.'

'Too many coming inside as well,' Renny added, her German accent soft as marshmallow. 'Not a good place for babies.' Looking at me she added, 'Did you mean to get pregnant so quickly?'

'No,' I said, 'it just happened, but we're glad. I'm doing my best to catch up with you!' That made us laugh, but Renny looked serious as she said, 'I would rather be back on the farm when we have the next one.'

Kathleen was looking after the farm with a manager while Tony and Renny were at Galana. Tony's career and Ian's too were focused on those areas of wildlife that most interested them. Conservation and hunting being interdependent, Ian went on to make conservation his life's work, while Tony joined Ker & Downey and became a leading figure in the field of professional hunting.

While we were still with them at Galana, Ian put up a leopard bait (a dead gazelle) in a tree, hoping to attract a male leopard that had been spotted too near the camp for comfort when there were so many young animals running around. A 'hide' was hollowed out in a patch of bush with a clear view of the tree across a strip of open land, and the plan was for Ian, Adam and myself to conceal ourselves in the hide an hour before sundown, waiting for the leopard to come and feed on the bait. Adam and Ian took rifles, while I would have preferred simply to watch the leopard feeding, rather than use the opportunity to shoot it. We had to creep into the hide well before twilight to make sure we were not observed, and remain crouched inside, neither moving nor speaking except in whispers. We had taken cards to pass the time silently playing and waiting for the sun to go down. As it sank beyond the scrubby horizon and light faded in that interlude of almost mystical relief from the day's heat, which is how night comes in Africa, as if on cue the leopard materialised at the base of the tree. It paused for a moment, looking around, and we froze, hardly daring even to breathe. Then, with extraordinary ease and grace, it seemed to glide up the tree to where the bait was wedged in a fork. We watched for a few minutes as it started to feed and I hoped there would be no need to shoot it, but the angle was ideal, and very calmly and carefully one of the rifles was raised. The shot at such close quarters was like a thunder clap in my ear, and instantly the leopard fell from the tree, landing heavily with a thud on the ground, inert.

Ian and Adam scrambled out of the hide to make sure the leopard was dead, but before they got close, it leapt up and made for a thick patch of bush a short way off where it disappeared from view. They approached cautiously, rifles pointed ready, and when they were still a few yards off the leopard broke cover. It doubled back, making for the next patch of bush, which was our hide, with me still inside. Instinctively I rolled into a ball like a hedgehog, expecting that within moments the desperate animal would plunge in on top of me. Two rifle shots cracked out simultaneously at that point and I looked up. The leopard was stretched flat on the ground some feet from the hide, quite dead this time. Crawling out, I felt shaken and not at all triumphant, while Adam and Ian inspected the carcass for bullet holes and exclaimed over the excitement of the past few minutes. The leopard was transported back to camp to be measured, admired and skinned, its glorious coat staked out on a wooden frame, while all I could feel was emptiness at the destruction of such a magnificent life force in its proud wild form.

After nearly a month away we were impatient to get back and start life in our own home where some of our wedding presents were still waiting to be opened. Arriving at last after several more stops along the way, we parked the Land Rover in its usual place beside the big pepper tree at the back of the house, outside the kitchen. Everything was quiet, and before calling for Mungai to come and help unload the car, Adam led me to the back door, determined to carry me over the threshold, laughing that it was the last time I would be such a lightweight.

The first room inside the back door was a narrow lobby which had been converted into a small kitchen for me, and leading off it was the dining room. The lobby was so narrow that I had to be carried head first through it, and when I was back on my feet at the dining room doorway, a chaotic scene brought us up short. This was incomprehensible as it continued on through the house with rubbish and smashed glass everywhere and a couple of doors off their hinges: the house had been trashed. 'Where the bloody hell is Mungai?' Adam yelled, and ran to the servants' huts down the drive beyond the pepper tree.

There was a lot of shouting and banging from that direction before Adam returned, furious. 'The bastard is dead drunk in his hut. Can't even rouse him. We'll have to go and find out from the parents what's happened. We've got to collect my other woman from them anyway.' The other woman was his black Labrador gun dog, Ruin, a very well-mannered, kind animal, who had been staying with the parents among their pack of nervy Pointers while we were away. She had earned the name 'Ruin' from her ruinous chewing of shoes, slippers and rugs when she was a puppy.

Cen and Alison were sitting on their veranda smoking and sighing over the latest farming reports when we arrived. Both stood up, seeming genuinely pleased to see us, as Alison said, 'Oh Ad, here you are, we weren't sure when you were getting back. It's awfully dry and the river is down, so tedious. Anyway,' she said, 'come and have a drink.' The Pointers had jumped up to scrabble at us with their front paws, whining with welcoming noises, while Ruin, too polite and well trained to jump up, pushed her wet nose into my hand to show how pleased she was to see us. Adam crouched down to fondle her ears and stroke her affectionately. 'How's my girl then,' he said softly to her, as her tail beat to and fro and she shivered with pleasure at his touch.

As soon as the dogs had dispersed to chase each other around the lawn, Adam turned to Alison, angrily enquiring: 'What the hell went on at our house while we were away?'

'Oh yes, I meant to go and check before you got back. Johnny said after the wedding the party decamped to your house, and the more reprobate of your friends went and fetched yet more crates and bottles from town, which turned things into a mighty bash. And there was some damage, Johnny said, but nothing serious that couldn't be fixed before you got back.' Alison stopped as she recollected that probably nothing had in fact been fixed. 'Johnny himself wasn't there, at the party,' she said. 'He was feeling too crook. He wasn't himself during the actual wedding. But he did his best. Poor Johnny.'

'Well, the house has been trashed, and Mungai is drunk,' Adam said tersely, 'we haven't got time for a drink. We'll have to go and clear up as much as we can, and hope there is at least a bed to sleep in for the night.'

Ruin had already jumped into the car, making sure she came with us this time, and as we climbed in ourselves, Adam said, 'We must go and say hello to Merry at the stables first, make sure she's all right and let her know we're back.' Merry Legs was his new polo pony, half-Arab she had the fine bones, spirit and fire of that breed. 'You can help exercise her, and the others too if you like.' He and Cen had several polo ponies alongside Merry in the stables. 'Keep you in trim,' he teased me. 'Get the passenger used to stops and starts, in training for polo later.'

Ruin was so glad to be home again she ran around in and out of the house, sniffing for new scents and bounding back to us, excited and happy. There was still no sign of Mungai. Picking my way through the debris of the rooms, I dreaded what I might find in the bedroom, but Mungai must have succeeded in one of his more lucid moments to tidy it and put clean sheets on the bed. I felt a wave of relief that it was made up and ready to get into later. Looking at the bed made me realise suddenly how tired I felt, and still queasy. Hoping the new bathroom was habitable, I went to have a look, grateful to Adam for installing it, and was even more grateful to find it decently clean and working despite the ravages of the drunken party, with clean water coming out of the basin taps as I filled a glass to drink.

I heard Adam calling from the sitting room and went through, glad to sit down in one of the camp chairs (armchairs had not been included in Alison's auction lots), ignoring the rubbish scattered around us. Adam was pointing to a stack of envelopes on the stone mantelpiece – someone must have collected our post and brought it down. Lots of wedding cards were there, still unopened, some bills, and a letter from the hospital.

The letter was from Matron, telling me that I was to report for night duty, starting the next night at 8 o'clock. Adam was incensed. 'You can't go onto night duty now we're married,' he protested, as if this were a personal affront to his marital rights.

'All the nurses have to do their share, and I've been allowed my entire year's leave all in one go, for our honeymoon. I can't refuse,' I explained, and added, 'we need my salary, you're not earning enough for me to give up work.' I didn't want it to be an issue, but Cen was only paying Adam £25 a month, which even in those days was a pittance. I thought wistfully of Avondale with its fat milk cheques rolling off the rich pastures, then quickly put the thought out of my mind.

CHAPTER 4

Milking times were at 4 o'clock in the morning and 4 o'clock in the afternoon, allowing a twelve hour rest for the cows in between, and time for Adam to attend to other work on the farm. Johnny, with his degree in agriculture from Massey, was now employed on the farm as arable manager, with his own house two miles from ours. This was near the farm offices and workshops providing a hub for farm activities, with Cen and Alison's house even closer to the hub so Cen was able to keep a firm grip on everything.

My night shifts ran from eight in the evening to eight in the morning, and when I got home I was able to sleep during the daytime while Adam was working, but he was very peeved about spending nights alone which he thought was entirely unreasonable now we were married. He had to be up by 3.30 each morning, ready for milking at 4 o'clock, then would come home for breakfast at 9 o'clock. I was back from the hospital by then so we were able to have breakfast together before I went to bed, tired after spending all night working, which I was not enjoying but had to accept as part of my job.

These breakfast times were magical, sitting out on the veranda with great views down to Lake Nakuru surrounded by mountains touched with gold by the sun. The colours and shapes at this time of day were still intense before the sun climbed high enough to drain them and I never got tired of gazing at this inspirational landscape. For breakfast we always had avocado pears sprinkled with salt and vinegar, and coffee from the small plantation that Cen had planted. Kenya coffee is mild and ours was almost ersatz in flavour due to the harsh growing conditions of our dry climate, added to which Mungai's roasting process depended on how sober or otherwise he might be when the beans arrived. The colour of the coffee in our breakfast cups, once milk had been added, was greasy grey, emphasising the indifferent taste. But it was our own coffee so we didn't mind, just as we tolerated the imperfections of the house, because it was ours, with its deficiencies still glaring, waiting to be fixed. While I was sleeping during the day, the house needed to stay quiet, so repairs had to wait. Household duties inside the house were suspended as well, pleasing Mungai, and Adam resorted to his parents each day for lunch.

I was relieved that my body was not reacting to the passenger as much as before because I needed all my energy for night shifts on a busy isolation ward filled with cases of hepatitis. These were highly infectious so a system of barrier-nursing was in place with staff wearing gowns, masks and gloves. Many patients were seriously ill and needed close attention. Unlike a normal ward at night when most patients are asleep, these were not sleeping patients and the degree of nursing required was quite intensive. I was concerned about the safety of my pregnancy among so many infectious cases, wondering if I should discuss this with Matron, but suspected she would think it very irresponsible of me to have got myself in this predicament in the first place, so I kept quiet. Apart from the Seth Smiths and Parkers, no one else knew, and in any case we would have to break it to the parents before telling anyone else. It was still too soon to tell them; they would not have thought it decent to announce this kind of news too early.

Other news was stirring excitement at home as Elaine had at last found her soulmate and was getting married in September. Fa was giving her away and Ros was to be her one bridesmaid, in a short blue dress that Ros made herself, with a matching blue cap perched on her head, making her look like a waitress. The crystal coronet I had worn for my wedding was posted back in time for Elaine to wear with her veil, and Muz commented in a letter: 'Elaine is going to be such a bonny bride, glowing with health and happiness, she has filled out in these last few months at Bible college and is quite rounded.' Proper food at Bible college then, I thought, unless she is pregnant, which would be surprising if something like that happened alongside Bible studies.

Another surprise was to hear that the reception would not take place in the back garden at Redhill, but in another new home that Fa had found after deciding that the Redhill doctors' practice was not challenging enough for him, which any of us could have predicted. Having sold up in Kenya there was now enough money for him to indulge in a new flutter of house-buying, hoping to find another modern blot, half-built like High Torrs (a previous hideous purchase). Memories of this formidable bargain drew him back to East Grinstead where house-finding forays led him to discover new houses being built at a private residential estate called Dorman's Park. The estate was scenic and wooded with no through traffic, quite different from noisy High Torrs on the other side of East Grinstead choked with busy main roads. Some of the houses in Dorman's Park were well-established, handsome and secluded behind gates and drives. One of these was the residence of the Bush Davies Ballet School, adding to the genteel character of the place. But what attracted Fa more than anything else were new plots from which boxy red-brick houses were rising out of piles of builders' rubble. Among these was one completed house of no special merit but already named Forest Lodge and ready to move into. The purchase was quickly made and the family bundled in, the new address gracing wedding invitations handwritten by Ros in gilded calligraphy.

Elaine had met her future husband Les at Bible College, where he was preparing to become a flying missionary with MAF (Missionary Aviation Fellowship), an organisation that provided medical and supply services to foreign missions. They were ideally suited and everyone was relieved and happy that Elaine's life had found its path, while for Fa and Muz, two daughters married in the same year was an undoubted success for a family much in need of some happy events.

Spindle, now aged twenty, was still locked up at Netherne Hospital in Surrey, where he was classed as schizophrenic and treated accordingly with Largactil and other powerful sedatives. These had side-effects, turning him into a zombie with shakes and tremors that were distressing both for him and for others when he went home for weekends. I had noticed before I left that he was becoming institutionalised, walking with a stoop as if too demoralised to hold his head up, shuffling along with his hands folded in front in a way seeming to emphasise that there was nothing for those sad hands to do. His clothes never seemed to fit properly, his body too bent and wasted to provide the right sort of framework, while his skin looked as if it was never touched by sunlight. I had wanted to see his shy smile again, and light come into his eyes at any mention of those subjects that still held a keen interest for him, but the drugs had erased his personality and enthusiasms. We all felt helpless now in attempting any course of action that might offer a chance of rescue from the pit of hopelessness that had engulfed him, but the drugs and nihilistic culture of mental hospitals had already destroyed any potential for rehabilitation he might once have had. Perversely, he now felt safer in the hospital than outside, sometimes wanting Muz to take him back during weekends at home when the stress of trying to fit in with normal life was too demanding, since hospital life required nothing more than submission.

In a brutal environment where violent patients terrorised timid ones like Spindle, injuries were common and sometimes severe. His teeth had been knocked out during one attack, so he now had dentures. On another occasion his hand had been deliberately crushed in a door, leaving him with a crippled hand. Worst of all was the acute trauma of an attack that fractured his right femur, caused by a maniac jumping on top of him, but despite all this horror the hospital was now the only home he knew, however monstrous. It hardly seemed right that the rest of us should be happy, out in the world pursuing our own hopes and dreams, while he had been, as he put it: 'written off'.

In my new home I was gradually adjusting to an upside-down routine of day and night and, despite stringent precautions against cross-infection in the hepatitis ward, within a few weeks I fell ill with a fever that quickly progressed to jaundice. I was very ashamed to become a patient myself, evidently having failed in the barrier-nursing technique. Somehow I must have slipped up.

As a member of staff I was put in a private room rather than the isolation ward and Bunny was called. As soon as I told him I was pregnant, he said it was impossible for the pregnancy to survive the effects of the illness but he was more concerned about another effect he was detecting, which was an irregular heartbeat. It was bad enough having an inflamed liver, making me feel very ill, without having a heart problem as well.

Adam was dismayed and upset by all this, and blamed the hospital. He said he was writing a letter to the matron. 'What about?' I asked, alarmed, as I still felt guilty about becoming infected.

'I'm telling her that, as your husband, I am withdrawing your services and giving in your notice with immediate effect.'

'You can't do that, I have to give a month's notice. I owe them that after letting me have so much time off for the honeymoon. And anyway it was my own fault, catching hepatitis. If I had been carrying out all the precautions correctly, it should have been impossible for me to get it.'

'Bunny said being pregnant could have lowered your immunity. Did you know that? You should not have been working on a ward with highly infectious cases.'

'I didn't want to tell Matron about being pregnant, not yet. So it's my own fault whichever way you look at it.'

'Bunny said you are almost certain to miscarry, but if you don't, he will have to do a D&C anyway as the virus is so toxic that the baby will be damaged.'

Talking about it made me feel even more guilty and a bit hopeless with everything going wrong so soon in our marriage. 'It's miserable for both of us, darling,' I said. 'I feel so bad about it. I'm turning out to be a dead loss as a wife, getting sick, losing a baby, and now having to give up my job.' I wanted more than anything to feel a reassuring touch from him, but we couldn't reach out to each other for a hug. He had to stand well back from the bed to avoid catching the disease. Visiting was limited for the same reason and it was a lonely time during the long days waiting to get better. Bunny kept coming to check my heart and was kind and attentive, consoling me when I had the inevitable miscarriage, saying it was for the best and next time, he was prepared to guarantee, everything would be fine.

Despite my objections Adam wrote the letter to Matron who came herself to my bedside with sympathy and understanding, so I was able to feel less guilty about what had happened. Best of all during my time in hospital Adam had the damaged doors at home repaired and fixed back on. The worst of Alison's derelict furniture was disposed of, and those pieces that could be salvaged were screwed and glued and hammered into service, so the house was quite presentable by the time I got back. Other good news was waiting, as Cen had suggested in lieu of a pay rise he would give Adam and Johnny bonuses at the end of the year, if the dairy and crop incomes improved under their management.

Now I was back home and no longer working at the hospital, it was a new start for me with a place of my own, making curtains and organising the household just as Muz had done throughout her own married life of shifting circumstances. Simple domestic activities helped to fill the void left by the little passenger who had departed with a minimum of fuss or physical trauma, but nonetheless had been recognisable in its tiny form as the first stage of a miniature human being when it was taken away.

Adam said, when he told his mother what had happened, she had been indignant. 'Wendy must have been pregnant before you got married, otherwise how could she have had a miscarriage so soon. You better not let on to people or they will think you should have had a quiet wedding.'

'I hope you told her in no uncertain terms that I was *not* pregnant beforehand. Don't you think her remarks are rather objectionable?'

'Yes, of course I told her, but I don't think she believed me. She was quite scornful of the notion of a honeymoon baby.'

Later when we met up at the main house and were carefully avoiding mention of this subject, Alison took me aside and said, 'I hope you will wait now before getting pregnant again. Elizabeth has been trying for years and it would be very wrong if you went ahead. It's only right that the first grandchild should be hers. It would cause great distress if you jumped the gun.' I was astonished. Did Alison really expect that I might be willing to hang around indefinitely waiting for Elizabeth to come up with the favoured grandchild, or that I might agree to remain childless in deference to her if she failed to bring forth this family treasure? It was nonsensical and I was outraged at such a suggestion. When I told Adam, he patiently explained to me that Elizabeth was what, in farming terms, was called a 'shy breeder', and it was a sensitive subject in the family. Anyway we would be having a pause now, he suggested, giving time for Elizabeth to get a head start.

I still had dozens of letters to write, thanking people for wedding presents, and in addition Adam wanted me to start a clinic on the farm, providing a basic health service for the workers and their families. There were more than a hundred workers who, with wives and children, lived in a 'compound', consisting of rows of huts, with communal latrines. Water came from stand-pipes operated by pressing a stud that opened a valve so water could flow. Initially, wash rooms had been provided with standard taps, but no one seemed able to remember to turn the taps off, so they were left permanently running, wasting precious water. At one point Cen, who genuinely wanted to improve the living conditions of workers, built flushing lavatories in a pilot scheme to replace long-drop latrines. These ceramic wonders were greeted with much excitement, but there was a problem as stones and mealie cobs were traditionally used instead of toilet paper, so the system soon got filled with these and broke down. New pits were then dug to reinstate the long-drops.

I started my clinic in a store room behind the farm office where there was already a sink for washing veterinary instruments, and a cupboard full of medicines used for cattle and horses. I checked with the vet that some of the ointments were safe for human use as a few of these were more effective than anything bought at the local chemist, and I was able to get a small budget from the farm for other medicines. Remedies like cough mixture I made up myself with honey and lemon juice. Coughs were the most frequent complaint among both adults and children, probably due to smoky conditions inside huts where food was cooked on open fires. Another common complaint was *nyoka*, literally 'snake', in this case meaning worms. Alison had her own remedy which she told me was the best treatment, proved by the fact (she said) that no one ever came back for a second dose. This was a mixture of castor oil and Epsom salts with a pinch of chilli powder. The chilli, Alison explained, irritated the worms sufficiently to make them want to jump ship, aided by the evacuants.

I asked Adam about some of his mother's more eccentric remedies and he admitted that he was dubious about her doctoring skills. 'That's why I wanted you to start a proper clinic. It's good having a trained nurse on the farm and saves endless trips to the hospital.' When there were cases of pneumonia or other serious illnesses, or surgical emergencies, trips to the hospital were still necessary. This began to be a problem when people started coming from other farms to the clinic after hearing that a nurse was giving out medicines. 'You're not to use farm transport for anyone who doesn't work here,' Alison told me, annoyed at the way that the clinic was attracting strangers. Unable to leave them without help, I took them in my own car, and Nakuru General Hospital soon became as familiar to me as NWMH as I escorted patients to wards, often staying with them long enough to make sure someone was looking after them and treatment had started.

I wanted to find common ground with Alison so we could develop a rapport, but it was difficult as she never seemed to relax or let down her guard. She appeared permanently harassed and wearied by all her responsibilities, so I thought if I could help her with some of these, she might see me as an ally instead of someone who had imposed themselves on her family. One evening when I arrived to open the clinic, I found Alison standing by the door looking stressed and muttering: 'So tedious, so utterly tedious. Cen's taken the Pugget (Peugeot pickup) and gone off with the house keys.' These sorts of irritations seemed to be constant, but some were of her own making.

One of the self-imposed trials was a 'postal round' that she had invented to save stamps, and when I offered to help, she got me driving round on this task which then became maddening as I discovered how pointless it was. In order to save money on stamps, Alison decided it was cheaper to drive around the town and countryside delivering letters and packages by hand. This could take all morning and sometimes all day. Eventually, exasperated, I insisted that she explain the logic behind the scheme, as the amount of petrol used on all this driving far outweighed the cost of stamps, and my little car was clocking up a huge mileage. 'The petrol is free,' she said, waving a hand towards the farm fuel pumps. I asked Adam about this. 'Of course it isn't free,' he said. 'The farm has to buy it just like anyone else. I think it's simply another way of distracting herself, like going to auctions. Maybe it eases her mind in some way.'

Why does her mind need easing, I wondered. She's got everything she needs right here in front of her. She has plenty of help, so she's free to do what she likes. Why can't she just enjoy living a happy healthy life among the animals and natural beauty of the farm? I thought about the Hemsteds and how every day was greeted with enthusiasm and purpose. I felt a pang, missing them, but my life was here now.

Adam took a day off when things were quiet and he could leave his African assistant, Arap Milgo, to look after the dairy. He didn't have regular days or weekends off but would make time for polo on Sundays, and on weekdays I went with him when he was exercising the ponies. We would ride to the top of the farm checking on herds and pastures along the way; inspecting water troughs, fences, gates, all the usual things, while stopping to watch birds and any other wildlife we came across. On telegraph wires there would be lines of bee-eaters, waiting to intercept flying insects when they would swoop down in a graceful arc snapping their beaks on the bee or whatever it was that might have been passing. In that dry country all kinds of small or larger animals and birds flourished among the trees and bushes. Sometimes guinea fowl or partridge flew up with beating wings, startled by our approach, or quail scurrying in small flocks along the path. Occasionally a reedbuck lifted its head to stare as we went by, unafraid, seeming not to recognise humans on horseback as threatening.

On the way back we always looked forward to giving the ponies their heads on the flat ground of Cen's new landing strip. At the age of nearly sixty he had learnt to fly, and had bought his own plane, a 5-seater Cessna, to avoid the tedium of driving hundreds of miles to board meetings around the country. As a successful commercial farmer he held several directorships. A hangar was built at one end of the strip and every time the plane took off or landed, children would run from the nearby compound to watch.

At home, Mungai was becoming more erratic as home-brewed beer took hold of him and his dark moods increased, so that even when he was able to shuffle into work, his presence was often more disturbing than helpful. When he started coming to work with a *panga* (machete) grasped in one hand as he plodded around the rooms, this became increasingly alarming. He was in a particularly belligerent mood one morning as he faced me with bloodshot eyes, disputing something I had asked him to do, and raised the panga menacingly. That was enough for me this time: he had to go. When Adam heard about the incident, he sacked Mungai on the spot and I think he was glad to go, grumbling that when the Memsahib arrived, trouble came to the house and the bwana should be sending her away instead of him.

There were always itinerant job-seekers who turned up each day at the back door looking for work, so replacing Mungai was easily done and a very cheerful, tall, respectable man called Juma took over. He soon had the household under control, which was a relief as we now had steady numbers of visitors coming to stay, or calling in. As soon as it was known that Adam's house had a new cook (me) and new beds, those friends who came from distant farms to do their shopping in Nakuru were glad of a room for the night, or refreshments after a long drive. These included Adam's bachelor friends who came to town on the prowl for unattached girls and would call in for a few beers and the latest chat on who was getting off with whom. They would also be on the lookout for a bit of bird shooting with Adam, or fishing on the river, or, best of all, buffalo hunts.

When preparations were underway for a hunt one day Johnny arrived to join the group, and just before everyone was ready to leave, not wanting to be caught short later on, he strolled to the old long-drop that still stood halfway down the garden. The others were impatient to go and there was a shout: 'Where the hell is Johnny?'

'He's in the thunder box,' Adam said, 'taking his time.'

'I've got a solution for that,' someone said, and went to open the boot of his car. Inside there was a small stash of thunder flashes. Taking one, he walked down the garden to the back of the long-drop where there was a large rat hole at the base of the wooden hut. Lighting the fuse he pushed the thunder flash through the hole and waited for an explosion that would eject Johnny in short order. Everyone watched in expectation of a bedraggled Johnny being blasted out, but there was a hang-fire and nothing happened for a few moments. The force of a thunder flash exploding in a confined space magnifies the effect and soon there was an almighty muffled roar, followed by the whole hut lifting off its base. It rose spectacularly in slow motion as the wooden seat inside shattered and Johnny flew out like a cork, the hut crashing to one side and falling apart. This was followed by further roars, this time of hysterical laughter and language as Johnny ran around disorientated until he was brushed down and placated, before being bundled into one of the cars with everyone else as they set off for more follies chasing buffalo.

I didn't want Adam to turn into a tame husband brought into line by new responsibilities as had happened, I noticed, to some of the other young Kenya men when they got married, their characters changed and high spirits subdued. I was happy to stay at home while Adam went off with his friends, not feeling as energetic as usual myself. I had recovered from the hepatitis but was not back to normal in the way I had been before. The queasiness had returned along with a depleted appetite, and I felt something was wrong.

It was at this point that a letter arrived from Fa saying he was coming back to Kenya with a new job as Medical Officer for Nakuru District Council, responsible for health services in rural areas. Kenya had achieved Independence this year with Jomo Kenyatta as President heading a post-colonial government and there was a feeling of hopeful optimism in the country. It was a new beginning and Fa wanted to be part of it, having abandoned his previously pessimistic view of the country's future. In true Fa style, he was arriving imminently, and would stay with us while he looked for somewhere to rent. Muz would follow later, he said, while Ros had now left home and was at Corsham College near Bath, doing a degree in Fine Art.

I was delighted with Fa's arrival and the novelty of having him as a guest in my own house, especially as he was unstinting in praise of my efforts at establishing the farm clinic, and transforming Adam's house with its spectacular views and garden full of birds. He lost no time in charming Cen and Alison, easing tensions in that direction, and former patients converged from every direction eager to see him again. He was happier than I had seen him in years, going off with a rod to fish for trout in the river, or striding across the wide acres of the farm with binoculars.

At the end of our garden the land dropped to a ravine, its steep sandy sides dotted with holes where bee-eaters had their burrowing nests, and this was a magnet for Fa. The ravine was the widest part of an earthquake fault that ran in a line across the lower reaches of the farm, where its deeper recesses provided a wilderness of tumbling rocks and undergrowth for hyraxes and other small mammals to flourish. These were visited at times by a solitary leopard who feasted on them before moving to the next site of easy meals. We knew when the leopard was in residence because we could hear his hoarse barking coughs at night, but we seldom caught sight of him. Rock pythons that normally lived close to the river also made visits to the ravine when food was scarce, and sometimes emerged from its depths to drape themselves in one of our garden trees while they digested a large meal, the bulge clearly visible among their coils.

All this was a joy for Fa after enduring long months struggling with the alien environment of English suburbia and the NHS, that he complained had become a production line with no time for doctors to look after patients properly anymore. In Redhill there had been no leopards or pythons at the end of the garden, and no breakfasts on a sunny veranda overlooking great views. At one of these breakfasts when my lack of appetite made me shudder as vinegar was being sprinkled on the avocadoes, Fa looked up and said, 'You know what's going on, don't you?'

'No. I don't know what it is. I just don't seem to have got back to normal after the hepatitis.'

'You're free of symptoms now, and your liver is back to normal. I'm surprised you don't recognise what your own body is trying to tell you. It's obvious to me that you're pregnant again,' he said.

'I can't be, it's too soon after the miscarriage. Bunny said nothing would happen for several months due to the effects of the illness.'

'Well, I'm telling you all the signs are present, and you should go to Bunny for confirmation.'

I went to Bunny and after examining me he shook his head in surprise, 'You're about ten weeks into another pregnancy. You can't have given yourself much time off,' he laughed. 'But all seems well and you should be able to deliver round about June next year if all goes to plan, and you avoid any more hazards.'

My first thought was how to tell Adam, but when the moment came, he said he had already guessed, and he was delighted to have the chance of a second shot so soon after the first one had gone astray.

CHAPTER 5

Fa had arrived in time for Christmas and was invited to join the rest of us at Glanjoro for Christmas dinner, which was really lunch. This annual event was what Adam called a compulsory parade, and now that we were married there was no suggestion that we would spend the day anywhere else, not just this year but every year into the future. Immediate family like Elizabeth and Peter, and Johnny, were automatically included, while aunts, uncles, cousins and various strays arrived for tea. Alison had a strict regime involving her larder which was kept locked, to be opened only at set times to dispense measured amounts of food to Benjie the cook. Potatoes were counted out and vegetables rationed in the same way. When it came to tea leaves, no matter how many people were to be served from a single pot, one teaspoon of leaves was thought quite sufficient. Alison liked weak tea, which was the genteel way to serve it in her opinion. Only gardeners and labourers drank strong tea. Pouring the tea and handing round cups on Christmas Day was a junior wife's role, so I was the one and learnt later to bring a small packet of tea leaves with me to add a few each time the pot was refilled, otherwise Cen would shout: 'Why are we having gnat's pee?' Blaming it on me, when he knew very well the effect of Alison's miserly rationing.

After Christmas, Fa announced he had rented a flat above Kishan Singh's garage on the main road into town and wanted me to go and see what might be needed to make it presentable for Muz, so he could send for her. Nothing should have been a surprise to me by now when it came to Fa's choice of places to live, but this was a slum, cramped and squalid, looking as if it might have been recently vacated by tenants in a state of dire poverty. Probably turned out for arrears of rent poor things, I thought, and when Fa cheerfully went on to tell me that Kishan Singh was doing him a favour by reducing the rent, I was certain my hunch had been right about the previous occupants. 'You can't live here,' I told Fa. 'It's a flea pit. You shouldn't even think of bringing Muz here.'

I felt fearful for my parents: what had happened to them? Becoming drifters, ending up in a shabby flat, with Fa in a dead-end job. And what of Babs? Had she at last packed herself off and that was why Fa and Muz were making yet another new start? Forest Lodge had not been sold and would be kept as a base in England. 'Just in case,' Fa said.

I had a friend, John Fulcher, whose mother lived on the outskirts of town and had a guest cottage in her garden, where no guests came to stay any more since she had become elderly and frail. The guest house was small and quaint, with its own kitchen and sitting room, just right for Muz I thought. It was arranged that Fa could stay there and Muz would join him in due course. Mrs Fulcher was glad to have a doctor at hand, and the situation was ideal for all of us as the little house was on my route into Nakuru for shopping, so I could call in. A letter was sent to Muz telling her that all was ready for her to join Fa, but she replied that it would be several months before she was able to leave Forest Lodge as tenants had to be found.

Meanwhile, another arrival caused much excitement, and speculation, as a friend of mine from England, Andrena, wrote to say that she was coming to Kenya and would like to stay with us while looking for a job. She explained this sudden appearance after a long gap in communication by saying that she had broken up with a boyfriend and needed a complete change of scene. Adam was suspicious. 'Do you think she's pregnant?' he suggested 'Needing to come here where no one knows her, while you as a good friend will look after her.'

'Andrena is one of the most sensible people I've ever met. I can't see her getting pregnant by mistake,' I said, 'but it could happen to anyone I suppose.'

When we went to Nairobi to meet her off the plane, we joked about checking on her waistline as she came down the aircraft steps, Adam being wary of the possibility that he might have two pregnant girls to look after. But Andrena looked as trim as ever, and instantly captivated Adam with her robust personality and golden-girl looks. It was going to be a pleasure having her with us. She would be a great addition to our circle of friends, we both agreed.

One of these friends was Veronica Finch, known as Finchie, who was the organiser of wild weekend parties generally held at those game lodges where uninhibited behaviour was tolerated. Finchie was hosting one of these parties the next weekend at Samburu Lodge and had invited us, but Adam refused to go as he said there would be a lot of childish behaviour which he didn't approve of. However, he said, if I wanted to go and misbehave with the rest of them, taking Andrena with me, then it was up to us and we could take the Land Rover.

It was a perfect opportunity to show Andrena some spectacular areas of countryside as we drove the many miles north, passing Mount Kenya and the great undulating highlands of Laikipia which were sparsely inhabited except by wild animals. Then into thorny scrubland where long-necked gerenuk (a type of gazelle) thrived, looking sleek and supremely graceful as they stretched on their hind legs to nibble the tops of spiky bushes.

When we arrived at the lodge there was Finchie presiding over an unruly collection of young unattached singles that included Johnny, with bucolic events well underway. The only married couple were Hugh and Jo Trent who seemed curiously out of place and were making valiant efforts to raise the tone of proceedings, marshalling everyone into a game-viewing excursion as a sober alternative to other revels.

Andrena needed no persuading on the game trail suggestion, but while we were following tracks some way from the lodge, there was a sudden downpour of rain and a ravine that we had crossed earlier became choked with mud. One of the vehicles got stuck and Jo, with the sturdy voice and figure of a sergeant major, took charge, rallying us to push. Andrena was anxious about my delicate state and told me to sit by the side of the road while others did the pushing. I tried to fade into the background, but Jo, looking up after another heave on the stuck vehicle, spied me not doing anything, and shouted: 'What are you doing loitering over there? Come and do your bit.' Andrena squared up to her, 'Leave Wendy alone. You've got me instead.'

Later when everyone was back, bathed and dined, skinny dipping in the dark swimming pool lit by stars was the next attraction. Dave Dewar had driven his pick-up close to the pool so headlights could be switched on just as Johnny was positioning himself for a dive off the board. Arms raised, he was caught in the spotlight, not an inch or detail of his pale white body escaping exposure. Not that he cared, he was fully tanked up, and so was Dave. The only person not drinking was me, and being sober gave me a clear view of proceedings so I was able to enjoy them in a voyeuristic kind of way. Adam was right, it was childish, but it was part of being young, fit, and untroubled. Time enough later for burdens, as most of the people at Finchie's weekend parties would be shackled by family responsibilities all too soon.

Andrena fitted into Kenya life as naturally as she would have done anywhere, whether in London or the outback of Australia. Undaunted by odd challenges she got herself a job at the coast typing letters for two off-beat characters, Robin Bewg and Muff Becker, who were building a small hotel on Turtle Bay at Watamu. There was no office at the building site and Andrena sat with her typewriter on the beach, wearing a bikini. The emerging hotel was named Seafarers, and next to it along the beach was Ocean Sports, owned by Ian and Dulcie Pritchard. These were the first hotels built on the bay, which up to that time had few buildings or inhabitants of any sort living beside its crystal blue waters, sheltered from the open sea by a coral reef. A coral headland divided the bay into two parts with a small cove known as the Blue Lagoon on one side and, on the other, Turtle Bay itself, distinguished by a turtle-shaped island lying close offshore, inside the reef. The coral reef remained pristine, as yet undiscovered by tourists and others who would later take the shells of living creatures as souvenirs, or to sell, destroying the exquisite submarine world that had remained untouched for thousands if not millions of years.

Ian knew every shape and crevice of the reef, and the bay with its tides and moods. Building the small laid-back resort of Ocean Sports provided a base for him to pioneer new forms of recreational sports in and on the water. One of these was a novel type of water ski: an alternative to the standard ski, it was a single disc, towed by a power boat. It worked well in deep water, but there was an incident in shallow water when Ian was skimming close to the beach: the disc flipped and struck sand, flinging him backwards. He was carried out of the water, conscious, but could not stand. It was said by people who were there, that he could still move his legs, so it was thought that his spine was undamaged and he was put in the back of a vehicle and driven to hospital in Mombasa. Tragically, he did not recover those initial movements and was paralysed from the waist down for the rest of his life, a very cruel fate for someone so vigorous in body and mind. Dulcie was determined to press on with the development of Ocean Sports and Ian gave directions from his wheelchair, a depleted figure, but never defeated. He adopted a Giriama puppy, naming him Dudu. Giriama dogs are a small, spotted coast breed, and this tiny animal sat on the tray of Ian's wheelchair keeping him company during the long hot languorous days when he would gaze out to sea, watching the fishing boats going out early and coming back at sunset with coloured flags indicating their catch. The small beach hotel of Ocean Sports became known to Kenya residents as 'Open Shorts' for its informality, and was a popular place to stay, with Seafarers next door.

Our mail at Glanjoro was collected from the post office each day by Cen or Alison, and any letters addressed to Mrs A. Hill she assumed were intended for her, leading to some confusion as I was now Mrs A. (Adam) Hill. The confusion was made worse by Alison thinking it was helpful to reply on my behalf to invitations that arrived addressed to me in this way. One of these was from the Rocco family who had a farm on the north shore of Lake Naivasha where they sometimes gave lavish parties. The invitation was picked up by Alison and the next time she saw me she said, 'An invitation arrived in the post for you and Ad from the Roccos, for one of their parties, and I've replied for you, declining. You wouldn't want to go. I'm sure you don't really know them.'

'Yes, I do know them, they have been friends of my family for years,' I said, indignant at her presumption. 'Have you still got the invitation?'

'No, I didn't keep it, thinking it could not be of any interest. And by the way I've had a letter from Joan Curry, an old family friend. Her daughter

Pam has left finishing school in Switzerland and embarked on a life of travelling. She wants to come and stay while she is in Kenya. I thought, as she is more your age and Ad's, she could stay with you.'

The subject having switched so nimbly from the Roccos to this Curry friend, infuriated me with its further presumption, but I bit back my anger, reminding myself that I was trying to be on good terms with Alison. I agreed we would have Pam, and it would be interesting to meet her. I was aware how low in spirits Alison had been lately since Elizabeth and Peter were selling their farm (for African resettlement), and were leaving Kenya to go and live in Ireland. Alison had a very close bond with Elizabeth and this move was a heavy blow.

I was thinking about this when Alison continued, 'The Currys like to come over from England during the shooting season, inviting themselves. We've had them several times. But when we asked if we could go and stay with them one year for the Royal Show, Joan made excuses. So I don't feel inclined to have Pam.'

'When is she arriving?'

'We don't know yet. I'll reply to Joan saying that you will be glad to have Pam, and maybe she will let us know when to expect her.'

I had been worried about breaking the news to Alison that, despite her advice, I was pregnant again, and wondered if this was a good moment to tell her. I took a breath and plunged in. 'Will you be going to the Royal Show this year? Because it seems we have another baby on the way and June is the month Bunny thinks it might be due.' I finished in a rush, nervous about her reaction. Alison looked at me, astonished. 'So soon?' Her startled gaze assessed my shape. 'Are you sure?'

'Yes, Bunny has confirmed it.' I felt as if I needed to apologise, but my happiness and Adam's at this unexpected event was too great to allow any disapproval from Alison to spoil it. She recovered herself slightly. 'Well, it's a pity it clashes with the show. In any case, we couldn't be here when the child arrives as poor Sis (her name for Elizabeth) will need propping up. It would be too awful for her to think of us here with your baby arriving when she can't have one of her own, and so far away, stuck in Ireland. I will have to go to her.' Alison looked forlorn as she added, 'She will have to be told, of course. Oh dear, it's very unfortunate.' It seemed to me even more unfortunate that Alison was unable to express pleasure at the prospect of a grandchild, even if it wasn't produced by Elizabeth. Seeing her standing there dejected and distracted by this latest setback, her nickname 'Auntie Glum' (unkindly spoken by others behind her back) seemed cruel but apt.

There were many weddings that year among my friends and the marriage of Storm Lyons was a major event. She was sparky and popular with everyone, fending off her many admirers while enjoying life as a single girl. She could afford to be choosy, so we were stunned when she announced she was marrying one of the more languid members of the bachelor set, who somehow had captured her over a single weekend, taking her on safari and during this brief interlude claiming the prize coveted by so many. Those who had fancied their chances included Johnny who was one of the hopefuls, along with John Clarke and Robert Howden (a Robert Redford lookalike) who, among others, joined the mournful throng of rejected suitors at Storm's wedding.

It was a grand wedding at Mweiga, where Storm's family had a large accommodating home that is now the Aberdare Country Club. Many of the other guests were friends of ours and I looked forward to being part of this gregarious circle. There was a general air of excitement among my age group now beginning to pair off and start their own families, and this was a dizzy time.

At country weddings, guests were accommodated by friends on farms nearby and we were allocated as house guests to an adorably eccentric host, Sandy Birkbeck. His father was a major general and the family illustrious, but Sandy was very self-deprecating and insecure in himself in a way that was endearing but baffling, as every advantage in life would seem to be his. He was a wildly generous and completely disorganised host. When we arrived at his house late that night in some degree of fatigue after a boisterous post-wedding party, no one could find which rooms were theirs or how many people were expected. This led to a scrum as a situation of multiple occupancy developed with many guests too inebriated to be aware that they were climbing into a bed already occupied. Sandy, well past midnight, attempting to disentangle couples finding themselves in the wrong room, wandered in a state of extreme agitation between guest rooms, wearing a diaphanous negligee he had borrowed, explaining that he had no pyjamas. At one point, becoming exasperated, he seized a bull whip and ran around cracking it in a vain attempt to restore order. The sight of Sandy with a whip in one hand while the other clutched at nylon frills attempting to cover a naked hairy frontage, remains a memorable image of that night. It was a long time before the sounds of heavy feet and querulous voices subsided long enough for sleep to take over.

The next morning after an epic and very late breakfast, rugs and cushions were taken outside to spread on the lawn so people could rest their throbbing heads. I stayed inside looking out into the garden from the window seat of a wide bow window, glad to be sober and glad to be alone in my vantage point after a whole day and half a night of noisy exertions. Adam had gone off somewhere, wanting to clear his head, he said. A short distance from the window there was a flag pole, planted in the lawn, and this became a focus of attention as Robert Howden attempted to climb it, egged on by recumbent figures scattered on the grass. A pineapple had been tied to the lanyard which normally hoisted a flag, and the object of the exercise was for Robert to place the pineapple on top of the pole when he got there. Everyone was cheering and taunting him: 'Weak knees, Robert, get a grip, shin up the bloody thing.'

When he was halfway up, the pole started to tilt, very slowly at first, and then without a moment to prevent imminent catastrophe, it came thundering down and crashed through the window where I was sitting, missing me by inches. I was covered in glass fragments and pieces of pineapple that had shattered on impact, with Robert deposited among the debris, while a crowd of curious faces appeared at the smashed window anxious to see if we were all right.

After brushing ourselves off, neither of us was found to have even a scratch, but I was shaken and wanted the reassurance of Adam beside me. Sandy was very solicitous, 'You need looking after. Where the hell is Adam?'

'He went to one of the barns. With Finchie,' someone said helpfully.

'Oh, *really*,' I replied, going off to look for them. But it was not what anyone might have thought as I found them reclining in a stack of hay, laughing and joking with transparent innocence. Finchie was never a serious flirt. They did look bashful though when they heard what had happened, and we all went off for a drive around the farm to revive ourselves.

Pam had already arrived when we got home, and had installed herself in our one spare room with quantities of luggage and instructions to the staff on the attentions she required, being used to English country-house standards. This was a very different kind of visitor from the usual straggly ones who arrived dusty and dishevelled with possibly one change of clothes. It became evident that the accommodation offered in our rather spartan house was not the kind that Pam was accustomed to, and friends of ours invited for lunch or dinner were not much approved of either. She seemed to have a particular animosity towards male guests. Instead of being pleased to meet young men of her own age, or older men with whom she might perhaps share an interest in travelling or world affairs, she was ready with a sharp put-down if any of them tried to engage her in conversation. Those around the table at dinner often included Andy who was a frequent visitor, and Johnny who came several times a week, as he had no cook. He was a kind, charming and thoughtful person who I imagined Pam would particularly enjoy meeting, but she was as dismissive of him as the others, and was only slightly less condescending to female guests. Normally it would be thought bad manners to behave rudely in someone else's house, but Pam remained aloof from such considerations.

When she had been with us a number of days, she explained that she was waiting for a money order to arrive from her father as she had run out of funds to continue her travels and, needing a place to stay meanwhile, it was convenient to remain with us close to Nakuru where one of the banks would receive her money. She didn't seem to have any plans for a career or a job, instead relying on financial support from her family. I had never met anyone like her before and was fascinated. Her presumption that she was entitled to a cash supply on demand, her air of superiority, her absorption with herself, how she looked, her expensive clothes and cosmetics, all this was intriguing. Apart from which, as a friend of the family she was welcome to any hospitality I could provide, though I noticed she took this for granted, believing that we were honoured by her presence.

'How are you getting on with Pam?' Alison asked.

I was careful to be circumspect. 'She's very independent for someone her age, travelling alone; quite fearless in fact.'

Alison sniffed. 'It's easy to be fearless when you are cushioned from the normal realities of life. Her mother has money, you know, as well as her father. Family money in each case.'

When I didn't reply, not knowing what to say to this, she went on, 'Cen and I will be leaving soon for the show, staying first at Howleigh (Cen's family home in Somerset), then on to Ireland for Sis and Peter. You will have to send a cable when the baby arrives.'

I would have liked to have Alison near me for the birth as Muz was not coming over in time. I was nervous about this first experience of childbirth and felt the need of an older woman who had been through it herself to be with me. At least Fa was here, I reassured myself, and if anything went wrong he would know what to do.

All the rooms in our house were set out in traditional Kenya fashion facing a veranda along the front, doors opening onto this space for ventilation and easy access. With a steady stream of guests occupying the second bedroom, it could not be used as a nursery and the only suitable space for a baby's cot and equipment was a small lobby between the two bedrooms and shared bathroom. Alison unearthed from long years of storage an heirloom cradle that had served generations of Hill babies (or it might have been Blacks), and this was set up in the lobby with a chair and small cupboard for baby clothes.

The cradle was Victorian with a traditional A-shaped canopy above a rectangular frame balanced on spindly metal legs crossing in an X-shape like a deck chair. Suspended from the frame was a sturdy canvas cot-base and mattress, the whole thing designed to be easily folded up when not in use. Muslin drapes completed the final effect when all had been assembled. I felt privileged to be handed an heirloom, along with a wicker hamper of Victorian baby clothes. These included a vintage christening gown, hand-sewn with layers of lace and frills, it even had tiny starched epaulettes edged with lace on the shoulders like little wings.

Muz had been busy knitting and sending parcels of matinee jackets and bootees, so these were put in folded piles into the small nursery cupboard, with flannel nightgowns and terry-toweling nappies that I was able to buy in Nakuru. Babies did not wear all-in-one garments covering most of their bodies, and the nightgowns were designed to be loose to allow air circulation. Latest advice on baby care was that they should be placed on their stomachs for sleeping but I felt instinctively that this was wrong, and babies should be placed on their sides as had been done at the hospital during my training.

I was having a very trouble-free and easy pregnancy, able to continue with all my usual activities, running the clinic and exercising polo ponies, but not joining in buffalo hunts. Adam wanted to fit in one last safari before the baby arrived and when he heard that Gerry Edwards at Rumuruti was having lion problems again, it seemed a perfect opportunity. I could come too, he said, since there was a good comfortable camping site on Gerry's ranch which was familiar territory after his many hunting expeditions there with Tony. Pam had departed the instant her money arrived, and we had a free run with no more imminent visitors. It was decided that we would take a gun bearer but no camp staff as I could stay in camp and look after it, while Adam and the gun bearer Kibee went after the lions that had been killing Gerry's beef cattle. The safari this time would not include the luxury of a tent or camp beds, because sleeping out under the stars would be more romantic, Adam said. Kibee, however, would not share this romantic experience, and would sleep in the Land Rover.

Gerry invited us to spend the first night at his house, glad of the company as he lived alone, constantly at war against lions and other besetting problems in the immensity of that wild region. He lived a sparse life and his guest room demonstrated this, but he was very proud of an addition to the guest bathroom that he had designed himself. This was a bath sculpted out of cement like a huge grey tank occupying most of the room, with hoses delivering hot and cold water. Gerry explained that it took a couple of hours to fill the bath so this would be started in good time for us to bathe and change before dinner.

When the bath was ready, having been filled by house staff almost as worn and gnarled as Gerry himself, I stood on the bathmat wondering how I was going to get in, or get out, scaling the sturdy walls reaching to waist height. 'I'll give you a leg up,' Adam offered. 'Like getting on a horse, but be careful you don't drown.' The walls were gritty, and so was the whole inner surface of the bath as the cement had the consistency of mortar used for laying bricks. Not a situation for lingering, but there was room for both of us to have a good splash as we marvelled at Gerry's ingenuity and the novelty of it.

It was surprising to find, next day, on the great scrubby plains of the ranch an unexpectedly cool and shady campsite beside a natural pool bubbling from rocks. The water was deep and clear, but Adam had no time to stop and admire it, being impatient to set off with Kibee to track the lions. My own task was to organise a rough kitchen ready for cooking game meat they expected to bring back. But first I must lower bottles of beer, tied together on long pieces of string, into the pool to get cold. When a camp table and chairs had been set up, I could then indulge my own impatience which had nothing to do with hunting: the pool glimmered blue and sublime, waiting for me to slip into its inviting depths.

Mid-morning is a time when sounds become more intense as the sun climbs and the bush starts to hum and crackle with heat, while insects buzz among dry leaves. Easing myself into the pool's deliciously enveloping water and dipping down to submerge myself, I missed the sound of a vehicle approaching until it stopped at the campsite some yards away. I was puzzled, thinking that Adam must have come back early, but the vehicle was not ours, and the men emerging from it were wearing camouflage instead of khaki bush gear. When they got closer to the pool, I saw they were British Army personnel, presumably from a training team in the area. They would not expect to find a solitary girl bobbing about nymph-like in this pool, and must have been even more surprised when I clambered out exposing a bulging stomach above skimpy knickers and nothing else. But they were gentlemen, betraying no hint of discomposure. When I had wrapped myself in a towel, they introduced themselves and asked permission to swim, as if the pool were my own personal preserve on which they had intruded. Later, refreshed, they handed round beers from their own supply, and ration packs, eager to chat about the locality and what I was doing there.

Adam and Kibee did return earlier than expected, streaked with dust and sweat, after a fruitless time following old spoor that petered out where a scuffle had taken place, but they would return next day to pick up new tracks. As no meat had been shot, it was a tin-can supper and an early night, so the hunters could start again at first light. I struggled to get into my zip-less sleeping bag, finding that it didn't adapt easily to my shape, needing an extra pair of hands to strain at pulling it over the bump. 'Bugger that,' Adam remarked helpfully. 'You'll have to do it standing up, like getting into a sack for a sack race. You'll have to jump up and down, pulling at the same time,' he advised, and with a few jumps I toppled over like a porpoise, the bag reaching to my armpits. Lying there on the iron-hard ground, I tried to conjure Adam's promised sensations of romance from the great firmament of stars above, and attempted to roll over towards him, but he was already asleep.

I woke later feeling cold, and my back, flat against the baked earth, ached. Turning onto my side was no better as the ground grated against my hip. Lying there, planning to scrape a little hole next day in that spot to accommodate my hip for the following nights, I became aware of something small and scratchy wriggling inside my sleeping bag, and another crawling creature trying to get in, out of the cold. What were they? Might they be scorpions? I decided to lie very still after that, remembering a friend who had been sleeping on the ground, camping al fresco like us, when a snake slithered in and curled up on his chest. Terrified that it might be venomous and sink its fangs into him if he moved, he lay rigid all night. At last, when dawn came, the snake uncurled itself and on sliding out, its beady eyes came face to face with his wide-awake ones. They stared at each other tight-lipped for a few seconds before the snake decided one look was enough, and shot off.

There was no sympathy for my night terror from the hunters at day break as they boiled tea and set off again, but I resolved to be better equipped in future. In any event there would be no more safaris for me before the baby arrived, as once back home, I was due to have a final check-up with Bunny whose estimate now was a birth date of 16th June 1964.

CHAPTER 6

A letter arrived from Muz with two pieces of news. Elaine and Les had been posted to Nairobi where MAF had a base, and Elaine was expecting a baby in September just three months after ours. Fa was very excited about this, hoping it would encourage Muz to come and join the rest of us soon. The Fulcher guest cottage was ready and waiting to receive her. It even had a small tidy garden that she could adopt and transform, putting down roots along with new plants, I thought hopefully. She and Fa were still young enough, in their fifties, to reassemble the strands of their life that had become tangled and disorganised by Fa's restlessness. Babs would not be able to follow him to Kenya, I reasoned, as he and Muz had too many devoted friends who would not tolerate any incursion. Our family was coming together again after so many years in the wilderness. We were back in Kenya, and now our babies were being born here, they would be Kenyans.

Feeling exceptionally well and healthy I was certain the imminent birth of mine would be easy and quick. There was an obstetric fad in vogue among doctors at the time for inducing babies on the day they were due if all other indications were favourable. Bunny, who always had his finger on the pulse of any new developments, was keen to practise this latest trend on me. My own maternity training tended to rely on leaving babies to come when they were ready, so at first I was dubious about intervention, but expectant mothers are impatient after nine months waiting, so any chance to hasten the arrival is tempting.

The first induction stage was what Bunny called a 'sweep'. Nothing very drastic, just a bit of a delve, giving some flicks to the sac holding the baby, intended as a wake-up call, like a few brisk knocks on the door. If this produced no result after twenty-four hours, then it was a 'stretch and sweep', repeated as often as necessary to prod things into action. After a couple of these I started having a few desultory pains and Bunny decided I should go into hospital to await further developments. The maternity unit at NWMH was in a separate wing, with private rooms and a nursery where rows of identical cots stood in line, the labour room tucked away at one end. Having installed me, Adam went back to work expecting to return in the evening to greet two of us. It was now Thursday, 18th June, and nothing much happened all day, so that when Adam arrived later with flowers, we both felt disappointed at the delay. He joked that the baby was making us wait for the sake of a grand entrance (imagining the kind of theatrical entry he himself liked to contrive on special occasions), but I just wanted a quick arrival with no flummery or drama.

By the next evening when Bunny came on his evening round there was no doubt that labour had begun in earnest and all seemed to be going well. Fa had come to visit but appeared nervous, which surprised me. I felt a need to reassure him and thought what a strange reversal it was, since normally he would be the one giving calm reassurance, but this time he was not in charge of the birth and it may have been unnerving to find himself side-lined as a bystander.

All Saturday and Sunday, Fa and Adam stayed beside me as this truly laborious process dragged on, but there was no sign of the baby appearing and the lack of progress began to be worrying. Adam was getting steadily more anxious as I became exhausted and delirious with pain and drugs and, in extremis, he started swallowing Purple Hearts from the supply Joan had given me after what she perceived as proof of their success at the wedding. He now sat beside my bed in a trance, pretending to read a book in order to appear composed, while holding it upside down. George Swannell, the vicar who had married us, arrived after Sunday service to say prayers for me and give a little homily.

'Childbirth is a great danger for women,' he declared in a voice heavy with doom. 'It is the greatest danger that women face in the whole of their lifetime.' Pausing with a polite cough to make sure I was listening, he continued, 'I will pray that you are delivered safely,' and went on droning similar platitudes as I convulsed with another contraction. He stood over me with two fingers placed on my forehead, saying prayers as if I were dying, and it spooked me through the haze of brain fog as I tried to fight another pain. I just wished he would go and leave me to die in peace without sanctimonious accompaniments.

Evidently it was a day for priests to be out on Sunday visits as no sooner had George left, than Father Prunty, the Roman Catholic priest who was a good friend of mine, after a few jaunty knocks at the door, bounced in. He settled himself on the bed, and without any preliminaries, launched into a round of the latest jokes doing the circuit of Irish religious orders, recognising that the mood in the room called for an antidote to the tension holding me in a vice of agony and terror. Gradually it worked, at least partially, and I felt immense gratitude and affection for this young man who understood without hesitation what was going on, and what was needed. A matter of simple empathy requiring no theological underwriting.

I had first met Father Patrick Prunty at a party where he was standing with a cigarette in one hand and whisky glass in the other, at the centre of a group of animated girls, laughing and chatting, looking entirely at ease. When I could talk to him alone I asked how he, as a celibate, was able to avoid feeling attracted to so many pretty girls. His reply has stayed with me as it was said with real sentiment:

'Yes, that is a very particular question, and a particular sacrifice that I make for my calling, but with no regret.' He was only twenty-five.

When Bunny came later on his evening round, it was noted that I had been in labour for more than two days and was still only at a halfway stage. Bunny was not in good shape himself, looking crumpled, crestfallen and uncertain what to do, his face blotchy and hands shaking. 'I need another drink. Then I'll come back,' he said, not very convincingly. Fa had become extremely concerned and was checking the baby's heartbeat with the midwives to reassure himself that it was holding up. It was, so far, and this was a good sign but was not a reason for inaction as Fa knew very well; babies need to be extracted before any crisis point is reached. With Bunny in charge, Fa was in a difficult position, unable to take any action himself, waiting for Bunny to come back. He didn't come back that evening and was not answering his phone. The midwives were busy with another baby arriving, and when I heard the first cries of that baby I felt a pang, wondering if I would ever hear mine, or if either of us would survive.

All that night I felt myself getting weaker, as if my body was giving up, having done its best, but the baby was stuck and no amount of muscular power was ever going to be able to move it. Adam had been sent home for a sleep as there was nothing for him to do, and when Fa arrived in the morning he decided to take charge since there was still no sign of Bunny appearing. Some of the other mothers in the wing were patients of Geoff Bird, Fa's former assistant, who now had his own practice in the town and was very well thought of. Fa wasted no time once it was obvious that Bunny was out of action, explaining the situation to Geoff and asking him to come and take over urgently.

When Geoff came into the room there was an immediate sense of relief and after examining me he said, 'We need to get you into the delivery room straight away, and as soon as everything is in place, your baby will be born in less than ten minutes.' I was amazed, hardly able to believe such a sudden and decisive outcome was possible after the interminable days and nights of inaction. The midwives were ready with a trolley and swiftly wheeled me off to the room that I had been waiting so long to reach.

Within minutes of arriving Geoff gave me a mighty injection of something that floated me up to the ceiling where I revolved in a state of weightlessness, seeming to look down on myself being hooked up to poles on the delivery bed. Geoff was putting together a ventouse extractor and when this was ready he clamped it, not at all gently, onto what I assumed was the baby's head stuck somewhere higher up than where it should have been. The force of this action brought me down from the ceiling with a thud, landing back in my bloated body where a tugging and pulling of unimagined agony started, like the 'drawn' part of being hung, drawn and quartered, I thought. I yelled at Geoff to stop before some terrible damage was done, and tried to kick him away with my foot. He shouted back at me, and then with a final hefty pull something gave way and there was a spluttering cry as a navy blue slippery figure of fury was caught and bundled onto my chest. Eyes tight shut, mouth wide screaming outrage, no need for any suction, a very loud arrival announced itself.

'Congratulations, it's a girl,' I heard above the screams as this small, madly indignant person, cleared her own respiratory passages. It was Monday, 22nd June 1964, and she had arrived just in time for lunch.

Geoff was so skilled I needed no stitches, and after a wash and strong cup of tea I was walking around with the baby in my arms by the time Fa and Adam arrived. There was relief and wonder on their faces as they took turns holding her, now pink and peaceful, eyes open, already looking interested in whatever there was to see. We had names prepared: Louise Katharine. Louise for a friend of ours, a granddaughter of the redoubtable Ingrid Lindstrom, close friend of Karen Blixen whom I admired for her powerful intellect with its philosophical insights; and Katharine for a favourite aunt of Adam's. It was also the title of a historical novel that I had read at an impressionable age and decided I would name a daughter after the heroine: Katharine. We had not announced any names in advance, as Alison had strictures on names.

'You can't call a daughter anything like Bridget or Rose,' she had said. 'Those are maids' names. And do remember,' she continued, 'it has to go with Hill.'

Immediately after the birth I did wonder if Adam would have liked a son, as according to Muz it was the desire of all men to have sons. These in her mind were rated more highly than daughters; her father's profound disappointment at having two daughters and only one son having impressed her from a young age. With each successive pregnancy of Grandad's tiny frail worn-out wife, he had made known his longing for another son, a brother for Stanley the eldest. But whether they were girls or boys, all later babies died and sorrowful visits were made to their forlorn little graves in the churchyard each Sunday. One of these dead babies was held in particular regard and always referred to as 'The Boy', with flowers laid on his small headstone and birthdays remembered.

Adam, possibly as a result of growing up in a family of three boys and only one girl, seemed to have an entirely different perspective and told me, on a high of euphoria after Louise's arrival, that he had been hoping all along for a girl, he loved girls, and this was *his* girl.

Even Fa was euphoric, congratulating everyone, even the staff. His smile wider than ever, he was behaving as if it was his baby, and in return he was being congratulated by everyone on his own new status as a grandad. He couldn't stop gazing at Louise, wanting to hold her, counting her fingers and toes, saying, almost in awe: 'Every detail is perfect, look at the shape of her head, the symmetry, even after ventouse.' When one of the nurses came to take her away for a rest, saying, 'Too much excitement, being passed around like a parcel, this little one had a traumatic birth and needs to be allowed to sleep,' Fa followed, beaming like a beacon. When the door closed, Adam and I were alone, holding onto each other with relief and barely believable joy, trying to concentrate on composing telegrams so he could go to the post office and send them off.

The nurses wanted me to stop fidgeting around the room and have a proper rest, so as soon as Adam had left, I lay down obediently on the newly made bed with fluffed pillows, and thought how easy it was to sink into a deep untroubled sleep. Before closing my eyes, lying there facing the open window, I wondered why the light outside had turned suddenly dark. Birds had stopped singing and sharp gusts of wind threw dust and grit against the glass, rattling it. I got up to close the window, and as I did so there was a flash of lightning and crack of thunder overhead, so loud that its ferocity made me jump and left me shaking. Within seconds, rain swept across the window as more thunderclaps reverberated like gunshot from a leaden sky and lightning forked to the ground. It was as if the momentous event I had just been through was being marked by a natural phenomenon of similarly awe-inspiring proportions. There would be no chance of sleep now while the storm continued, and back in bed, propping myself up with a writing pad on my knees, I began a long letter to Muz describing all that had happened, and how miraculous it was that the baby had arrived safely at last.

After a quick recovery I was allowed home the next weekend, to coincide with a couple of days off for Adam so we could be together for the first time as a family, settling in with Louise and receiving visitors. The day after she was born, Adam had planned to take the day off, intending to spend it at the hospital with me. But Tony, calling with congratulations, suggested a celebratory buffalo hunt as Renny had produced a son, Martin, just three weeks before and he could think of no better way to celebrate the two births. This was too tempting for Adam to refuse and I had no objection as I was feeling tired that day, glad for him to have a break after spending so many hours patiently sitting beside my bed during the long labouring ordeal. Going on a hunt with Tony was precisely what he needed. I was not alone, as word of the baby's arrival had spread and visitors came with armfuls of flowers: the Hemsteds and McCubbins hotfoot among the first.

Louise, from the start, was a very self-possessed baby and her composure even in testing situations surprised us, along with the further surprise that we had produced such a perfect-looking child. All new parents are famously blind to any imperfections in their infants, but we could not ignore the reactions of people meeting her for the first time, and concluded that they were probably just as surprised as we were. Fa in particular with his extensive experience of newborn babies, was especially captivated, and the nurses told us they couldn't keep him away from the nursery while Louise was there, exclaiming to them on her loveliness. I was impatient for Muz to see her, and disappointed that in reply to my long letter written on the afternoon of the birth, Muz had sent just an ordinary card with a brief message inside, expressing no particular emotion at the news.

The telegram that Adam sent to his parents somehow became abbreviated in transit and arrived with the words: LOUIS KATHA ARRIV AL SAF 22. They thought it referred to a visitor coming to stay. Visitors did come in such numbers it was a scramble trying to keep up with household management while allowing myself enough time for successful feeding of Louise, closeted in the tiny nursery. This kind of activity was, by social convention, only done in private behind closed doors out of sight of guests, especially male ones, or anyone else likely to squirm.

It was lucky for us that Louise continued to be an easy-going baby with all these people dropping in, staying the night, or several nights. Our visitor book, a wedding present, shows among others during that time:

Pippa and Lucinda Howden from Wami, Konza; Simon Fletcher from Naro Moru; Clare Fielding from Timau; Ian and Pat Campbell Clause from Lumbwa; Trim and Kevin Lyons with baby Tana from Mweiga; Ken

Gordon from Ndurumo, Rumuruti; Biddy Blayney from Northumberland; Hazel and Theo Potgieter from Timau; Charles Moore from Nyeri; James Ashton from Australia: all staying one or more nights, and then more local callers like Angie and Tim Guy, John Sankey, Tony and Renny, and Johnny, who came in and out.

Elaine, with husband Les, arrived to stay when Louise was two weeks old, driving up from Nairobi where they were living at the MAF mission compound near Dagoretti, conveniently close to Wilson airport for Les who was piloting MAF flights. Their baby was due very soon and excitement was intense, but we were sad that Muz was still held up in England, and suspected that she felt guilty about leaving Spindle. I could see the dilemma for her, pulled two ways between him and Fa, both needing her.

Andrena brought a new friend, John Clarke, when she came to stay, meeting Louise for the first time. John's family had sold their farm at Dundori where they had been neighbours of Elizabeth and Peter, and had bought another farm at Londiani, next door to Avondale. This coincidental proximity reignited my frustration at losing the chance to have had Avondale for ourselves, particularly as Andrena and John seemed more than casually involved, and he had already taken her to meet his parents.

'I'm sure he's on the verge of popping the question,' Andrena enthused, with none of her usual disdain when discussing men. She had that glow and faraway manner of love-struck fixation: 'We're going on safari and it will be just the two of us, miles from anywhere.' I had never seen her like this before and was impressed. John had been to Cambridge and was ambitious; she would not be marrying a Kenya cowboy. But his mother, Audrey, had a formidable reputation.

'How did you get on with Audrey?' I asked warily.

'It wasn't what I expected,' she said. 'I was on edge because I had been warned about her. But she was splendid, rock solid, old school, no frigging about, we got on like a house on fire.' This was a surprise, but I could see Andrena's directness, common sense and practicality, would not go unrecognised by Audrey, and similarly Andrena would connect with the same characteristics in Audrey.

When Alison and Cen returned from the Royal Show, after coming to our house to inspect Louise, the first question they asked was about the christening. I explained that neither of us wanted a christening. We couldn't see any necessity for a ceremony we saw as outdated and meaningless, with godparents making vows they could never keep. Alison was shocked. 'No christening! You can't have a child who isn't a Christian.'

'Louise can choose for herself when she's old enough,' I said, thinking that sounded entirely reasonable.

'Rubbish, it's not a matter of choice, it's what matters to the family,' Alison said so firmly that Adam visibly wilted, and I decided it wasn't worth upsetting everyone and making the situation with the parents worse than it already was, so I climbed down and said we would reconsider.

Fa agreed that diplomacy was the better course, and moreover it might bring Muz over if we asked her to help set a date so she could be with us. I wrote to her with this suggestion, and meanwhile engineered a compromise on the issue of godparents. Our vicar, George, conceded that parents could themselves act as godparents, so we need choose only one other person besides ourselves. This was easy with Andrena as the obvious choice, and when we were arranging the date, Tony and Renny suggested a joint service to christen Louise and Martin together since they were the same age. Muz had replied and promised to be there, so all seemed to be turning out well.

While Andrena had agreed to be Louise's godmother and said it was an honour, she added that she didn't want us to invite John. This was surprising as the last time we had seen her she was full of excitement about the safari and future prospects together. She looked far from love-struck now, as she told us that the safari had been a disaster. It had started well, at a good campsite where they were enjoying days out in the bush, watching game and shooting birds for the pot. But early one morning, leaving the camp fire doused when they went out, it later flared up and spread through the camp in their absence so they returned to a scene of complete devastation. Everything was burnt to the ground. All the camp equipment had been John's and they were left with just a vehicle and the clothes they were wearing, the shock erasing all visions of romance along with their possessions. John was so shaken by the experience it left him out of sorts, grieving for the loss of safari gear he would be hard pressed to replace, while Andrena took the ill-fated safari as a bad omen.

She was not a girl to hang around, and when she heard that the Tea Hotel at Kericho needed a receptionist she applied and got the job straight away. This in due course led to Jon Low spotting her since all the tea planters were regulars at the hotel. He wasted no time in getting to know her while John Clarke was hesitating, and within the year she was engaged and married to Jon, reorganising his household and garden with a dairy on site where they milked their own cows. Andrena created wonders in her new big kitchen with all the home produce, assisted by a modern machine I envied desperately: a Kenwood electric mixer that had been a wedding present. The tea estates had their own club and a young vibrant community where Andrena thrived, entertaining lavishly in a fun-loving social circle.

During this time I was still having a fall-out with the church and only agreed to go ahead with Louise's christening for the sake of peace and harmony with those people for whom this ritual held significance. After many happy years for me at St Christopher's when a much loved all-embracing vicar, Gordon Mayo, had packed the pews with a lively flock, those pews were now sparsely occupied. Gordon had left for a different ministry at Lee Abbey in Devon, and everything had changed. The new brooms officiating at St Christopher's were eager to impose a stricter regime and lost no time in sweeping away Gordon's dynamic innovations, disapproving of those elements seen as frivolous with people having fun and being joyous, instead of grave and earnest. No more social or sporting activities were allowed in the church hall, only prayer and Bible study groups, while the Youth Fellowship was to admit only true believers into its membership. Particularly upsetting for me, on a day when I had gone to put flowers in the church, was to find it stripped of ornamentation and memorials that now were seen as distracting from the real business of litany and worship. It felt like a puritan takeover of our warm loving liberal church, forcing it to become exclusive instead of inclusive. While the previously large and enthusiastic congregation gradually dwindled to a very small number, there was much rejoicing by the new hierarchy presiding over what they saw as a cleansed church.

Someone I had been friendly with, John Fulcher (whose mother owned the cottage that Fa was renting), joined the others in this clean sweep and I was perplexed at the change in his character. From being a slightly ramshackle but engaging eccentric when I had first met him years before, John was now a crusading visionary having had a Damascus-type conversion under the auspices of the new system. He had been a solitary figure previously, and it was a surprise when he invited me, back then, to visit his farm to see round and have lunch. His mother joined us for lunch, appearing to be on hand to chaperone me in a way I found quaint, but slightly odd. She may have hoped by her presence to contribute a measure of refinement to the event, as John lived sparingly in two mud huts joined together, one providing living space and the other presumably for sleeping, though I did not get to see inside it. He was an Old Etonian and this kind of austerity seemed almost a hallmark of some, scorning home comforts.

John's style of dressing was equally unorthodox as he wore his khaki shorts long and wide, with a pistol strapped to one thigh, its brown leather holster suspended from a belt around his waist. 'For snakes,' he explained. I hoped this didn't mean that any were likely to appear during lunch, and hoped also that he was not intending to make a pass at me, so I was relieved when it turned out that the real reason for inviting me was to solicit an introduction to my friend, Jane Gomersall. Jane was in the group of friends who had engineered my long-ago blind date with Adam and all of them were honoured guests at my wedding, but none of them seemed to be anywhere near getting married themselves. Jane was twenty-eight, the age at which girls were said to be on the shelf if still single with no immediate prospects. John seemed a most unlikely suitor. I wondered if he might have been under some pressure from his mother to settle down and improve the standard of his home life, seeing Jane as a suitable wife: a sensible organised Yorkshire girl, from a different background, but respectable. I could understand John being attracted to her, as many men were, but she was fastidious and aloof, confident in herself and her willowy good looks with a striking combination of dark hair and milky complexion that never goes unnoticed. John, by contrast, was a brown nut of a man, whiskery and unkempt, not Jane's type at all, I thought.

An introduction seemed pointless and I made excuses, but John had set his sights on Jane and possibly by the power of prayer, or divine intervention, in due course he captured her and transformed her into a born-again Christian. I hardly recognised the new Jane after this metamorphosis. All makeup had been wiped from her face, her beautiful glossy hair had been cut very short, and instead of looking stylish in the way she always presented herself before; her clothes now looked droopy and drab. I was not invited to the wedding and neither was anyone else from our previously close and friendly group. Elaine, though, had mysteriously appeared on Jane's radar. 'I've met your sister,' she said, 'at a church meeting in Nairobi.' I was surprised Elaine had not mentioned it, but understood the parameters of this different world that Jane had now entered, of fellow evangelical Christians, and when she added, 'I've come home now,' I could see it was real, and was glad for her.

Friends of mine who had been single were getting paired off in a rush. Even John Clarke, recovering himself, sneaked off and got married in England without telling anyone. This caused much indignation among Kenya boys like Adam who were anticipating a stag night revenge on John for the savage rituals they had been subjected to when it was their turn. John's escape was regarded as cheating, and bad form to go and get married safely out of reach.

Those English girls who came out by ship in search of husbands were called *The Fishing Fleet*, and, if going home without success were then called *The Returned Empties.* John Clarke's new wife was not one of these, and did very well when she arrived back with him to make a home at Grove Farm, next door to glorious Avondale, holding her own against the matriarchal Audrey.

As well as *The Fishing Fleet* there were *The Ground Sheets*. These were a flighty set of girls who preferred British Army officers to local boys. Instead of being seen as eligible if unmarried, British Army types were not always looked upon with favour by young males of the settler community. The status and sophistication of professional soldiers with fat salaries possibly presented a challenge. There was a sizeable British Army encampment at Gilgil where the Officers' Mess ran a disreputable (but very popular) night club called The Sack of Screws. This was a magnet for many of us, as any relief from the banality of provincial night life was not to be sniffed at.

If we went out at night, Louise came with us, sleeping in a carry-cot on the back seat of the car. Vehicles parked outside people's houses during dinner, or public places such as hotels and restaurants, always had *askaris* (guards) who kept watch, alerting parents if there was any problem.

In September Elaine's daughter, Rachel, was born with no fuss, and Fa was elated for a second time, shaking the hand of everyone he met, wanting to share his news and good fortune. He was especially relieved that it had been an easy birth, the baby was another perfect specimen, and Elaine was radiant. Motherhood suited her tender nature. I was surprised on my first sight of Rachel that her skin was light brown instead of pink. 'She doesn't look exactly English,' I commented in a sisterly way.

'Well, she's not altogether English,' Elaine said pertly, recognising my dig. 'Only half. The other half is Celt. Les is a full Scot. You know that.' I quickly said how pretty the baby was, and how lovely for the two cousins to be so close in age.

CHAPTER 7

It was surprising and disappointing that Muz kept postponing her arrival. We thought the excitement of meeting her first grandchildren would bring her over as fast as her tiny feet could run up the steps of the plane. But even this prospect seemed insufficiently tempting, and for someone as devoted to Christian ritual as she was, it was baffling that she could bear to miss the christenings. Especially after a date was set and she promised this time that she would be there.

'What do you think is going on?' I asked Elaine.

'I expect she's busy,' was the vague reply. I noticed that Elaine, as time went on, increasingly avoided any difficult subject.

'She can't be too busy to come and see her own first grandchildren,' I said rather sharply. 'They're growing so fast, she'll miss the best early stages.'

'Well, she's got Spindle to think about. We mustn't put ourselves first.'

Oh Lord, I thought, forcing myself to resist a curt response. There was no point trying to get an opinion out of Elaine if it involved any criticism, implied or otherwise. So I left it at that and resolved not to enquire of Fa what he thought either, since he was tight-lipped now that the delay was becoming embarrassing.

I was soon distracted from worrying about Muz as one of Adam's cousins, Susie Dunlop, asked me to look after her baby while she went to England to visit a friend. A male friend, Adam suspected, as Susie was in the process of divorcing her husband and enjoying new freedoms as a sensational redhead with few inhibitions. Her husband, David Dunlop, was a DJ on Voice of Kenya radio, his quips and chat familiar to thousands of listeners. He was popular and was a local celebrity among households tuning in to his daily radio show. Away from the microphone, relaxing at home with Susie, the camaraderie could turn volcanic when the two of them, both volatile characters, fought each other like fiends. This had been witnessed by a terrified Adam on several occasions when staying with them in Nairobi, having to shut himself in his room to avoid getting caught in the crossfire.

Their older child, Angus, had already been deposited with someone else and the baby, known as Boo, would come to us with a Seychelles nanny, so they would be no trouble, Susie assured me. I was happy to take them as, unexpectedly only ten months after Louise's birth, I was pregnant again and could do with the extra help. Unlike most European mums I had deliberately chosen not to have an ayah for Louise, wanting to look after her myself. This had been nothing but a pleasure, but as she was now beginning to get more active it would be good for her to have Boo as a playmate, I thought, while Maria the nanny could help look after both of them.

As well as operating the clinic twice a day, I had taken over a backlog of farm office work for Adam, typing letters and writing up cattle records. A daily record was handed in to the office each evening reporting all herd movements: births, deaths, illnesses, inoculations, vet visits, milk produced and any noteworthy incidents. Each animal had a card with its ear tag number or name at the top, and any information arriving on the daily record was entered onto its card. There were more than three hundred animals on the farm so this could be time consuming, and needed to be accurate. I liked detail so this suited me, and with Maria now in charge of the young children I could enjoy getting out of the house and having a job again.

The office was the farm's hub and being there gave me an insight into how it worked, or didn't work. One area of concern was the high death rate among calves, with less than half surviving the first few weeks of life. This was causing problems for Adam who needed heifer calves as replacement stock in the milking herd. Calf-rearing was Alison's job and she was very proprietorial about it. But Cen, with his strictly commercial attitude to farming, backed Adam when it was suggested that I should take over the calves and apply proper standards of hygiene, nutrition and general care. Alison was furious at what she perceived as further interference from me when I was already seen by her as a very unwelcome intrusion, undermining her position and authority.

Susie's mother Constance (known as Consie or Coss), was Alison's twin sister, and their conversations around the subject of my invasion of the Hill family were relayed to me by Susie, mimicking Alison's angst, impatient to tell me the latest. 'You're called *The Wretched Wendy* now,' Susie told me delightedly. 'According to your dear mother-in-law you're nothing but a damned nuisance and a wretched blight on their lives.'

Alison and Coss were identical twins, but completely different in personality while looking like two matched string beans. Coss had always been very decent to me and her husband Cyrus was a true gent who tipped his trilby whenever we met and was a charming cultured man. Susie was the cousin closest to Adam in age and affection, the families living on farms not very distant from each other as the children grew up with English nannies who were close friends. They kept each other company in the peculiarly amorphous world of nannies whose social status remained below par whether in England or the colonies. I never heard their first names mentioned. They were known simply as Nanny Babbage and Nanny Snow.

Nanny Snow was the Hill nanny who had looked after Cen and his sisters while they were growing up, later joining Cen and Alison in Kenya when Elizabeth was born, and staying to look after her and the boys as each one came along. Nanny Snow lived with the children in a 'nursery' house in the garden, separated from the main house, and Adam often spoke about this arrangement which he thought very odd as most other children lived with their parents. He recalled a sense of isolation, along with times of acute hunger as a meagre diet in the junior household was thought adequate for nannies and children who were not expected to eat very much. As soon as he was old enough to learn to shoot, and allowed to have his own air rifle, he went out shooting mousebirds in the vegetable garden to supplement their meals.

By the time Louise was born, Nanny Snow was back in England, too old to work and homeless, as she had never accumulated any money or property of her own. She appealed to Granny Hill at Howleigh for a room, offering to assist their live-in maid with small chores in return for board and lodging. This was granted rather grudgingly by Granny who insisted that Nanny was not to think of herself as part of the family and must keep to kitchen quarters as, after all, Nanny was still a servant, even if in this case she was a retired one – living on their charity.

Adam said that when Nanny was a young nursery nurse in the household at Llandaff, before the family moved to Howleigh, she fell in love with the coachman's son who wanted to marry her. But Granny made it clear that her duty was to the family and she could not marry while she remained in their employment. So Nanny gave up her own prospects and devoted her life to successive generations of Hill children; but this was not unusual for girls in her situation at a time when duty and vocation came before personal inclination.

When Louise was born, Nanny sent a letter and little jacket she had knitted, thrilled that she had lived long enough to celebrate the arrival of a new Hill baby. Granny Craddock (Fa's mother), was similarly delighted and, almost as if released from further service now the next generation was assured, she and Nanny Snow each died within months of Louise's birth.

Fa had been anxious about his mother's declining health after a letter came from the matron of the Methodist Home where she was living, warning that Gran's chronic bronchitis was finally getting the better of her. He had been pondering whether to go back and see her, at the same time using the opportunity to check up on Muz. As soon as Muz heard about this, the prospect of Fa paying a visit to England propelled her into booking a flight to Kenya, pre-empting any visit by him, no doubt suspecting that during the visit he might sneak off to see Babs.

So it turned out that Muz didn't miss the christenings after all, but she was not herself and christening photos show her looking morose and blank, as if her body was there while somehow her spirit was absent. She's left her heart behind in Forest Lodge, I thought; she now feels more secure over there than back here trying to make the Fulcher cottage feel like home. And Fa himself has probably left his heart behind with Babs. This could have explained why the much anticipated reunion envisaged when Muz arrived was not a success, and the cottage, despite its charms, seemed to hold no comfort for her.

The one person, Dick Johnson (Fa's old partner in the Nakuru doctors' practice) who, by the merest sound of his voice could magically bring back her sparkle, had died of stomach cancer not long before; his loss felt deeply by his many adoring patients and friends. He was not yet sixty and had carried on working right to the end.

'It was that third wife of his that was the death of him,' Muz complained, lamenting bitterly that he had married again and she had been replaced in his affections. 'That Joycie woman, no heart, all bluster and booze, never looked after him properly.'

Muz would have looked after him properly, I thought, she would have loved him to death, so he would have died happy. 'Dick loved you,' I said, 'and would have married you in an instant instead of Joycie, if you had let him.'

'We did discuss it, Dick and I. That may surprise you, but we did. One of the difficulties, for me, was that he scorned any concept of binding vows such as Fa and I had made to each other when we married. Dick seemed unable to understand why I felt that unshakeable loyalty, despite all that had happened. When you have stood up in church and vowed "till death us do part", you can't just walk away. It's not only a matter of how you behave towards the other person, it's how you behave towards God as well, obeying or disobeying, and if you are a Christian you have to obey.'

'Well, it doesn't look exactly as if Fa is going along with that, if what the Bible says is true: that your thoughts have to be as pure as your deeds.'

'I can't do anything about your father's thoughts. I can only do what I think is right in my own life. It wouldn't have been right with Dick. I did love him, but I love your father more.'

'Maybe true love means sometimes having to let go. You might be doing Fa a favour by letting him go, so he and Babs can be together, if that is what he wants.'

'That would leave me with a complete sense of failure, letting him and Babs go off together.'

'Yes, it would be the ultimate sacrifice. For love. As in "Greater love hath no man, or woman ..."'

'That's death, not love.'

'Maybe they are the same in the end.'

Dick was buried in Nakuru cemetery where a parallel road and railway ran past the lines of graves held in a parched treeless open space behind a low wall. Despite its uninviting state this forlorn depository was not, to me, at all forbidding. I had been introduced to graveyards from an early age by Granny Craddock who took me along on visits to cemeteries after Sunday church whenever she was staying with us. Impressing on me the importance of keeping a friendly eye on those who had gone before, she said those of us who were still here had a duty to look after these final resting places. Muz and I consoled ourselves by taking flowers to Dick's grave, and visited others like those of Enid Grant's parents, and the pitiful small plot of Venice Molony with her unborn child. Who would remember her story later on, we wondered, and who would know that Enid's father had at one time been the keeper of the King of Siam's elephants. It was there in the palatial Royal Compound that Enid had been born and had lived as a small child. She now lived in England and was relying on me to look after her parents' graves. Their headstones and those of Dick and Venice had brass plaques with their names and dates marking them, but the brass in time became too tempting for thieves and all were taken, so that nothing marked the graves any more after a few years.

I hadn't dared tell Alison that another grandchild was on the way so soon after Louise, further eclipsing Elizabeth, but there was no need to worry as great news arrived just after Christmas 1965, that Elizabeth was 'expectant' at last and the baby would be born in Ireland where she and Peter had bought a farm at Ballinasloe, in Galway. Alison was transformed by this news, making plans to be with Elizabeth for the birth, even taking up knitting and chatting happily as I helped her dismantle the Hill cradle with its muslin drapes, to be taken with her to Ireland. Louise had now been promoted to a cot, which she and Boo shared, as well as a big pram that Susie had lent us.

At weekends and night times when Maria was off duty, I had both babies to look after and felt very responsible for Boo who was not a robust child. Despite Maria's attempts and mine with spoonfuls of body-building food, she remained frail and milk-white, her arms and legs like twigs. I wondered if she was pining for her mother and began to be concerned as no word came from Susie about when she might return. I sent letters with photos of Boo as the weeks and months went by, hoping the photos would prompt feelings of nostalgia, but no reply was received and we began to think maybe she would never come back. Her mother had no more knowledge of Susie's intentions than we had, while Alison reported with a sniff, 'Consie let Susie do whatever she liked as a child; she's always been headstrong, so it's no wonder she's gone off like this.' Then one day Susie suddenly reappeared and took Boo and Maria back home again, with the big pram, but no explanation for her long absence except that she had needed to get away from all her problems for a while.

I missed Maria's help but had no trouble taking Louise with me when I was working on the farm as there were always willing hands to help look after her. Since Alison had become preoccupied with anticipation for Elizabeth's baby, my involvement in farm activities was less resented, so I could begin to enjoy these more and feel a sense of belonging. The small details of life on the farm were the ones that gave me most pleasure as I watched gentle routines like the *uji gari* (porridge cart) drawn by two oxen, creak slowly along the dirt roads carrying a midday meal for labourers out in the fields. *Uji* was what they would have at home, and the big metal drum of sloppy porridge carried by the cart was infused with a certain amount of an alcoholic concoction, to provide stamina and motivation it was said. It certainly seemed to have that effect as it was slurped from enamel bowls with enthusiasm.

Farm ox carts and wagons were ubiquitous, cheap to run and heavy duty. The most spectacular of these on Glanjoro was the *kuni gari* (firewood cart) with its long line of spanned oxen patiently trudging the roads. Odiambo, the driver, was as old and bony as the oxen themselves and spoke to each of them tenderly by name, using the reach of his thin hippo-hide whip to deliver occasional flicks of encouragement over the brindled backs as the team plodded on, shouldering their yokes in a timeless way that seemed as natural to the landscape as the dusty road and parched grass.

Each morning before dawn the first sound was not bird song but the low whistling of herders as they called the cows for milking. The thin air of altitude carries sounds over long distances before sunrise brings eddies of warmth and disperses the calls. Adam would already be gone, sliding out of bed in the dark after turning off the clock alarm that I never heard. Just as he never heard the cry of a child in the night, a similar form of editing made me deaf to the alarm while allowing me to hear any noise from a child. The wife of a fireman had once told me that she and her husband were able to filter night time noises in the same way, so that she never heard the fire bell, while he slept through every other sound in the house however loud or insistent. It was a mystery how this was possible, but was certainly very convenient. I loved to wake to the whistling herders each morning, then go back to sleep until the great chorus of birds at daybreak, which is one of Africa's special wonders, woke me again.

I was feeling particularly well and thinking how pregnancy suited me when, without any warning or provocation, the baby miscarried. Even worse, there were complications and I had to go to hospital for an operation. The anaesthetist was Satch (Dr Satchwell), a peppery Irishman who had been a dancing champion as a young man and still twirled at parties, demonstrating fancy footwork. Less accomplished was his skill in the operating theatre on this occasion as halfway through the procedure, with Bunny at the performing end, the cylinder of anaesthetic gas ran out, and I woke up. My instinctive reaction in a fuddled state was one of panic, attempting to climb down from the table and run away. Theatre staff grabbed and held me while Satch administered a powerful shot of something to knock me out. Later, back in my room, I started coming round with the weird sensation that I was lying at the bottom of a well, with people shouting to me from the top. Someone slapped my face and shouted even louder, 'Wake up. Open your eyes. Don't go back to sleep.' It took me hours to surface, and then there was only disappointment in realising why I was there, and that the baby was lost. This experience made me wonder how it was that Louise had hung on when I hadn't even known I was pregnant, exercising no care or caution, riding horses and generally racketing around. Now here she was, a splendid baby, a power-house walking and talking. She even came on buffalo hunts with us, and Renny came too with Nettie and Martin.

On one of these hunts in the Nakuru lake forest, Adam and Tony went ahead with the Nderobo trackers and dogs, while Renny and I found a clearing where we could spread rugs for a picnic under the shade of tall fever trees. It seemed a safe place to sit with the children as we set out our picnic and the hunt ran on into the distance A little while later we were startled when a commotion erupted some way off with gunshots and furious barking from the dogs. Renny and I looked at each other: something was wrong. In the distance we could hear hooves pounding through the undergrowth, and soon realised that the sound was coming closer, and coming towards us. The buffalo herd must have been provoked by the dogs into a stampede and instead of galloping further into the forest, had turned on their tracks and were steaming like an express train in a straight line to our clearing, which was right in their path. Instinctively Renny and I pushed the small children to the ground and lay on top of them, trying to make ourselves as flat as possible. When the herd exploded into the clearing, what happened next was extraordinary. Showers of stones and twigs thrown up by the buffaloes' hooves pelted us as we lay prostrate, but instead of trampling us, they jinked at the small mound we had made of ourselves and passed like heavy armour on either side. I felt the rush of their bodies and smelt their rank smell as the ground shook and the massive bunched power of the herd thundered past, but it was all over in seconds, leaving us showered with dirt and debris. We raised ourselves gingerly, wary of stragglers following behind, but the herd had vanished as suddenly as it had appeared, leaving us shaken but completely unharmed.

The men and dogs limped back, ready to make tea boiled up with milk and sugar in the same pot, African-style, with slabs of bread dipped in, while discussing the retreat. When we told them about our close brush with the herd, their reaction was short on sympathy, being much more concerned with the annoyance of an aborted hunt.

It was at Tony and Renny's house that we met a new couple, fresh from England, who had arrived at Egerton Agricultural College where the husband, Joe, was lecturing in tropical agriculture. They seemed exotic and soon fascinated us with stories of life in the fast lane in Bristol making us feel like bumpkins in our isolation from the mainstream. We may not have been able to offer them glamour, but we did have our own versions of social recreation among a circle of friends who met up for dinner at weekends with pontoon afterwards, requiring much alcohol and general loosening of polite behaviour. These casual gatherings usually ended up at the Seth Smith farm where friends like Charles and Rosie Harris were regulars. Charles always fell asleep before we had left the dinner table, his head resting on the tablecloth, oblivious when the rest of us went through to the drawing room and remains of the meal were cleared from around him by the servants, leaving him still resting there. Later, he would wander through to our pontoon table, looking bewildered, 'Deepest apologies for being such a bad host,' he would mutter, collapsing into an armchair.

'You're not the host,' we pointed out. 'This is Tony's house.' Charles would blink in bemusement and be instantly asleep again. Rosie would have to drive him home in the early hours, their two small children, Simon and Georgina, on mattresses in the back of the car. Charles was not drunk, he was just permanently fatigued.

Joe was never fatigued, and whenever we called on him and Liz his wife, whatever time of day it was, they would emerge from the bedroom looking tousled, clutching towels. We teased them. 'You can't be in bed, it's nearly lunchtime.' (Or teatime or early evening). 'How can you spend so much time in bed? It's not civilised.' We may have been a little envious of so much free time, and the way they glowed and were so shameless.

'Do come in. Tea, gin, or champagne?' they would offer, whatever time it was.

It was normal to call on friends without warning as few of us had a telephone, so informal hospitality was a natural part of life.

We were always eager to hear how Joe was getting on at Egerton where his freewheeling liberal views were causing him some difficulty in adjusting and settling into campus life. He had wanted to demonstrate his belief in social equality by riding a bicycle instead of driving a car, reasoning that most African students had bikes so this was a way of bonding with them. After some weeks acclimatising himself to bike-riding at high altitude, a group of African students asked to speak to him.

'Sir, with respect to you, why are you riding a bicycle?'

'It is to show solidarity with you. To show that we are all equal.'

'Sir, we don't want you to be equal with us. We want you to be above us. Lecturers are not supposed to behave like students, sir. We want you to show respect like other lecturers driving a car, sir.'

Joe was abashed. He realised how foolish his notion had looked to the students, and told us the story against himself, knowing we would rib him about being a daft leftie.

Soon after this we heard that he was in hospital. The information rattled down the grapevine and sounded like another misadventure, so we were intrigued. Liz said it was too embarrassing for her to tell us what had happened, and we would have to find out from Joe himself.

Later, after he had recovered and was able to join our pontoon evenings again, we were all agog.

'Well, it's a slightly touchy subject,' he began, looking at Liz.

'Go on. We all want to know.'

'The thing is, you know how Liz and I tend to be more than a little enthusiastic in certain areas. Well ... actually it was all her fault the way it happened.'

'You liar,' Liz shouted. 'Tell them the truth.'

Joe corrected himself. 'No, of course, my fault entirely. Well, it was like this. We had gone for a siesta as usual, but on this occasion became somewhat over-eager. Somewhat carried away in the spirit of the moment you might say. The fact is that a certain portion of delicate anatomy got rather battered, not to put too fine a point upon it – got rather torn – you get my drift. Awful bad luck, simply couldn't keep up with that level of demand. Not boasting of course.'

We sat silent for a moment, imagining the scene before there was a general collapse into hysteria.

'It was an emergency, you understand,' Joe protested. 'So much blood, I passed out, and Liz had to call for help from the servants' quarters to drag me out to the car. Then it was a case of her driving like a maniac to Nakuru Hospital with me *in extremis* and straight into the operating theatre. A terrible flap. Sorry about the pun.'

'So, did it mean the full circumnavigation after that?' we wanted to know.

'No other option.'

'And what's it like now?'

'What might have seemed like a rare misfortune, I have to tell you, dear friends, now puts me in the unique position of offering you a before and after verdict,' Joe said, wanting to impress. 'Not many chaps get to have this particular insight, so you are privileged to be the recipients of my intimate opinion.

'Go on. Don't be coy.'

'Well, a bit disappointing really. Not a scrap of difference either way.'

'What about you, Liz?'

'As the master says,' she replied, 'except he's so proud of the new beast he wants to show it off all the time.'

'*Not to us,*' we implored, and Tony who had been to Oxford and acquired a store of literary quotes, added: 'As the Bard says, "*There's a destiny shapes our ends, rough hew them how we will.*" There was not much more to say after that.

The parents' household meanwhile had become animated with more than one excitement as, in addition to Alison's plans for attending the birth of Elizabeth's baby, Cen was preparing to lead a delegation of Kenya farmers to London to meet Barbara Castle who was the Labour Government Minister for Overseas Development. White farmers wanted the British Government to provide guarantees that the land redistribution scheme would be fair and sufficient funds would be allocated for the buy-out. When the delegation arrived at Mrs Castle's offices they were treated with scorn, 'swatted away like flies', according to Cen's description when he returned despondent, thinking their mission had failed. But their efforts were not in vain as the initiative was taken up by the World Bank along with funds from the British Government, and the resettlement scheme proceeded over several years with much success. White farmers had an option to sell for a fair price without compulsion, enabling African farmers to buy land with affordable loans.

In May 1965, the best news of the year was the safe arrival of Elizabeth and Peter's son Michael after so many years of hoping and waiting. That it was a boy was of prime satisfaction to Peter who had many times spoken of the importance of male heirs. In conversations around this subject, before they left Kenya, I had asked him if they might consider adopting if no child of their own appeared. He said this was out of the question. 'An adopted child,' he explained, 'would have unknown genes, quite alien to one's own family. One would never know what kind of child one was getting. It is far better to remain childless than to introduce uncertain qualities into the family.' When listening to Peter's opinions, I never argued as his self-belief was so fervent it was in a way endearing. If I hung on his words with rapt attention he warmed to a theme with increasing eloquence until his big round face shone and beamed at me most generously, grateful to have an appreciative audience.

Fa was very pleased to hear the news of Elizabeth's baby and allowed himself a sherry to celebrate when he came for an evening drink with us. He often came round when he had finished long days of driving to rural clinics, knowing he would find us on the veranda watching distant reflections of sunset on the lake, while drinks were poured and Adam would be there smoking his pipe in the break between milking routines. Muz didn't seem to want to come with Fa, and this bothered me. A family time like this needed her presence. Louise would be scuffling around and Fa would hoist her onto his lap, talking to her earnestly about things he had seen on his trips. She would look at him quizzically, as if he were relating strange mystical encounters and then, very precisely in a few chosen words of her own, reply quite sensibly, delighting him. His only criticism was that she didn't smile very much, 'She's a very solemn child, taking life rather seriously, don't you think? Not larking about very much.'

'Well, you're the same, so that must be where she gets it from,' I pointed out.

It was true, Louise was a serious-minded baby. In her pram each toy had its place and if any was moved, she would put it back in position again. Throwing anything out of the pram as other children might do was unthinkable. She disapproved of that sort of behaviour and if a visiting child was put in the pram with her, she would sit primly at her end, keeping herself to herself, and an eye on her toys. When she was six months old she had pushed her bottle away and picked up a cup, drinking without help from then on, demonstrating a mind of her own from a young age.

The McCubbins and Hemsteds were frequent visitors, calling to see how we were getting on, Joan bringing armfuls of flowers and vegetables from her garden. She despaired of my garden which had no water supply so the only plants that survived were drought-defying types like Babu's Delight, spreading its cheap and cheerful clumps beside the veranda steps. This plant got its name from Indian station masters who planted and tended regiments of the species up and down the line where it grew like a weed.

'I'm sure you could grow cannas if you diverted the drain from your bath water and cultivated a patch out at the back,' Joan suggested. 'They like shade, so you could have a bed near the big pepper tree.'

I was enthusiastic, longing to have a proper garden with flowers that could be cut and arranged in vases in the house.

'I'll bring tubers next time,' Joan promised.

Expecting a modest number I should have remembered that Joan didn't do modesty and arrived with a truckload of enormous tubers like giant sausages. All were attached to lumps of heavy soil ready for planting, and later when I had toiled with the gardener to accommodate them all, we had a sizeable plantation. Sturdy green stems rose from the tubers over the next few weeks with broad leaves and buds that soon burst into glorious red, yellow and orange waxy flowers. For some reason these began to attract dogs, so that by the time Ruin and various others had jumped and rolled and gone wild in the canna bed, it was in no state for Joan to be impressed the next time she came.

She stood outside the back door, her stout body tight and square, hands on hips, surveying the result of my efforts, screwing her face up at the sight of the mangled plants lying in a mess of slime. Never shy about being forthright I could see that Joan was not going to let me off.

'You've done a very foolish thing,' she growled, 'you've planted the cannas on top of the cess pit, and furthermore, diverting the bath water into it has made it overflow. No wonder the dogs love it, rolling around in all that filth.'

'It was the garden boy who said the canna bed should be dug there.'

'Don't blame the servants,' Joan said archly. 'You're supposed to be the one giving orders. He will simply have put it there because the soil had already been turned when the pit was dug for the new indoor lav. Don't you see?'

'Yes, I do now, but cesspits and drains have not been a topic very much discussed by Adam or anyone else in the general scheme of things I'm supposed to know about on the farm.'

Joan laughed, 'No harm done then. But the plants are contaminated so they will have to be thrown away and burnt with the rubbish. You still need a proper garden. You've got a good borehole. There should be enough water for a certain amount of irrigation if you organise it properly.'

'It's the cost of anything like that. The farm won't pay.'

Joan looked annoyed. 'You and Adam can't go on living like poor whites. Your house isn't even finished. No plasterwork inside so you can't paint the walls or hang pictures properly. And now it seems you can't even grow your own flowers or vegetables. It's not on. We did warn you.'

'I know. But we still have a good life here, and we've got Fa and Muz not far away.'

Having said that I felt a pang thinking about Avondale, and looked away in case Joan noticed and said something. She must have read my thoughts, putting an arm round me as we turned towards the house. 'You know Avondale is rented out now, to some Italians, but the new Settlement Board is looking at all the farms in the area so I expect we will sell if they offer enough; it seems like the most sensible thing to do.'

'Maybe it's just as well that Adam and I didn't take it on, then, if the farm is going for resettlement.'

'Look at it another way,' Joan said, 'after getting it as a free gift, you would now be in line for quite a bonanza if you sold to the Board. It's not often that sort of windfall comes along. Then you would have a nice big nest egg to play with. You and Adam could do whatever you liked.'

'Don't remind me,' I said wistfully.

CHAPTER 8

The next excitement after Michael's birth was Andy Hill's arrival home from Cheltenham College, this time permanently, so all three brothers were now back in Kenya. I had been looking forward to seeing Andy again. He was part of a generation, like Ros, let out into a world embracing more liberal times, easy-going in the new breeze of the sixties, making some of the men of my own age look stuffy and unenlightened. Andy was refreshing and popular as a new bachelor joining the social scene with his public school dash and polish. He had plenty of charm like his brothers, and was also a good dancer. He and I quickly established a rapport of frivolous banter and enjoyed dancing together at parties where we deliberately behaved in a flirty way designed to raise eyebrows. Adam encouraged this as he liked to circulate among different partners without any obligation to keep me company – after more than two years of marriage we didn't need to be plugged into each other all the time.

Johnny was absent from these parties, preferring to spend evenings at the Rift Valley Sports Club in Nakuru where the conviviality among drinking friends too often resulted in him feeling flattened the next day. On such mornings, when Johnny's labour force was gathered outside the farm workshops waiting for him to arrive with the day's orders, Cen would storm up, shouting, 'Where the hell is Johnny?' One of us always had an alibi for him, and Cen always accepted whatever it was. He and Alison were very protective of Johnny and he was allowed liberties which Adam could never have got away with. Susie said they couldn't bear to send Johnny away to school in England because they would miss him too much, so he went to school in Nairobi instead of Cheltenham like the others. He later felt this had disadvantaged him and that he had missed out on the broader education and experience he might have gained from public school. There was a melancholy in his expression when he spoke about it. He may have lacked some of the style and confidence imparted by a school like Cheltenham, but he had something that other men his age seldom possessed: a sweetness of soul that was demonstrated in small acts of kindness and thoughtfulness, presented with no trace of affectation.

Unusually for a young man at that time, he created a garden full of colour around his house, somehow devising a system to keep it watered. Often when he came to call at our house he would bring posies of flowers, carefully arranged in concentric circles of different colours and tied so they could be put straight into a glass. I had no fresh flowers of my own to brighten the house so Johnny's posies were much appreciated. His thoughtfulness drew girls to him and a series of them fluttered around his house intermittently, causing disapproval from Alison.

'That strawberry-blonde girl, what's her name? One of Johnny's hangers-on. She even left some of her clothes behind last time. *In his bedroom*, would you believe it – so shameless.'

'She was probably staying overnight and intending to return another time,' I suggested mischievously, provoking more indignation. 'Anyway, how did you know about the clothes?'

'I always go and tidy Johnny's drawers and cupboards at least once a week. He's never been good at looking after himself.'

Oh, I thought, she's using the excuse to spy on him, and warn off the girlfriends, wanting to keep him firmly in her orbit. No wonder his girlfriends never last. It had puzzled me why they left so soon as he was certainly eligible and his physical attractiveness was more than just average. He was tall, tanned, blond and broad-shouldered, the kind of man any girl would want to know better. His loneliness would draw them to him all the more, and he needed a good woman to hold instead of a whisky glass. The Africans on the farm were very much of the same opinion and talked about it. They knew everything that was going on, often with insights that were a great deal more perceptive and practical than ours.

Johnny's looks contrasted with the other brothers who, just as good-looking, were dark and lean, while of the three of them the one displaying the most distinctive Hill physical feature was Andy, who had the Hill nose: large, bony and beaky. Cen's was the most splendid of these specimens, followed by two of his sisters, Katharine and Monica, with slightly less pronounced snouts.

Andy needed a job and wanted one with good prospects, presenting himself to the African Highlands Tea Company for a position on the first rung of their managerial ladder. He was accepted as an assistant on one of the estates near Andrena and Jon, quickly becoming absorbed into that vivacious society but not too far away for frequent visits and stopovers with us, preferring our company and food to that of his parents.

European employers were often given nicknames by their workers and Cen's was *Nzige* (locust) because he nibbled away at their wages by fining them for any misdemeanour or error. Adam's nickname was *Sigara Mwanzi* (smoking reed) due to being tall and thin like a reed, while incessantly smoking either a pipe or cigarettes. A cigarette was the first thing he reached for in the morning (instead of me), and last thing at night. Sometimes as he dozed off, the cigarette would fall from his lips onto the bedclothes where it would smoulder and flare up before one of us became aware that the bedclothes were on fire. Another bed-related hazard was the Walther pistol he kept under his pillow at night in case of intruders or stock thieves. There were times (I suspected as a consequence of experiences with Mau Mau) when he had nightmares, and on one occasion in his terror grappled with me, thinking I was attacking him, while my terror was that he might reach for the gun and shoot me. On another occasion he did grab the pistol and sat up in bed shouting unintelligibly before letting off a couple of rounds through the ceiling. After that the roof leaked and we had to move the bed.

The Kenya dairy industry was going through changing times since the government had introduced milk quotas, and Cen decided to build a cheese factory to provide a commercial outlet for the surplus milk. The factory was built on farm land alongside the main road to Nakuru so customers could stop off at the factory shop. An old wood-fired steam engine drove the machinery that powered big stainless steel vats imported from Denmark with all the other cheese-making equipment. A Danish couple who had experience in producing different kinds of cheeses were recruited to run the factory, and proved so quiet and diligent they became known as the 'cheese mites'. Four kinds of cheese were produced: Tilsiter, Gruyere, Stilton and Danish Blue. All these fat round cheeses sat on shelves in the cold store maturing, and people who came to buy were given a tour and samples to try. All four varieties of cheese quickly became very popular and soon the factory was exporting to other African countries.

Cen's plane was useful for marketing trips and Alison usually accompanied him, reluctantly. She complained about aggravations on these trips: 'It's all very well for Cen when we're flying because he can pee into a carafe to relieve himself, but no such relief is provided for me,' she said.

'Can't you come down wherever there's a bit of flat land with a few bushes?' I suggested, tongue in cheek.

'Don't be crass, we might never be able to take off again. Cen would never take that sort of risk, and anyway you can't just land a plane to have a pee.'

'Why doesn't he take Adam instead of you? They could both use the carafe, and you would be spared.'

'Yes, it might well be an idea for Ad to go with Cen on these trips, and even more usefully, when he goes on his big trip to England. You've heard about that no doubt. It's his latest craze, flying the Cessna all the way to England to see his mother and sisters.'

Adam had not so far been included on any of the business trips and we had not heard about this latest proposal, which surprised and thrilled us. 'What a cracking idea,' Adam said. 'I'd love to come with you. When are you planning on going?'

'It would be no good you coming,' Cen said bluntly. 'For such a long trip I need a co-pilot. I'm putting the word round for someone.'

'I could learn to fly,' Adam volunteered eagerly. 'I've always wanted to fly. It's a perfect opportunity.' His elation was so infectious it communicated itself to the dogs who looked up expectantly, thinking an outing was planned that might include them.

Without so much as a flicker of an eye Cen replied, deadpan, 'You're not clever enough to learn to fly, but Johnny might manage it.'

'Johnny won't want to,' Alison put in firmly. 'And anyway he and Ad both have to be here on the farm while you are away.'

Adam said nothing, but I wished he would challenge Cen's monstrous put-down and not allow him to get away with it. Later, thinking about it, the remark was revealing in that it exposed an attitude of father to son that may have explained Adam's reticence in asserting his own entitlements within the family.

When no one could be found among Cen's contacts to go with him, he advertised for a co-pilot. There was just one reply and this was from a missionary who needed a cheap trip back to England, but said that he would have to pray about it first. Cen was impatient, questioning how long the praying was going to take, and how reliable the missionary was likely to be if he needed to apply for divine approval on every action. When the reply did come it was affirmative, but with certain conditions. Cen was an atheist, so any instruction from a source he regarded as illusory was likely to be scorned, especially if it was allowed to delay his own preparations. 'He's a damned fool, that missionary,' Cen grumbled. 'How can anyone with enough intelligence to fly a plane, believe such twaddle.' According to instructions from above, the missionary said they must have an inflatable dinghy stowed on board in case they had to ditch over the Mediterranean.

'Does he have any idea what a rubber dinghy weighs?' Cen raged. 'We'd be lucky to take off at all.'

'Maybe the missionary would agree to life jackets instead,' Alison suggested.

'The man's a lunatic. Having him on board would jinx the whole trip. I think I'll take Jean instead, if she agrees.' Cen said.

This remark fell like an unexploded grenade into the silence that followed. Jean was a family friend who would be amusing company, certain to spice up any trip and make a co-pilot seem redundant, but it would cause a scandal.

Alison was irate. 'You're not taking Jean. Think of the gossip.'

'Do you have any other suggestions?' Cen asked and, without waiting for an answer: 'That's all right then, I'll ask her.'

I found Cen's atheism intriguing and was unable to resist taunting him about it, especially when he launched into one of his diatribes on the subject of life after death. This always brought on spasms of distress from Alison who was stolidly Anglican. 'I do wish you wouldn't go on about it,' she groaned. 'It's too tedious. And for others, like me, it's blasphemous.'

Cen, ignoring her, continued, 'I've killed so many animals in my life, it's plain to see, after they're dead, they're gone, finished, nothing else. Why would we be any different? When we die, we're snuffed out, that's all there is to it. Nothing to suggest otherwise. Eh, Alison?'

She knew the bait too well and was not going to rise to it. I, however, was more than ready. 'You might get a nasty surprise if you find that you have not been snuffed out after all, and there you are, in a fix, completely unprepared, because you haven't read the handbook and found out beforehand what it's all about.'

'That's enough, the two of you,' Alison would interrupt at this stage. 'Isn't it time Wendy went home?'

It may have been my lack of deference that meant I was not included at the parents' regular Thursday night dinners to which Adam was invited and attended dutifully each week. Johnny was invited too, but seldom turned up, much to Alison's annoyance. She knew he spent most evenings at the club and was aware how this was affecting him. 'What Johnny needs is a sensible girl from a good family to settle him down,' she said, 'but he keeps bringing back the most unsuitable ones.'

Dairy work hardly ever finished before eight and evenings were short and precious, so I resented the obligatory dinners when Adam went straight from the dairy to the main house every Thursday night. I asked him to find out why I wasn't included, and, in case there was a misunderstanding, to explain that I would like to go too.

'What did they say?' I asked when he got back.

'Mum said Thursdays are family evenings,' he replied, slightly apologetically.

'What do you mean, *family evenings*? I'm their daughter-in-law. I am as much family as you and Johnny.'

I knew this was an awkward subject for Adam and he was torn between loyalty to me and loyalty to them, but he was married to me, not his parents. Loyalty to the marriage had to come first. I was not prepared to back down, and stated this fact as plainly and reasonably as I could, not wanting to have a row about it.

'I entirely agree that our marriage comes first,' he said, 'but we rely on my job to support us, so it's really the job that comes first, and Dad is my employer. You know what he says, *"Kazi kwanza"* (work first), so, because we're living here on his farm, employed by him, he calls the shots.'

'We could always go somewhere else,' I suggested.

'And get someone worse?'

Elaine came to stay later that year, bringing Rachel so the cousins could get to know each other. Of all the quiet calm people I had ever met, Elaine was the embodiment of a type of serenity that was almost disturbing in its worthiness, as she never raised her voice or expressed displeasure with any situation, person or thing. This placid persona had not been passed on to Rachel, however, as she was a restless, tense, hysterical child, throwing herself into tantrums, screaming with rage as she convulsed on the floor. We were mystified as to how Elaine could have produced a child so different from herself, and Les as a laconic Scot, was never likely to exhibit any loss of composure, so there was no explanation for the disparity. Louise would have been a more likely progeny of theirs, causing Muz to remark that the babies should be swapped for a more logical balance of personalities. Putting them in the pram together would send Rachel into a frenzy, and when this happened Louise went into china-doll mode, remaining expressionless while Rachel in contortions of fury tried to propel herself over the side to escape.

Elaine's method of dealing with this and other tantrums was by speaking gently to Rachel: 'Now, Rachel, dear, we don't want to make this kind of noise, do we. It's not very nice. If you are upset, we can talk to Jesus about it.' This approach seemed only to increase the paroxysms, and I began to wonder if it was in fact Elaine's sugary handling of Rachel that provoked her to these extremes.

I was to discover that even Elaine could be provoked if the case was serious enough to rouse her. One of the reasons for her visit was to check on Fa and Muz and see how they were getting on at the Fulcher cottage. I had warned her that Muz seemed depressed and vibes between her and Fa were strained, the Babs affair still clouding their lives I volunteered by way of explanation. Any suggestion of impropriety was unthinkable to Elaine who refused to believe anything like that could happen in a family like ours, and Babs was a good friend to all of us she insisted. This pretence held up until, on a visit to Fa and Muz one day, the conflict between them shocked her so much that, unable to contain her feelings, she blurted out: 'The atmosphere between you two is evil. You can't go on like this!'

Returning to us at Glanjoro she reported what she had found, and what she had said. It was hard to believe she would use such a strong word as 'evil' to describe that household. 'Did you really say that?' I asked.

'Yes, and it was true,' she replied, in a quite un-Elaine-like tone of voice.

'What can we do?' I asked, wanting to use the chance to try and find some solution to the impasse. 'While Babs is there hovering over them, they will never be able to go back to how they were.'

'They need to talk to a minister about it, so they can pray together and follow what it says in the Bible about Christian marriage.'

'I think it's too late for that. Maybe they need to get divorced so Fa can go off with Babs. Then Muz could settle down at last and concentrate on her music. She might even find someone else.'

Elaine was shocked. 'She could never do that. They can't get divorced. The Bible doesn't allow divorce.'

Les had been on a flying trip taking supplies to mission stations in Ethiopia and had come to join us on his return. The Peugeot Taxi Service with regular fast transport between Nairobi and Nakuru was very useful as it was comfortable and reliable. Elaine and Les had no car of their own, so they used the taxi service and while they were with us I took them on trips in my old Anglia, or they borrowed it to drive around visiting friends.

We had planned a visit to the Hemsteds one day and collected Muz to go out to the farm, all of us packed into the Anglia with me driving. Les was in the front seat with Louise on his lap, the other two with Rachel in the back. It was a trip of about thirty miles to the farm at Subukia and we were driving on a long flat stretch of road beside forest slopes shelving away to the top of the Rift escarpment, when a large buck sprang from bushes at the verge, aiming to cross the road in front of us. It jumped high in the air to try and miss the car, but didn't make it and crashed into the windscreen, shattering it and showering us with glass. The buck's body, wedged in the windscreen, blocked my view as I braked, hoping not to run off the road or hit anything. We did hit something, causing enough of a bump to dislodge the buck as the car shuddered to a stop, its front bumper rammed against an anthill some yards off the road, with the buck, showing no signs of life, lying alongside.

We all sat stunned for a moment looking around, before noticing that Louise was almost buried in pieces of glass where she was sitting on Les' lap. Her face was covered in fragments and there were even some small flakes in her eyes, which we washed from the bottle of drinking water always carried on trips. She didn't cry or make any fuss at all, the sudden appearance of the buck landing almost on top of her seemed to be of more interest as she looked around to see what had happened to it. Even Rachel in the back on Elaine's lap failed to have a tantrum, all of us wanting now to climb out and shake the glass off ourselves.

As we were doing this, several Africans came running down the road towards us which we thought was kind, assuming that they were coming to see if we were all right. But when they got close they completely ignored us and instead, seizing the dead body of the buck with shouts of triumph, each taking a leg, they ran off with it as fast as they had arrived.

Joan laughed so much when we told her about this, she got a stitch and had to bend over, her whole body wobbling with stifled groans as we told her how we had heaved and sweated to push the car back on the road, driving gingerly the rest of the way, nearly suffocated by dust swirling through the empty space where the windscreen had been. We were still brushing remnants of glass off ourselves as Joan, with her skill at treating all kinds of ailments and injuries among staff and animals, examined Louise's eyes with a magnifying glass and irrigated them again. When we had all had a wash and cups of tea, sinking ourselves into Joan's lush armchairs and sofas while the small children rolled around with her tribe of pugs on the carpet, we felt revived enough to tackle the gargantuan lunch that was infallibly produced whenever visitors appeared. It was a special occasion this time, celebrating the successful breeding of Louisiana crayfish that Joan and Stephen had imported from America, nurturing them in tanks on the river with a view to supplying hotels and the export market.

Muz never felt entirely comfortable with Joan whose hearty boisterous manner made her nervous, but this time Joan sensed Muz's discomfort and was solicitous. 'What you need to do, Fay, is talk sense into Alfred, get him to put his brass plate up again. Bunny would jump at having him back, the poor man with such terrible shakes he's barely able to function half the time. Everyone wants Alfred back. All his old patients are desperate to see him at the surgery again. He's only fifty-five years old. What's got into him with all this to-ing and fro-ing? Ants in his pants and bees in his bonnet.'

'Yes, you're right of course,' Muz seemed glad to have the case put so bluntly by Joan, 'if only he would make up his mind what he wants to do and where he wants to be. But nothing seems to satisfy him anymore. Any discussion on the subject only gets him irritated. And there's still Ros to think about, back in England, with Andrew stranded in that ghastly hospital.'

The McCubbins too were worried, unable to understand why Fa, who in normal times never lacked decisiveness or a clear sense of purpose, was now wasting his talents in a humdrum job that was leading nowhere, while Muz followed on, trying again to create a new home for them both. Pat and Hugh had their own worries since Hugh's anticipated promotion to managing director of The Kenya Farmers Association had been blocked by Cen who was on the Board of Directors. Other members of the Board backed Hugh's promotion, but Cen had a preferred candidate and somehow was able to get his man elected. Hugh then resigned, unwilling to continue in a job that held no prospects for advancement, and feeling that it was time to leave Kenya he and Pat started looking elsewhere. This was very disappointing for the rest of us and did not enhance my estimations of Cen. I was perplexed by the contradictions in his character. Some of his actions were entirely laudable in pursuit of aims like the cheese factory and acquisitions of land, while in others he could be ruthless, demolishing the ambitions of others, such as his recent remark crushing Adam's dream of flying.

This latest demonstration of aggressively controlling behaviour towards Adam made me feel furiously defensive of him, wanting to find ways to boost his self-belief, to counter the denigration which inevitably must have an effect however casually he tried to laugh it off. I began to question whether love alone, however committed, passionate or tender, could make him feel secure enough to transfer reliance on his parents, to reliance on me. This thought came more sharply into focus when Muz remarked one day, 'I know things are not always easy for you on Glanjoro, but don't ever try to take Adam away from his parents.'

'What do you mean?' I asked, startled.

'Just bear in mind the relationship,' she replied enigmatically.

Whatever the presentiments, nothing too serious was going to get in the way of simply enjoying ourselves as the sixties blasted away old cobwebs, replacing these with new energy and ideas across societies around the world. Music and dance were the life-blood of our age after two decades of constraint and nothing was going to stop us now, shocking as this might seem to pre-war generations like those of Muz. Observing the unashamed gyrations of current pop stars accompanied by amplified rhythmic strumming of guitars and drums, she declared, 'That kind of music and behaviour comes straight from the devil, infecting all our young people with the wrong ideas.' She was right about how it infected us, with everlasting joy, the wrong ideas however were all hers.

Adam and I were both members of the Nakuru Players, a theatre group with its own theatre and regular productions in which Adam always had a leading part. He was a natural actor and performer, able to transform himself into any character just by the way he moved and spoke. Playing Thomas Cromwell he displayed such menace it actually scared me to see him turn vicious. When he was into a part like this it was as if he immersed himself in a disguise, feeling more comfortable in the skin of that identity, escaping from his own for a time. His acting talent was not limited to period drama as he could just as easily play one of the ugly sisters in pantomime, or a fool in comedy; his versatility much celebrated and appreciated by the group. When he was on stage I was usually backstage helping props or dressers, and Louise would be sleeping or lying awake in her pram parked in a corner, unbothered by the tension and scurrying about.

The first time Adam played a pantomime character in drag, he sent me to buy an outsize bra from one of the Indian outfitters and when I asked for the largest size bra they had, the shop assistant looked at me dubiously. 'Oh, it isn't for me,' I explained, 'it's for my husband.'

'Does he have a problem?' the man asked.

'No, it's just for his costume.'

'We have large size costumes,' the man offered, pointing to a rack of suits of the kind that Joan wore.

'I'll just take the bra,' I said quickly, and the assistant went to look through boxes at the back of the shop, eventually producing something that looked grotesque enough to be suitable. He wrapped it carefully with pitying glances at me, and remarked as I took the parcel, 'I hope this will give satisfaction, Madam.'

'Oh yes. My husband will be very pleased with it,' I said, making a quick exit.

One of the producers, Bernie, kept pressing me to take a part. 'You have to overcome your nerves and appear in at least one production, even if it's just a walk-on,' he urged. 'We all know you can sing. I'm going to audition you for a part in the panto. I really must insist; you can't go on hiding back stage.'

Eventually I relented and found myself cast as the Ice Queen, encased in a shiny white satin tube, supposed to look like an icicle, shaking with terror on the first night as I waited in the wings for my cue to go on and sing an eerie solo. The costume had a low neckline, which in its slippery satin, slipped even lower as I waited under the lighting platform where members of crew worked switches directly above me, and whispered lewd comments on the view down my front. Seconds before my cue, a handful of ice cubes from above was dropped with deadly accuracy down the drooping neckline, so that my entrance as a regal queen poised to deliver a siren song in high soprano, descended into farce as I stumbled on stage, clutching my chest as if I'd been shot. My ice maidens, who were skipping demurely on tiptoes in a dance around iceberg scenery, stopped abruptly in alarm. The audience took this as part of the act, so I waved to the maidens in a queenly command to resume their dance, hoping to rescue the scene from comedy as the piano down in the pit struck up with the opening bars of my song. Lights dimmed and a spotlight came on with dazzling effect in front of the footlights, where I was to stand and sing in a beam of intense heat. Standing rigidly on my spot, I could feel the ice cubes melting as I sang in a high-pitched strangled voice, and trickles ran down to spread in a puddle around my feet. Mercifully the minute my song was ended the curtain came down. After that I made my entrance from the other side of the stage well away from the lighting platform.

My part was a very small one, so I was relegated to a communal dressing-room shared with other bit players while Adam, elevated to stardom, had a superior room with other stars. Some of my dressing-room companions were young men cast as Viking slaves, all of us thrown together in this cramped space. One of the slaves was a skinny pink Englishman called Wally to whom, inexplicably, I felt attracted.

The business of theatre in crafting imaginary characters out of flesh and blood people, creates a world of make-believe where reality is suspended together with normal inhibitions among a collection of diverse personalities: all edgy, all talented in varying degrees, some distinctly neurotic. It was in this surreal atmosphere that Wally timidly held my hand backstage while I waited to be called, whispering encouragement and compliments, smiling shyly at me. Adam was too engrossed with the leading lady who was blonde and brash, to notice or be interested in anything passing between Wally and me, so that when Wally invited me to have lunch with him at the Stag's Head hotel on one of my shopping days, I accepted without a second thought. Bearing in mind that Adam often went for a late drink with the blonde actress after rehearsals when I had gone home with Louise, it seemed entirely reasonable.

On the day of the lunch date I arrived at the Stag's Head and was steered to a table in a far corner of the dining room where there were no windows to illuminate whoever was there. It was pure theatre again, doing incognito stuff, talking in low voices, peering at each other in the gloom. As my eyes became adjusted to the lack of light I noticed a man and woman sitting at the next table, and then noticed that the man was staring at me. Help, I thought, I've been recognised. Who is this person? He was an older man and, as I glanced sideways at him, not wanting to show my full face, I realised with a shock that it was Cen. His companion was a woman I had not seen before. She appeared entirely at ease as if they knew each other very well. She looked elegant, with natural grace, toned and chic. The look Cen gave me before he turned back to her was one that said, 'Neither of us has seen each other.' I understood that perfectly.

The next time I saw him was at polo when of course nothing was said, but the incident had unnerved me and made me feel guilty for sneaking off with Wally and being discovered in such a situation, so I confessed to Adam and told him about the strange encounter with Cen and the mystery woman. 'No mystery there,' Adam said, amused. 'That's Billie. She and the parents have known each other for years. She's a widow with a farm at Gilgil on the Malewa (river) where we rent grazing. Dad goes over once or twice a week to check on our steers.'

'Why would he be having lunch with her secretly at the Stag's Head then, instead of the club, if they are all good friends?'

'For purposes of diplomacy maybe? Like you and Wally?'

That put me back in my box, and it was a relief that he took it as a joke and would probably tease me about it whenever the subject came up.

Polo occupied most weekend Sundays with Adam increasing his handicap and the number of ponies shared by him and Cen. Johnny and Andy were not polo enthusiasts. Play varied between two main clubs in the area, Njoro and Kinyatta. Njoro was more convenient for us, as the ponies could be ridden and stabled there by the *syces* (grooms), while matches at Kinyatta near Gilgil meant they had to go by train. The sport had strong support from ex-Indian army colonels and brigadiers who had retired to the uplands of Kenya and were fierce traditionalists, not shy about castigating young players like Adam if they were clumsy or shoddy. Brigadier Tuck (known by everyone as Friar) had a habit of pouncing on any lapse, and hissing through his teeth with annoyance while delivering caustic reprimands.

One Sunday when Adam was mounted and waiting to go on the field for a chukka and I was holding the pony's head to steady her, Friar approached. In the same way that Fa's twitchy smile was a preamble to some kind of penetrating observation, Friar stood there, hissing with fierce breaths. Drawing himself up to the fullest height his ancient figure allowed, he spoke through clenched teeth: 'Your tack is an abomination. *Look at it!*

Falling to bits. Chewed to hell. Damned dangerous. You wouldn't drive a car without brakes, *would you?*'

It was true about the tack. Rats regularly gnawed it back at the stables, the leather as tasty for a rat as biltong.

'Rats!' hissed Friar. 'That's a damned silly excuse. Put your dogs on the buggers. Terriers. You need terriers. *D'you hear?*'

'Yes, sir,' Adam replied, chastened. But Friar hadn't finished.

'And when you've seen to the rats, get yourself some new tack.'

We watched him stalk off, his back stiff with indignation. Adam and I looked at each other and the reins, tatty and almost chewed through in places. Fat chance of the farm paying for any new ones, we thought. Cen was as tight as Fa where money was concerned, but made sure that his own tack was serviceable. Aside from these disparities, polo was a great leveller, a time when everyone was part of a team, either on the field as a player or, like me, among helpers and spectators, wives and girlfriends, assisting in numerous ways.

Of polo couples, Mary and Don Rooken Smith personified those qualities that make the sport noble and fun and inclusive. Don, a high handicap player representing Kenya at home and abroad in tournaments, had that mixture of athletic good looks, charm and skill, that marked out the players. Mary was no mean player herself but was modest and preferred to join others of us in supporting roles. She and Don were both from settler families with relatives and friends all over the country who, in common with other similarly deep-rooted families, mucked in with everyone else. Mary's two little girls, Zoe and Sally, would be there running around on the dry grass with other small children, Louise trying to join in, just starting to get her balance on stumpy little legs.

The heat and pace of chukkas, the air dense with dust and swearing, players galloping off the field to change sticks or ponies held ready for them by assistants like me with not a moment of play to be lost, often left me feeling a mess while Mary remained poised with a physical and inner radiance. She still played polo occasionally, but it was more often her brothers, Robo and Fuzz (Robert and Francis Foster) who, unlike Mary, were hefty and thick-set, who thundered past on small ponies visibly sagging under their weight.

There was an airstrip next to Kinyatta polo ground, so Cen and other players who had their own planes could fly in, some coming from Nairobi or Nanyuki, always a source of excitement for Louise when she spotted a plane. She was familiar with the comings and goings of Cen's Cessna at the farm, and most exciting of all for her was being hoisted up into the cockpit by Adam to look at the instruments. Cen didn't approve of children getting anywhere near the controls where they might fiddle with something vital, but Adam encouraged Louise's enthusiasm while making sure nothing was interfered with. He was a very attentive, loving and tender dad, fully engaged, swinging her up onto his shoulders to go and look at anything that might interest her, or lifting her into a saddle to have a ride on one of the ponies.

'It won't be long before he starts her with a stick and ball,' Mary commented. 'We need young ones coming up now the old colonels and brigadiers like Friar are hanging up their spurs.' It was true, those ex-Indian Army cavalrymen who had introduced polo to Kenya were now a dying breed, still coming to polo but no longer riding, though sometimes acting as umpires, like John Graham. The cream of the old guard such as Will Broadfoot and Johnny Nimmo who along with Friar had been champion players in their time, were now reduced to the ranks of spectators.

Our weekends were planned around farm work, meaning that polo, theatre or parties, had to be fitted in. Having no telephone caused difficulties when organising events or keeping in touch with friends. Cen and Alison had a phone but would not take messages for us. John Clarke called them one day trying to get an urgent message to us about a camping weekend at the Mara that we were planning together. Cen replied (very rudely, John said), 'We do not take messages for Adam or Wendy. Do not bother us again.' Consequently the camping trip went ahead without us which was a considerable disappointment at the time as such trips were rare events.

Calling at the Fulcher cottage when shopping in Nakuru was the best way to keep in contact with Muz, who was languishing there in a state of limbo. She was not a sociable person, and kept herself occupied in the absence of a piano by organising the little cottage to make it as homely as possible, trying her best to pacify Fa and meet those needs of his that appeared so consuming. It was a complete surprise on one of these visits to hear that they had given notice on the cottage and were going back to England, just like that, quite suddenly, without any warning.

The next evening when Fa turned up at drink time, as usual without Muz, I confronted him as he was getting out of his car. 'What's all this about? Taking off again. Is it something to do with Babs? What about Muz? Her plight in all of this.'

'What do you mean – plight?' he asked indignantly.

'She's stuck in an impossible position, trying to keep up appearances for your sake, while at the same time you are keeping Babs on toast. It's despicable.'

'How dare you use the word: *despicable*. You don't even know what it means.'

Fa was furious, literally hopping mad, his feet jerking up and down as he stood beside the car while whistling through his teeth in the way he did when particularly incensed. I stood in front of him, surprised at how calm I felt as very often my anger matched his when an argument provoked one of his tirades.

'Of course I know what it means, and I'm using the word entirely appropriately in this case.'

Fa slammed his fist onto the roof of the car. 'What do you expect me to do then? If you're so clever, what does the daughter advise the father to do?'

The moment had come that I had often thought about and agonised over, wishing like Elaine that everything could magically go back to how it had been before Babs.

'You have to choose,' I said. 'Either Muz or Babs. It has to be one or the other. It's the only honourable thing to do.'

Fa said nothing, but I could see his hands shaking as he got back in the car, sitting very still for a few moments to collect himself before driving off, not stopping for a drink this time.

Fay (Muz) at the time of her engagement to Fa

Fa, whom Spindle resembled so much at the same age

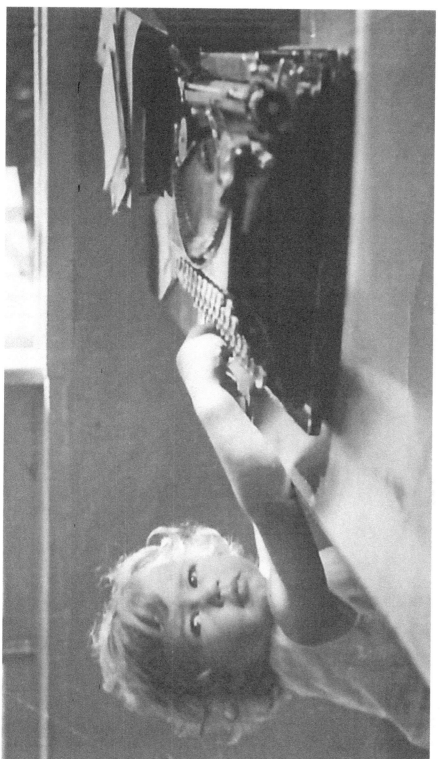

Wendy getting started

Wedding day

Getaway car

Louise and Piglet

Under the fig tree 1969

CHAPTER 9

Saying goodbye to Fa and Muz for the second time in less than three years was no less wrenching than all the other times when one or more of us set off on journeys that separated us by thousands of miles. The difference this time was uncertainty about their future since my confrontation with Fa had forced exposure of the issue causing the current crisis. After Fa and I had each calmed down and reconsidered, we were able to have a reasoned and conciliatory talk about the situation.

He described candidly the emotional turmoil that had racked him for so many years with the torment of conflicting pressures, often driving him to the edge of despair. 'It's a torture of the mind as well as the heart,' he said, 'when one begins to doubt those principles that have been paramount in guiding one's life, but no longer seem as dependable as before. We may believe ourselves to be the person we think we are, or should be, and then something comes along that blows apart that whole concept. We grapple with the unfamiliar sensations that have entered our being, no longer having the surety of standing on firm ground, or knowing what we believe any more. There is no logic to feelings that invade and then inhabit one's very existence, every hour of the day, and then by dreams at night.' He stopped as if weighed down by the burden of these thoughts. 'In clinical terms it might be classed as an obsessive condition, resistant to free will.' He brightened on the appeal of this theme. 'Magnificent Obsession! That's the title of a book.'

'I think it's a film as well,' I said. 'Have you seen it?'

'I have,' he replied, and that surprised me as he never went to the cinema, at least not with any of us, which suggested he might have gone with Babs. I was wondering whether to ask him about this, when he interrupted my thoughts with a question posed so mildly it took me by surprise.

'Do you think it is possible to be in love with two people at the same time?' he asked. I could see what he was driving at.

'Yes. But probably not equally. Maybe each in a different way.' I felt sympathy for him and relief that our conversation was proceeding without rancour, confidingly. 'Maybe there is some sense in societies that allow more than one wife, recognising that one woman may not be all things to one man, and vice versa. But if that were the case then women should be allowed to have more than one husband,' I suggested.

'Do you have an additional husband in mind?' Fa asked provocatively.

'No, of course not,' I laughed, 'and I don't think most women would want to have to cope with more than one husband. It's easier for men to skip between different partners, while women are tied down running the home and looking after children.'

'Do you think it's that easy for men to skip around?' he replied archly, and a long pause settled on the conversation as the conundrum confronted us both again.

Changing the subject Fa turned to me with a look of concern. 'Before I leave I need to know that you are fully well again after that odd episode, experimenting with amphetamine. Not a good idea at all. I can't understand why you did it?'

'Bunny prescribed it for me, for losing weight, after I got so large with Louise.'

It was ironic that my initial concern, before getting married, was that I was too thin and when I asked Bunny for advice he put me on a course of anabolic steroids, with bizarre results. He then reassured me that once I was married and pregnant I would put on weight automatically, and he was right as I observed with growing satisfaction my size ballooning to gratifying proportions while expecting Louise. I assumed that my body, minus baby after the birth, would reduce in size while keeping some pleasing curves, but did not expect to turn into a Rubenesque figure far bigger and flabbier than could have been imagined. This became most evident when squeezed into the icicle costume for the pantomime, inevitably presenting an irresistible target for the ice cubes. It was this incident that sent me back to Bunny for new advice on how to shave off the bulges, and he prescribed a course of amphetamine as an appetite suppressant. This had dramatic results almost immediately as I was barely able to sit still long enough to eat, and food lost all attraction, while a kind of manic energy took hold so that I was unable to sleep or rest, too jittery and jangled to settle on anything for long. Adam was very unimpressed with this latest drug regime. 'First of all you turn into an Amazon on Bunny's pills, and now you're twitchy as a cat with fleas. Why can't you just accept the way you are, and be normal?'

I had lost a stone and the inches were still falling off so there was no reason to carry on with the pills, especially as Adam was getting fed up with my fidgets, so I stopped, and was able to reassure Fa that I was back to my usual healthy self. What I didn't tell him was that I was pregnant again, knowing it would pain him to be leaving at such a moment, especially if he felt a need to be on hand for the birth in case of complications as before with Louise. I was nervous about facing another trauma if Bunny was incapacitated, and would have liked both Fa and Muz with me. It was wretched having to let them go, but would only prolong the parting if they stayed with no resolution of the problem between them.

The conversation with Fa questioning the nature of love as a lifelong bond, providing for all needs in its exclusivity, made me question my own emotions. My previous expectation of a lifelong bond with Lanner through the certainty of a love I thought indestructible, raised the question: was that love now completely extinguished? Could I be sure of it? There must not be even the smallest flicker that could unexpectedly flare up and cause doubts. I knew that Adam was sensitive on the subject of Lanner and covered this with sarcastic remarks at any mention of him, so I was careful to keep his name out of conversation, especially since Lanner and his wife were now back in Nairobi after various overseas postings. I hoped I would not meet him by chance on a shopping trip to the city, nervous about how I might react. Memories were everywhere, impossible to avoid. On the road, if I caught sight of a red DKW passing by, without any conscious thought I would find myself glancing at the driver in case it was him, then in the next instant feeling furious for being so stupid. Other tugs like a piece of music or song could bring him back, but of all these the most persistent was also the most prosaic: a whitewashed milestone on the side of the Nairobi road with the figure 74 painted on it. This had been the number of Lanner's RAF squadron, a symbol for him of what he said were the best times of his life, so it had become a magic number. All these memories were irrelevant, I was determined to believe, as the life I had now was the life I wanted, with my own family of three, soon to be four.

Louise was intrigued about the baby she imagined was going to spring out fully formed as a playmate. She was just two years old and able to hold a conversation and express some quite bold opinions. She was sceptical about Muz and Fa going away when I explained they had gone in a plane to England. She had never seen any plane larger than Cen's Cessna with its limited range. 'They can't go very far,' she told me earnestly. 'They will come back soon. They will be sad in England.' I thought she might very well be right. She had developed a close bond with them, while remaining cautious in the company of her other grandparents Alison and Cen, who were still wary of the discordant effect of a grandchild in their household. Cen was intolerant of small children with their piping voices and sudden squalls. 'Don't bring them in here until they learn to be civilised,' he had complained at Christmas when Louise opened a present that unexpectedly squeaked when it was pressed. His aversion to unwelcome sounds did not extend to the dogs I noticed, who were allowed to make incessant disgusting noises scratching and scrabbling, farting and barking, all behaviours fondly indulged by him and Alison.

Once when I was banished to the guest wing with Louise after she had inadvertently banged a toy on the floor, Alison came with us and offered to stay and read to her so I could go back and join the others. This was a surprise but it soon became clear that Alison's reluctance to engage with Louise was softening and when left alone with her, the two of them quickly developed a rapport. I would find them chatting happily on walks around the garden or visiting the stables. It helped that Elizabeth, Peter and baby Michael, were due to visit and preparations were underway assembling toys and a nursery, Alison's mood brightening with grandmotherly sentiments as the time drew closer.

Another key event coming up was the Nairobi Show. This was the highlight of the farming year for us when Adam and I became fully occupied looking after show animals: washing, grooming and preparing them for the ring. The show was an unmissable opportunity to exhibit our best animals and win prizes, adding to the prestige of the herd and sales of breeding stock. It was also a time when friends from all over the country would be there, converging on the Agricultural Society's members' tent for energetic socialising. Women wore hats and men compulsory jacket and tie while drifting between hospitality tents like that of Muthaiga Club where dress codes prevailed whatever the circumstances. This meant that we had to keep a change of clothes at the cattle stalls where we spent most of the time in overalls.

Each evening when events had finished and animals were bedded down (African attendants in the stalls with them), we went to Muthaiga Club for the night, dead tired but somehow up for more socialising. Club rules did not permit children on the premises and somewhere had to be found for Louise for the week. There was a children's residential nursery in Nairobi and other parents recommended it, so we booked a place for Louise and took her there on the day before the show with her little suitcase of clothes and teddy. The nursery was housed in an institutional building like a hospital and Louise was placed in one of the metal cots in a room with rows of cots containing other babies and children. It felt wrong to leave her in such a grim place; to see her standing there in her cot holding onto the bars watching us go, looking abandoned. Explaining to a small child that it's only for a short time and you are coming back, does nothing to allay the fear of being left with strangers in a barren place with parents having disappeared. I could see in Louise's eyes that she had no understanding of why she was being left there. It was a very bleak moment, but Adam was pragmatic saying that we needed a break and would be so busy with the cows there would be no time to worry or fret. It was an important showcase for Glanjoro Friesians and dairy products, a commercially valuable time and, as I was constantly reminded: '*kazi kwanza.*'

Dairy cows look their best just before calving, glossy and rounded with physical features in peak condition, which Adam maintained was the same for humans. 'Women never look better than when they are in the late stages of pregnancy, about to give birth,' he would say. This was not a view shared by most women who, unlike cows, have to carry the bloated accessory of an infant stuck out in front instead of slung more comfortably underneath. Despite this possible advantage for bovines, I felt sorry for the cows having to be shunted on and off trains, and then being coaxed to plod around a show ring in their advanced state.

When one of our heifers showed signs of labour while being paraded around the ring, I watched from the side in a sweat of nervousness hoping she would not give a mighty heave and groan at the moment that the judge went to inspect her. She was a pretty heifer with a large black patch on one flank in the shape of a Mickey Mouse face. This was distinctive, and she was a favourite of mine so it was a triumph when she won her class, standing quietly for the judge and waiting until she got out of the ring before dropping her calf.

There were no milking machines in the cattle lines, so cows were milked by hand and this usually presented no problem, except this time with one stroppy animal called Maua (meaning flower in Swahili) who refused to be hand-milked. The only machines at the show ground were those on display at the Fullwood stand, none of them actually functioning as they rested on gleaming plinths. It was decided that I should approach the salesmen at the stand and ask in a persuasive manner if they would agree to plug in one of their machines and let us use it for Maua. It would be a splendid demonstration for potential customers to see the equipment in action, I suggested. The Fullwood salesmen, who at first were not enthused, eventually agreed, and Maua was led on a halter through the show crowds twice a day to be milked at the stand. This attracted large groups, not all of them Fullwood customers. The attention was gratifying for all of us, including Maua who was a sociable animal and, trained for the ring, knew how to play to an audience.

These prize animals were pampered excessively in preparation for showing. First they were washed down with a hose to remove all dust and dirt from their coats, then they were shampooed, brushed, hooves polished, tails combed, and any obvious defects disguised. Tufts of white hair appearing in a black patch were dyed black, and any black hairs in a white patch were bleached or covered in a paste normally used on tennis shoes. If it rained, there was a risk that dye could run down causing streaks to appear in the wrong place, requiring a bucket and sponge close to hand so this could be dealt with quickly.

In between chores like these we sat on straw bales among the cows, chatting and drinking tea from a big pot brewed on cooking fires a safe distance from the wooden stalls and straw bedding. These were some of the best times, when we could rest for a while as visitors strolled past or stopped to admire the animals. But I missed Louise and worried about her. The cattle lines were peaceful and this helped me stay calm, but one day there was a commotion as men in uniform came shouting and pushing people aside who were walking past our section. I could see a small knot of men in suits who looked like VIPs, walking behind the uniformed ones who were clearing a path for them. As they came towards us, one of the VIPs flourished a fly whisk in the air indicating that he wanted to stop, and attention immediately focused on him. It was Jomo Kenyatta and I was surprised at how small and dapper he looked, but that may have been because those around him were tall, and the uniformed ones were big and square. Kenyatta paused to glance at the cows as the rest of us rose to our feet and stood respectfully beside them. For an instant his eyes met mine and in that moment I noticed how sharp and alert they were, and also slightly bloodshot in the way that Africans who have lived in smoky huts for any length of time can develop this feature. None of us spoke, and Kenyatta moved on, inscrutably.

I liked taking Maua to be milked, threading my way through the crowds, leading her on a halter while carrying a bucket in my free hand. She attracted considerable interest from passers-by and one afternoon I noticed coming towards us among the throng of people, someone I recognised instantly with such a jolt it was like a shot to the head. I stopped abruptly, causing Maua to stumble as the halter jerked and the bucket dropped to the ground with a rattle. The 'someone' stood as transfixed as I was and the few yards between us yawned wide, until Maua pulled at the halter and this person smiled. It was the same lop-sided smile and same loose-limbed Lanner coming to pick up the bucket and carry it for me. Neither of us spoke on the way to the stand, and Lanner waited as I went through the process of connecting Maua to the machine. When she had settled, I turned to him, not trusting myself to speak first. He looked at me in the musing contemplative way that I remembered too well. 'Is it really you?' he said.

'No. I'm a different person now.' I wanted to sound offhand, while still feeling tense and guarded.

'You don't look any different,' he said, 'except rounder maybe, which suits you.' He laughed, breaking the tension, and then his expression changed, becoming more serious as he asked quietly, 'Are you happy?'

'Yes. Very.'

'I always hoped you would find someone to make you happy.'

'Thank you.'

'I'm working at head office now,' he said, casually, in the manner of old friends catching up.

'That's very grand. You've done well.'

'And I have a daughter, and a son.'

'Oh, a matching pair, like cuff links.'

He laughed in the amused way that had previously always disarmed me. But not this time. He noticed my discomfort and the laugh faded. 'I better be getting back,' he said, and held out his hand. Are we to shake hands I wondered as I stood and stared at his, the same smooth tanned hand waiting for a formal handshake. Seeing my hesitation, he leaned forward as if to give me a hug instead, but then turned abruptly and without a goodbye walked away into the crowd. I felt shaky, but glad that I had seen in his eyes a tiny glimmer of wistfulness that somehow was very healing.

On the last night of the show, revelry back at the club was well under way when we arrived after packing up at the cattle lines and loading animals onto the train to go home. There had been a wedding and some of the guests, well oiled, were looking for more sport after the bride and groom had left and regular Muthaiga members started coming in for drinks and dinner. Adam was easily persuaded to join an escapade with others and I didn't want to be left out if it was nothing too strenuous (remembering I was pregnant), or likely to end in any of us getting arrested. A plan emerged over more drinks at the bar when the wedding party stragglers produced remnants of confetti from their pockets, suggesting we roll these into small pellets to use as ammo, dropping these from skylights on the roof above the dining room onto the plates of unsuspecting diners sitting below with the object of seeing how many hits each of us could score. It was kids' stuff, frivolous and silly, but we were in a mood for giddy release from the week's labours. Fingers were dipped into drinks to dampen the scraps of confetti that were then rolled into pellets and replaced in pockets. As soon as dinner was about to be served, we climbed out of a bedroom window onto the roof and crawled to the open skylights where we could get a good view of the dining room directly underneath. 'It's a good thing you're doing this now, before you get any bigger,' Adam remarked to me. 'Good exercise for you too.' Any benefit of this kind meant nothing while I was trying not to fall off the roof and ruin the whole excursion. Taking position at the skylight openings, we aimed individual pellets through the apertures, targeting plates of soup on the tables below. It was tricky getting the aim just right, and most pellets went astray, but a few found their mark and there was immediate consternation at these tables as agitated voices floated up to us:

'God dammit. Something has fallen in my soup. Look. It's happened to you as well.'

'Bird droppings!'

'Waiter. This really is too much.'

'Quick. Shut the skylight. *Mara moja*' (at once).

We didn't wait around for long after that but descended in short order, brushing ourselves off, ready to go and join the diners, feeling hungry now. It was our last night in Nairobi on top of a good innings at the show, so we were running on adrenaline and far from ready to slope off to bed after dinner. The same over-enthusiastic group of friends who had gone on the roof raid with us, suggested a nightclub, and later in the early hours of the morning as we crept back into the club, there was a light on in the men's bar indicating drinks were still available. Inside, dimly seen through a fog of cigarette smoke, hunched over a small table, were the same four poker players that invariably could be found there at this hour: Peter Fisher, Kim Mandeville, Patrick Walker and Bengie Bowles; so engrossed, none of them even looked up as we went in.

All I wanted next day (thankfully free of a hangover as I had not been drinking), was to go and rescue Louise, convinced she was feeling bewildered and forsaken. Adam tried to reassure me. 'Lots of people leave their babies at the nursery over the show and I've never heard any complaints.' When we arrived to collect her, she looked sad and forlorn, standing in her cot like an orphan. Stricken with guilt I snatched her up, squeezing her tightly as we both cried with relief. Adam took her while I packed her little case and then, as we walked away, it was harrowing to see the small anxious faces of other children left behind. We couldn't wait to get out of there and go home, promising never to leave Louise with strangers again.

Having babies and bringing up children was a more casual affair then, possibly because we were all much younger than many parents starting families now, and our childcare guru, Dr Spock, advised a common-sense approach with minimum fuss and fanfare. Pregnancy was seen as a natural process that women took in their stride along with child-rearing, and visits to the doctor were thought unnecessary unless there was a problem. This time I waited several months before going to see Bunny or telling anyone else about the pregnancy, until my changing shape began to be noticed. I had a strong feeling that all was going to be well, and when I told Alison she seemed genuinely pleased, and relieved that the expected date did not clash with the visit of Elizabeth and Peter with baby Mikey, which was anticipated with mounting excitement.

The guest wing at Glanjoro House was scrubbed and polished as never before in preparation for the visit. As the flutter built up so the mood of the house lifted and servants' chatter rose to such animated levels I could hear them from as far away as the farm office. The day before the family was due to arrive, Alison came to the office to tell me that she had invited Adam and Johnny for drinks the next evening to welcome them, and was sure I would understand that it would be better to restrict numbers to just family. 'They will be tired after travelling, and there will be plenty of other times for you to see them later on,' she said, quickly turning her attention to something else before I could reply.

It was not simply my disappointment at being excluded yet again, but Adam's defence of this behaviour when I confronted him about it. 'You can't allow your mother to go on treating me like this. Each time she gets away with it, the next time is worse, more damaging.'

'You mustn't take it personally,' he said. 'She doesn't mean to upset you, it's just her way. She is not the soul of tact.'

The morning after the drinks evening I was in the farm office as usual, keeping clear of the house until invited. The office door was open and Elizabeth, seeing me inside, ran in with squeals and hugs of greeting. 'Oh, I'm so glad to find you here. We were disappointed you couldn't come last night.'

'I wanted to come. I was so looking forward to seeing you, but Mum thought you would be tired and prefer only family for your first evening.' Elizabeth looked puzzled, 'Mum said you couldn't come, she didn't say why. But it doesn't matter now you're here. Do bring Louise down to the house. I can't wait for the cousins to meet. Mikey hasn't gone for his nap yet.'

Louise was playing outside with the farm children where their mothers stood around gossiping and making saucy remarks to the mechanics repairing tractors at the workshops. This disinhibition among African women was one of the things I loved about them: the irreverent humour and readiness to laugh that was part of an ability to make light of any difficulty, at the same time taking in their stride the care of numerous children whether their own or others, so that Louise was always safe and welcome in their company. Scooping her up after an exchange of greetings and thanks to them, I walked with Elizabeth around the side of the house to the garden where Peter was looking after Mikey. He was a cheerful smiling baby, busy crawling on the dry grass of the lawn in his romper suit, delighted when he found a discarded mealie pip and tried to put it in his mouth. Elizabeth quickly took it away as she picked him up and brushed him off, then introduced him to Louise who was keen to make the distinction that this was 'Baby Mikey', while she was already two and no longer a baby.

I was allowed to join the Thursday dinner that week and Johnny was to be there this time as well. Louise came with us in the usual way when we went out at night, accustomed to sleeping in the car. When we arrived for dinner Elizabeth was delayed and we were told this was because she always sat with Mikey until he went to sleep, which could take hours. This infuriated Cen who insisted dinner must be served at eight sharp and no one could sit down until Elizabeth was present, so there was deadlock. Alison was anxious to avoid a scene, 'Surely, Cen, we can delay dinner just a little. It won't make any difference. We're only having stew and that can't spoil.'

'Damn it, Alison, we can't have dinner held up by the demands of an infant.'

'Well, if dinner has to go ahead on time, you must allow Elizabeth to come later when she's ready.'

'Oh, very well,' he said, 'but the servants are not staying on to serve her at midnight if it takes that long.'

'Don't be ridiculous, Cen, it won't take that long. Mikey's a good easy child.'

Grudgingly, when Pedro announced dinner, Cen indicated our places at table and we sat down with Elizabeth's place left empty. Peter was apologetic. 'Elizabeth would be incapable of swallowing a mouthful unless she was satisfied that Mikey was safely asleep. It's normal for mothers to feel this way.'

'Why isn't Wendy sitting in the car with Louise then?' Cen said sarcastically.

'That's enough, Cen,' Alison interrupted, 'Elizabeth will be here soon.' But she wasn't, and the meal finished without her, all of us sitting through each course studiously ignoring the empty chair, while Alison glared at Cen to make sure he didn't comment on it.

Infant sleeping routines lay far from my own concerns, worrying about what was happening at Forest Lodge since Fa and Muz had returned. Usually Muz wrote faithfully every week when we were apart, but this time no word came from her which only increased my unease. No letter came from Fa either, but eventually there was one from Ros, with bad news.

Another Craddock disaster, I thought dismally, fitting an almost inevitable sequence of misfortunes since a train of them had been set in motion. It started this time with Fa and Muz's arrival home after a very long and complicated journey via planes, trains and buses. When at last they opened the front door of Forest Lodge they found the house devastated. A tank in the loft had sprung a leak and flooded every room. Ceilings had fallen, parquet flooring had peeled off, Persian rugs were floating in a tide of debris and worst of all, Muz' precious grand piano was a wreck. The tenants had left some weeks before without telling the agents, and neighbours had not realised that anything was wrong. All that Fa and Muz had left were the contents of their suitcases as they went to find somewhere to stay while the house was cleared and renovated. When it was habitable again they moved back in, each of them in a state of nervous exhaustion, particularly Fa who was wretchedly on edge and jumpy, more so than ever before, Muz said. She had become depressed and fearful in the face of this latest setback and Fa's despondent mood. He had always been the one directing their lives, but now seemed completely adrift.

The culmination came quite suddenly not long after, as he announced to Muz that he was leaving her and going by himself to take up a job as medical officer at RAF Marston in Norfolk. He explained that the decision was an intensely painful and conflicted one that rested on his conscience with no defence, Muz being blameless. This was no comfort to her, and Ros reported that Muz then took to her bed and was inconsolable. Spindle remained in limbo in hospital, and Ros hurried home whenever possible from Corsham to give what support she could. I was useless at such a distance and, stricken with guilt at having forced the issue with Fa, felt compelled to do something to help Muz restore meaning to her life now that Fa was no longer there as her guiding light. Escaping the confines of Forest Lodge where she endured daily the memory of Fa announcing his departure and driving off, seemed essential. I thought that inviting her to come over to us for the baby's birth might give her a new focus, so I wrote saying we needed her and would pay her fare. She could stay with us for as long as she liked, and it would mean so much to have her with us, I said. To my surprise she responded readily and started making plans to close up Forest Lodge again, leaving the neighbours in charge this time.

Adam suggested I should take a break from farm work to prepare for the baby and rest up a bit now that physical work at the calf sheds was becoming more tiring. My efforts there had produced worthwhile results and Cen, who needed convincing, asked for a report with evidence backed by figures. This was straightforward as all births, weights, diseases and deaths were recorded, so I wrote a report showing that in the two years that I had taken over management of calf-rearing, mortality had fallen to less than 3%. Alison was furious. 'This is all made up,' she stormed, shaking the paper in my face. 'How dare you try to say that the calves are doing better with you in charge.'

'I'm not trying to prove anything. I'm just producing figures as Cen requested,' I said, hoping to sound conciliatory.

'Well, Ad says you're going to concentrate on the baby now, so I can take over again. He knows what's best for the calves, and what's best for this farm.'

Elizabeth and Peter's visit with Mikey had temporarily soothed and calmed Alison, but now their visit was over she felt bereft without them and was turning her fire on me to counteract the loss, I thought. But a couple of incidents occurred soon after, that revealed another scenario.

I was in the farm office one morning when the phone rang and it was Billie. She sounded upset and breathless as she explained: 'My car broke down on the main road just past Naivasha and I got a lift to Gilgil where I'm phoning from. Please ask Cen to come and give me a tow, it's urgent. I'm getting a lift back to wait in the car so it doesn't get its tyres stolen.'

'I'll go and find Cen straight away, don't worry,' I told her.

Cen wasn't in the house and neither was Alison. After enquiring at the workshops, it appeared they had gone to inspect a water tank at the top of the farm. I drove up there and found them looking at the tank. Cen listened quietly as I relayed Billie's message to him, but Alison exploded. 'That bloody woman again, why can't she leave us in peace. I suppose you'll have to go and rescue her, damned tiresome and tedious.' It was the first indication I'd had that there might be someone other than me upsetting Alison.

Not long after this, Adam was asked by Cen to go and perform a post mortem on one of the steers that had died on Billie's farm and I went with him to help. The farm, Naitolia, was too dry for crops but ideal for ranching on its several thousand acres rising from the plains of Gilgil to the Rift escarpment. This mighty ridge formed a natural boundary on one side of the farm with, at its foot, the glorious Malewa river on its tumbling course, fast-flowing and full of rainbow trout. Billie's house stood in command of these majestic views while also looking west across acacia plains to the wide blue expanse of Lake Naivasha shining in the distance. The Malewa river was considered by fly-fishermen like Fa to be one of the most beautiful and prolific of all the many great rivers in Kenya.

When we had completed the post mortem – a messy one as decomposition was rapid in that heat – we went for a wash at Billie's house. She was not there and her African butler, a courteous man dressed rather splendidly in white *kanzu* and scarlet cummerbund, showed us to Billie's ensuite bathroom, handing us clean towels and closing the door. On our way out a few minutes later, passing through Billie's bedroom, we noticed something we had not seen on the way in. The double bed had been turned down and on one side there was Billie's nightdress carefully laid out, while on the other, just as neatly folded, was a pair of men's pyjamas. 'I recognise those,' Adam said, 'they're Dad's.' He didn't seem surprised. 'Dad spends a couple of days here every week to check on the steers, and stays the night, obviously. I know Mum doesn't like it, but what can she do? It's one of the reasons she gets so ratty. Dad being so friendly with Billie.'

'You said they were old friends, all three of them the best of friends. It looks like your dad is something more than a good friend, and your Mum is expected to put up with it.'

'It's a choice between that or forcing the issue and causing a major drama.'

I thought of Muz and Fa, and how forcing him to confront the issue with Babs had led to the present rupture with all its seismic consequences. It must be more healthy, I thought, to break away and build a new life with fresh purpose, rather than live drowning in perpetual unhappiness and frustration.

Occasional letters arrived from Fa, with no mention of Babs, while in true Fa style the letters were full of bright-eyed observations of the Norfolk countryside, and forays with binoculars exploring what was there amidst the captivating effect of novel surroundings. It was plain to me, if not to him, that the undemanding nature of the job at RAF Marston would not hold him for long, and the next move I suspected would depend very much on what Babs had in mind.

CHAPTER 10

The farm workers were always a couple of jumps ahead of us with intuitive awareness of all happenings on the farm, including what anyone's next move was going to be. Surmising that I needed now to employ an ayah, they sent me a plump jolly Kipsigis woman, Mama Elizabeth Laboso, who arrived at the back door one morning with her possessions carried in a suitcase on her head. She was a relative of Arap Milgo, our African assistant manager, and was warm and motherly, very black and very dear. I took her on gratefully, and Louise put her arms around Elizabeth's stout legs as if to say, 'She's ours now.'

Halfway down the drive a group of huts stood in their own neatly swept compound where Elizabeth was given one among those of the other staff. Her three young children came to live with her, soon becoming close friends with Louise, and in the quiet hot afternoons when Elizabeth went for a siesta, Louise went to nap on her bed with her in the cool dark interior of her hut.

Preparations for the baby were well underway and Louise had decided she wanted a sister. 'We don't want boys, do we,' she said, as if that settled the matter, but Elizabeth told her that God would decide.

Adam had his own expectations. 'If we're having another baby we need to have another dog,' he announced during one of these discussions. 'Mum says the Morralls' Labrador bitch has a litter ready weaned and I think it would be good to have a puppy growing up alongside our own new one, playing together. Good for Ruin too since she lost her recent litter.'

Ruin had mated by mistake with a stray mongrel, which meant that all the puppies had to be euthanised at birth as no one would take them with doubtful breeding when there were purebreds to be had. There was an exception to this view when one of the noble Hill pointers produced what Cen referred to as a bastard pup, just one, and as the pointers were so neurotic they seldom bred at all, this single offering was treasured and given to Adam as a birthday gift. He called the nondescript puppy Beetle for its shiny black coat, and when the Labrador puppy arrived from the Morralls, he was named Roger. The two of them were instantly adopted by Ruin, who perhaps thought they were her missing pups that had mysteriously reappeared none the worse for vanishing at birth.

Roger, from the first moment, showed himself to be remarkable in his abilities, quick to learn good behaviour and fetching skills, while having an altogether charming personality and gentle disposition. All three dogs were very much Adam's pack and went with him everywhere on the farm, the puppies scrambling to climb into the back of the Land Rover desperate not to be left behind whenever they heard car keys being jangled out of Adam's pocket. I felt jealous of this fawning attachment to him and thought it only fair that I should have a dog of my own, who would stay at home and keep me company. A small dog I thought, a house dog, and when I heard from the vet that one of his customers had Dachshund puppies available, I went to see them. I wanted a female, thinking I might breed from her as these were pedigree pups and Dachshunds were popular. There was just one female left, and when I got home with this tiny animated sausage lifting an enquiring nose to peer out of its basket, Louise was smitten and said we must call her Piglet because she was so small and looked like Piglet in the Pooh books.

She was a perfect size to curl up on my lap in the evenings and become my shadow, staying close and affectionate, my own little dog. But Piglet was a feisty small beast with ideas above her station, determined to join the pack as time went on. All too soon in the evenings, instead of sitting on my lap she jumped onto Adam's, her nose pointed towards his face as she gazed adoringly into his eyes. All attempts to bribe and cajole her back to my side were rejected, and in the dark early mornings when Adam left to go to the milking, she scampered after him. I could hear him releasing the chain that lowered the tailgate of the land Rover for Ruin to jump in, and then the younger dogs would be lifted up one by one, Piglet bouncing with excitement just like her namesake in the books.

When Muz arrived, Elaine and Les met her off the plane in Nairobi and took her to stay with them for a few days before putting her on the Peugeot taxi to Nakuru. We had built a guest wing onto one end of the house, ready to receive her by the time she arrived, so she would be comfortable and have her own space. Louise now slept in what had been the spare room, and the baby's cot stood waiting next door in the small lobby that doubled as an improvised nursery.

The waiting became prolonged as the baby was late, and Bunny was reluctant to interfere this time since the previous fashion for inducing babies on the date they were due had proved unsafe. Adam was impatient and took me for a long walk across rough ground in midday heat. 'It will make the baby feel uncomfortable and want to get out,' he suggested. He was right, as the exertion got things started by the evening and he took me to hospital confident this time that the birth would be easy and quick. Everyone said second babies came faster – first ones having blazed a trail. There was not much evidence for this theory however by the next morning, after a long night labouring through the usual process.

Bunny visited early, thankfully sober, and after a quick assessment said the baby was POP (persistent occipital presentation), which meant its head was bent forwards, impeding normal delivery, so it needed to be manipulated into the correct position. This scared me but Bunny was gung-ho, wielding the ventouse extractor with a flourish to demonstrate its efficacy. It looked very much like a bicycle pump and I said so.

'Yes, the principle is much the same, but it's a powerful implement and this is a tricky procedure so you're going to need knocking out with pethidine to get you through. We don't want you yelling the place down,' he remarked cheerfully.

The experience was a mighty struggle and no less of a torture than last time, but quicker, and by lunchtime I had a large strident boy in my arms, as different from Louise as cheese and chocolate. In the afternoon, when patients were settled for rest times with no visitors allowed until later, the boy was still making so much noise he was banished from my room to the nursery, where he continued to rage, making me feel anxious as I listened to him, unable to doze. I rang the bell, asking to feed him as I thought he might be hungry after such an ordeal of vigorous extraction, but when the nurse came she insisted it wasn't my baby crying, saying in any case it was too soon for him to need a feed. This only increased my anxiety as I knew it was him, I already knew his voice with the insistence of its sound, and that this new person was not going to be another Louise, calm and controlled. My friends had said Louise's temperament reflected my own unfussy attitude to pregnancy and motherhood, which I took as a compliment and felt quite smug about it, assuming this next baby would respond to my virtues in the same way, but it was obvious at the earliest stage that this one would not be conforming.

Adam didn't seem as thrilled to have a son as I had expected but later, back at the farm, I noticed in the cattle records that he had marked the event with the words: '*Today, 24th October 1966, Wendy had a bull calf.*' It was Johnny's birthday as well, so we took that as a good omen.

Along with the reversal in obstetric practice on inductions, another new concept had been introduced since my last stay in the maternity ward. Instead of ten days 'confinement' in hospital allowing blessed respite from the hurly-burly of home life, it was now thought unhealthy for new mothers to lie in bed risking deep vein thrombosis, and a four-day recovery regime was the new rule. I was still feeling tired at the end of four days and had a slight temperature, but Bunny pronounced me fit and I took the small pile of clothes I had ready for the baby to dress him for going home. One of the nurses said he must have his cord shortened before getting dressed, which surprised me as cords were usually left to detach themselves by natural process after a few days. She was a new nurse from Ireland and insisted this was normal practice 'back home', but she cut the cord so short it bled a great deal and needed a dressing which I knew could not be right, though she insisted this was entirely correct.

Muz, who was a qualified midwife and waiting at home for us, was incensed at what the Irish nurse had done. 'Telling you that's what they do in Ireland is in no way reassuring,' she said indignantly. 'When did the Irish start making up rules for the rest of us? Let's hope it heals quickly.'

Muz had many prejudices and Irish Catholics were up front, followed by jazz players, and anything she considered vulgar such as gladioli flowers. But I was grateful to have her there helping me and looking after Louise, with assistance from ayah Elizabeth who was proving as capable and unassuming as we could have wished.

There had been a lot of discussion on names for the baby as Alison had strong views. Adam and I both liked Evan, which was a family name, but Alison vetoed this. 'You can't call him Evan,' she said. 'It has to be something that goes with Hill. People will drop the aitch and he'll be Evan 'ill.'

'I don't see why people can't say Evan Hill without dropping the aitch,' Adam reasoned. 'We don't know many cockneys.'

Alison sniffed at the mention of cockneys. 'What about David?' she suggested. 'Granny Hill would be pleased.' Granny's maiden name was David, from a large extended family of Welsh Davids, and it was Adam's second name in honour of this connection.

My own view was that we needed something a bit more distinctive than David to go with a plain surname like Hill. To me, the name belonged to a whole clutch of plain names like Jim, John, Tim and Tom, none of which signified much of an identity when joined up with Hill, but these were the sort of names Adam thought safer than my preference for strong names like Roland, Ryder, Silas or Simeon. Adam dismissed these as fanciful, and when I pointed out that his own name, Adam, though unusual, went very well with Hill, he said he had never liked it and had been teased at school.

Louise didn't want a brother, but did have an opinion: 'I think Nigel is the best name,' she said. 'I like that one the best.' We didn't know any Nigels, so this was a surprise.

'That's no good, he would be called Nig,' Adam said quickly, and the discussion languished until at last after several days of deliberation, I agreed to three innocuous names: Simon Robert Evan, and everyone was happy. Except that the slightly raised temperature I had come home with got worse, and the hole in Simon's middle where his cord had been cut off became infected, so he developed a fever as well. Muz tucked the two of us in bed together where I could feed him lying down when I became too ill to sit up.

At this point Elaine and her family arrived to visit and the house became crowded and noisy with people coming and going, busy talking in loud voices. This would be a welcome sound at any other time, but the slightest noise jarred me now as the illness worsened and my sensitivities increased along with rising levels of pain and fever. Muz became alarmed, suspecting that I had puerperal fever, a complication of childbirth. She phoned Bunny from Cen and Alison's house, asking him to come urgently with injectable antibiotics, and to his credit he arrived quickly, looking concerned. He confirmed the diagnosis and injected me with a hefty dose of procaine penicillin, doing the same for Simon after looking at his infected wound. He said that cords should never be interfered with, but if it was common practice in Ireland, he had no comment. Louise was very upset when she saw the big needle going into Simon's small buttock and screamed almost as loudly as he did. The antibiotic followed by oral doses took effect so quickly that each of us was on the mend very soon, but sadly I was unable to continue feeding Simon myself as the fever had dried up the milk supply.

During the hiatus of my absence from normal household comings and goings, Muz took charge, so that meals were produced at the usual times and visitors looked after while I lay in bed with Simon. She had been the one rescuing me from crisis this time, while last time, with Louise, it had been Fa. What would have happened without either of them looking after me was too disquieting to think about.

For Muz, being busy was the best kind of therapy and diversion from her own anguish. She felt needed and valued again after the heartbreak of rejection by Fa, and with her many capabilities she provided stability for us at a shaky time. Elizabeth was a stabilising presence too, and doted on Simon whom she called: '*Bwana mdogu wangu*', (my little master). As soon as he was well enough to go out, she took him for walks in the pram, with Louise helping to push; reminding me of walks with Ah Pu our Burmese nanny when it was Elaine in the pram and me reaching to hold the handle with her.

During this time, Fa wrote long affectionate letters to all of us, including Muz, as if nothing had happened, hinting that he had never intended his job at RAF Marston to be more than a temporary position while considering other options. We speculated that he was biding his time while Babs rearranged her life to accompany him to some exotic destination where they could live together incognito. We waited breathless to hear the next revelation; it was still the sixties and couples in their situation who went off together were objects of scandal, especially if they were professional people where it could affect their employment status. Fa had asked Muz for a divorce, but she refused on the grounds that she was bound by her marriage vows, maintaining that since she had done nothing wrong, why should she suffer the shame of divorce, allowing Fa and Babs to skedaddle with the happiness they had stolen from her?

By immersing herself in our household of ceaseless visitors, the sorrow of her single state was eased while there were meals to be cooked and delivered to the table, children and servants to be cared for, dogs kept under control, and frequent emergencies attended to. Since Simon's birth, the farm clinic had transferred itself to our back door and Muz helped with the dispensing of advice and medicines, as well as driving people to hospital if they were too sick for our simple procedures.

What we dreaded most among those turning up at the back door were any victims of seriously nasty accidents, especially agricultural ones involving the kind of machinery that mangled hands or limbs. When a shout came from the kitchen one morning to warn us of a small procession coming down the drive carrying a shape slung in a blanket, I was apprehensive. I watched them approach, the blanket acting as an improvised stretcher with an inert bundle inside, and steeled myself for a sight I did not want to see or have to deal with. The blanket was lowered, none too gently, to the ground, but instead of revealing a lacerated figure, a demented one sprang out and leapt onto me with arms of manic strength clasped around my upper body. Tightening his grip, he shrieked that I was his mother and would save him now that he had found me. The servants gathered round enthralled, not wanting to miss any of the drama, wanting to know who the madman was, as no one recognised him. The general consensus, offered helpfully, was that he was most likely running away from the police after killing someone, or he might be bewitched after having a spell put on him. While this debate ran on, I remained pinioned in an iron embrace as the man wailed and slobbered, imploring me to help him.

Adam was away on the farm and we had no telephone for emergencies, so it was decided after much excitable discussion that I should climb into the back seat of the car with the deranged man still clinging to me, and Muz would drive us to the African hospital with an escort in the front seat. More commotion followed at the hospital as we arrived and were extricated from the car. The sight of me and the demented man joined like grotesque Siamese twins in a state of acute distress, being bundled into the casualty department, caused uproar with everyone shouting instructions or running for cover. Staff had to administer a sedative injection to the man before he could be detached and then, they assured me, he would be tied to a bed while waiting for the police to come and decide what to do with him. A few days later when I went to the hospital with another patient and enquired about the man, staff said he had managed to escape before the police arrived. I had to hope that he would not reappear at my back door, and the staff reassured me, saying that he would not remember how he got there in the first place.

At Christmas Adam was given a bonus which was hugely appreciated, enabling us to buy a larger car for the accommodation of two children plus varied passengers and cargo. We traded in the old Anglia which had not entirely recovered from its collision with the buck, and bought a nearly new Ford Cortina estate with room for all needs, including mattresses in the back for the children to sleep on when we went out at night. It was a valiant car with a gutsy engine and tough suspension that could ride the unmade roads with equanimity. This type of car also fitted in very well with polo on Sundays, when lunch for large numbers of players and spectators had to be prepared at home by polo wives like me, then transported to Njoro or Kinyatta Club. After several chukkas had been played, the players, in addition to urgent thirst, would have gargantuan appetites. I worked out how to meet this with the kind of food that could be wolfed down in quantities while standing chatting in groups on the club veranda; beer glasses balanced on the balustrade.

Thick slices of meat loaf went down well with beer, together with curry pies and sausage rolls, all home-made. These were served alongside big Tupperware bowls of cooked chopped potato mixed with chives and mayonnaise, various salads, and piles of hot garlic bread. Pudding was my speciality – I always made a hundred chocolate eclairs, and other wives brought their own signature pieces. Alison's contribution was a whole cheese from the cheese factory with crackers and farm butter, which was always popular. She never did any cooking herself, declaring, 'I am like Queen Victoria, I do not cook', but we noticed Cen's eyes lit up whenever good food was offered at someone else's table. Very occasionally he and Alison would accept an invitation to lunch or dinner at home with us, reluctantly, feeling uncomfortable in our house as if they were slumming. But once Cen had a plate of something enticing in front of him, he would exclaim, 'Damn good this. Eh, Alison?' It was a dig at her for the inadequacies of her own table, but she would hardly touch what was presented at ours, as if to endorse the indignity she felt when being expected to eat 'down at yours', as she put it.

Soon after the Cortina arrived, there was a polo tournament at Njoro Club and Adam went off early to meet the visiting team and help with arrangements for the match. The Cortina with its wide, flat, rear compartment, was ideal for stacking boxes and trays of food prepared for lunch. Muz helped, and when all was loaded including the children, Simon in a carry cot, we put the last trays of eclairs on top of the boxes and went back inside to get our handbags, ready to go. It was a hot day and I left the Cortina tailgate open for ventilation, failing to anticipate what would happen next. The dogs, shut in the house with instructions to staff not to let them out until we had gone, somehow escaped at this point. Not wanting to be left behind, they jumped into the back of the car on top of the food, bouncing around with excitement for what they thought was an outing, trampling and squashing everything including the eclairs which flew around scattering cream like confetti. Louise was outraged, shouting from the back seat, 'Look what the dogs are doing! Pieces of food are even going into my hair. And onto Simon as well.' I called the dogs and they jumped out obediently, well trained by Adam. Muz had arrived with her handbag, and together we surveyed the devastation.

'Most of it can be reassembled and no one will know,' Muz offered in her practical way. 'The meat loaves and other savouries can be moulded back into shape, and the broken eclairs piled into pyramids with more chocolate icing poured on top, so they can be transformed into profiteroles.'

With the dogs safely shut indoors again and staff helping to patch up the food, we later served the restored trays to players and spectators, with everyone exclaiming at the magnificence of the profiteroles (any imprint of dog paws thankfully undetectable).

Granny Hill and the Aunts back at Howleigh in England had been ecstatic when news of Simon's arrival reached them. The birth of a male heir to their line of the Hill family was seen as a significant event and excited letters arrived from Granny and each aunt, with pressing invitations to visit at our earliest opportunity with the children. Regular handwritten letters were a lifeline between families at this time as there was no other means of communication besides radio telephone or telegrams, which were used only in emergencies or for urgent news.

Muz and I waited each week for a letter from Ros who was due to leave college that year, and we hoped would come and join us in Kenya while deciding how her degree in Fine Art might lead to some kind of wage-earning future. Contact with Spindle came through the hospital social worker who sent Muz sporadic reports on his progress, or lack of it. We wished Fa would visit and report back on how he was, each of us aching for news of him in a more compassionate way than the clinical assessment of someone assigned to this task; besides which Spindle would be overjoyed to see Fa and have the reassurance that his family still cared about him. In replying to Fa's breezy letters, Muz urged him to go and see Spindle, but we knew Babs was not sympathetic. She blamed poor Spindle for 'unhappiness' in our family, so this opinion was unlikely to encourage any initiative from Fa to relieve Spindle's predicament, but as Fa made no mention of Babs, we had no idea what was going on between them.

After their last visit to us, Elaine and Les had been posted to Ethiopia where they faced a challenging missionary assignment in a much less developed country than Kenya, but were delighted that this offered them a more pioneering type of missionary work. Soon after arriving, news came that Elaine was pregnant again which was good news in one way, but not so good that the only medical help available was a rural African hospital where they lived, several hundred miles from more sophisticated services. Luckily MAF flights to Nairobi were frequent, so they had this connection, and were able to come and visit us again in the new year of 1967.

When they arrived we were startled to see that Elaine was already huge, although the baby was not expected for another four months. We were sure it must be twins, but Elaine said a Dutch woman doctor who ran the African hospital had examined her and said there was definitely only one baby. We were sceptical, and thought she should be checked by a doctor in Nairobi and get an X-ray. Elaine was adamantly against this on the grounds that an X-ray would suggest she didn't have complete faith in the Dutch doctor's expertise, who in addition recommended a home delivery for the birth, which she herself would attend, assisted by her partner who was a Dutch nurse.

'A home delivery in the wilds of Ethiopia!' Muz was aghast. 'That would be crazy, taking such a risk. Les can't be happy about that when you could easily get to Nairobi in good time, with proper hospitals.' She looked at Les for support.

'All the missionary wives, when they are due to give birth, fly to Nairobi a month before the expected date. It's normal practice,' he said. 'But Elaine wants the baby to be born at home, and the Dutch doctor is all for it. I'm not happy about it and ... ,' he broke off, looking at Elaine who was sitting calmly with her mind made up. 'Won't you listen to your mother?' he urged.

Elaine had a steely determination when she was set on something. 'I haven't decided on this without proper thought and prayer,' she said, quelling Les with a look. 'I've prayed about it and God will be looking after me so there's nothing to worry about. Anyway, Rachel's birth was easy and the doctor says it's a positive sign for the next one.' She looked around at us, smiling. 'Everyone should be glad and happy, not thinking about problems.'

That seemed to settle it, and though Les still looked uncertain, we all knew nothing was going to divert Elaine once she had God on her side.

Even with good medical services, in our case not too far away, Simon was still getting recurrent infections, mostly now affecting his ears and causing him to wake each night screaming in pain. Nothing seemed to relieve this: standard analgesics were only temporarily effective and repeated courses of antibiotics failed to clear the infection. If only we had Fa with us, I kept thinking. None of us were able to get a full night's sleep and we were all in despair watching him suffer. In between bouts he was a happy vigorous child, intent on exploring and investigating everything around him, not shy about making his wants known loudly and insistently. Louise didn't approve of such demonstration and made it clear that, in her view, Simon's arrival did not provide unmitigated joy for her. This kind of reaction is not uncommon when a second child arrives and steals the spotlight. To some degree Adam compensated for this in his devotion to Louise, lifting her onto his knee, saying, 'You're my *special* girl, and you're going to be *three* soon, almost grown up.'

The birthday party was an absorbing topic and Louise had definite ideas about it. She wanted a picnic on the farm: 'Where the big trees are, so we can be in the shade, and my friends can come.' The big trees were tall spreading acacias at the top of the farm in an area called Ngata where there was better rainfall for trees to grow large and bushy. Louise was impatient to go and choose a spot so it could be prepared if the grass needed to be cut. Ngata was on the other side of the main Nakuru to Njoro road, some way from the house, so we took the car and were driving up a track towards the big trees when we met Cen and Alison in their pickup, coming down. We stopped and I leaned out of the driver's window to tell them about our tree search, but before I had a chance to speak, Alison interrupted, looking annoyed. 'What are you doing on this side of the farm?' she said crossly, 'I wish you would keep to your own side.'

I explained about the picnic party, but this seemed only to irritate her further. 'We don't want you having children's parties on Ngata – strangers driving up there. This is a private road.'

I was taken aback at the unexpected rebuke, unable to understand what had provoked it, and didn't want Louise to be disappointed. Looking at the surprise on her face I said quickly, 'That's all right, we can find somewhere else,' and started turning the car around as Cen and Alison drove off.

'Where are we going now?' Louise asked, bewildered by the change of direction

'There are some lovely big trees near the river,' I reassured her. 'We won't have such good views from there, but it will be easier to get to, and Grandma won't mind us being there.'

'Why does she mind us being at Ngata?'

'She doesn't want strangers driving up there.'

'My friends aren't strangers.'

'I think she's worried about anyone else discovering nice picnic places on the farm, and then having their own picnics there without permission.'

'What's *permission* mean?'

'Letting someone do something that they are not allowed to do without asking first.'

'Like Simon wanting to play with my toys?'

'Yes, exactly like that, but he can't understand yet, so you will have to wait for him to ask permission later, when he's a bit older.'

'When is he going to get a bit older?'

'Oh, look, there are the trees,' I said quickly, pointing ahead, glad to interrupt that line of questioning.

I had a particular tree to aim for, not too far from a track leading to the river where its course was marked by some big acacias in a pasture where the cows often grazed. We parked the car beside a likely tree and got out to inspect it and the surrounding area. Louise walked around on her short legs, then stopped indignantly, pointing at the ground: 'There are disgusting cow pats all over the place. They've even got flies on them. My party can't be here.'

'We can get rid of the cow pats. They will be easy to scoop into buckets and take home for the garden. The grass can be cut nice and short and we can take rugs for people to sit on. It will be perfect,' I told her.

'I want Daddy to look at it first,' she said, unconvinced, 'and be sure there are no thorns fallen off the trees that can scratch.' For a three-year-old she was surprisingly fussy .

I asked Adam what Alison meant about keeping to our own side of the farm. Did that mean I was banned from the Ngata side, and if so, why?

'It seems to be a weirdly territorial thing with her,' he said. 'When you stopped doing the clinic and office work, and the calves too, before Simon was born, she was delighted to have it all to herself again. Not that she does anything useful in any of those areas, more's the pity. The calves are back to the old Belsen regime with her in charge, dying like flies.'

'I'm surprised your dad is happy about that,' I said. 'He's usually more concerned with commercial results than family dynamics, so I would think he is less bothered about who looks after them as to who does the best job of keeping them alive.'

'Quite so, darling. But he has to keep Mum happy, and now you're starting to come back to work again, at my request I have to say, Mum has got into a flap-doodle about you putting her out of a job. Turning up every day on what she regards as her patch. Even giving orders to her servants, she alleges.'

'You know I wouldn't do that. What does she mean?'

'She says you ordered Pedro to sweep the office one morning.'

'I saw him standing outside the back door with a broom, just standing there doing nothing. So I asked politely if he could do a quick sweep of the office floor which was deep in dust from the road. But it was tactless, I know. I should have realised Mum would be touchy about it.'

'She's more than ever touchy just now. The thing is, it's really Billie she's mad at. She can't attack Billie, so she attacks you instead, simply because you're nearer to hand and can't retaliate. We'll have to ride it out, and try to avoid doing or saying anything that provokes her.'

'That's all very well, but we have a family now and it affects all of us if she carries on like this. I do wonder if she is actually trying to drive me away. It does feel like that sometimes.'

He put his arms around me and it felt protective and comforting as he said, 'You know she doesn't mean it, not personally. She's very fond of you really. Be patient, it will blow over. Just tread gently in the meanwhile.'

Muz and Alison were opposites in temperament and upbringing, but had a grudging respect for each other whenever they met: like two cats on stiff legs, their backs not quite arched, but poised. When I told Muz about the encounter on the road to Ngata, and Adam's explanation, she was sanguine, with possibly some sympathy for Alison trapped in the Billie situation. 'Don't let the unpleasantness get to you, just carry on being yourself, making light of these difficulties,' she advised. 'You know what Fa always says: *nil carborundum* – don't let them grind you down.'

At the mention of Fa we both brightened, as he had told us that he was leaving RAF Manston and, astonishingly, had taken a job as resident doctor with Brooke Bond tea estates at Kericho, so he was coming back to Kenya. There was more good news as Ros was coming too, having left college with her degree, she had a job teaching art at Kaptagat School. So there we were, all of us soon back together again, except for poor Spindle, who still nevertheless clung to the hope that he would be cured and released to discover what real life was like.

If we thought that Fa would step off the plane in Nairobi and come straight to us at Glanjoro, we were disappointed. He was met at the airport by a Brooke Bond representative and driven directly to Kericho where a suitably smart doctor's house was ready and waiting for him. Whether Muz had been hoping his decision to return to Kenya might mean he was returning to her, she made no comment, and when I tried to ask in a roundabout way, she said she was much too busy to think about Fa's intentions. She was already fully involved in musical shows at Nakuru Players where she had been welcomed with jubilation on her return: come back at last to breathe new life into their piano and productions. Having a piano to play was always therapeutic for Muz who became transformed when playing at theatre evenings, with members buying drinks for her (non-alcoholic of course) and sweet-talking her: 'Go on Fay, give us a tune on the old Joanna.' She played numbers from current London shows and obliged with requests, but was ferocious with anyone treating the piano like a piece of furniture. She had been appalled by the state of it when she got back. 'It's quite scandalous,' she said, 'people propping themselves up on the piano with their beer glasses, then these get knocked over. Imagine the carelessness, spilling beer inside a musical instrument as highly strung as a piano. No wonder it was so badly out of tune, and some of the keys had gone dud. I had to get a tuner up from Nairobi, and pay for it myself.' But secretly she was delighted to engage and pay a tuner, and for her playing to be enjoyed and valued.

It took very little to make Muz happy. Her joy in having a piano at hand, along with the satisfaction of rescuing it from further abuse and restoring it to noteworthy health, was a delight to see. Her popularity at the Players further energised and liberated her after the calamity of Fa's departure. Most dizzying of all was the unaccustomed attention of men finding her attractive, in particular one man who was taking a close interest and refusing to allow his compliments to be ignored. Muz was not yet sixty and, no longer crushed by Fa, she had reverted to her natural state which was lively and carefree.

Her admirer, Len Allen, was an aspiring actor. Amiable and easy-going, his acting talent was more evident in the exercise of aspiration than in its execution. Wishing to be recognised as a serious actor he refused comedy parts, but inadvertently and unerringly by doing something daft on stage, he turned scenes of tense gravity into farcical mishaps. During a Robert Bolt play, while pacing about the stage as he declaimed a speech in full regalia of flowing robes and extravagant gestures, he strode through the footlights and off the platform, collapsing into the front row with such unconcern he made it look like part of the plot. The audience found it hilarious and the scene was ruined, but he seemed incapable of understanding what had gone wrong or taking any blame for it.

Muz and I wondered at this apparent mental block and other oddities. During the war, Len had been the rear gunner in a Lancaster bomber when the life expectancy of new recruits was about two weeks, but somehow he had survived numerous sorties and didn't mind describing in detail how terrifying these had been. Sitting for hours cramped in a freezing metal box, rattling and juddering under flak and the deafening roar of the engines, his responsibility was to shoot down any night fighters that came at him like darts flashing in the moonlit sky. Few rear bombers lived to tell of these experiences and those like Len who did, could easily be excused some post-trauma anomalies. He may have been left with a blip on his brain, but this could have been, for Muz, a comforting change from Fa's cerebral superiority.

Len adored Muz and took her to concerts in Nairobi and weekend outings when he wasn't working as manager of Unga Millers in Nakuru. Encouraged by his attentions she bought new clothes and even took off her wedding ring, becoming so confident in her new independence that she decided to rent a cottage: 'So Len and I can have some peace and privacy,' she said, and moved in with barely a backward glance. The cottage was on Ronda Estate, a sisal farm owned by our neighbours, Beryl and Richard Christmas, on the other side of the river. When Ros arrived she named the small house: 'Gooseberry Cottage', due to her embarrassment at being an intruder on Muz and Len's blossoming romance when she went to stay there.

The move to Gooseberry Cottage solved a problem for Adam and me as we could then have Fa to stay, but this was fraught with anxious moments when he went for long walks along the river, risking tricky encounters with Muz and Len. It did happen once but good manners prevailed and they behaved like old friends exchanging pleasantries. Muz was shaken however by the sudden appearance of Fa striding towards them, and the awkwardness of the moment. 'He didn't look all that happy,' she remarked later. 'In fact he looked quite gaunt and strained.'

'Starting a new job is a challenge,' I pointed out, 'even for Fa, and he doesn't have you looking after him, making sure he eats properly. It will have been a shock suddenly meeting you and Len on the road, I'm not surprised he looked strained.'

'I thought it would be good for him to meet Len, a war hero like himself, and see that I'm not doing so badly for myself.'

We were interrupted at this point by Juma delivering a note in Alison's handwriting. There had been a message from MAF in Nairobi asking us to contact them urgently. They had heard by radio from the mission in Ethiopia that something had happened to Elaine. She had given birth, but things had gone wrong, and Les was trying to get in touch with us.

CHAPTER 11

The Kenya telephone service was subject to frustrating vagaries and sudden disconnections but we were able to get through to MAF after a few attempts and were told a disturbing story. At first everything had gone well for Elaine and a healthy son was born without complications. Everyone was delighted and congratulations were being offered all round as the doctor completed the delivery with a routine injection closing down the birth process. This didn't go to plan as Elaine continued having contractions and when the doctor did an examination to see what was going on, she found there was another baby still inside trying to get out. These efforts were hindered by the effects of the injection and there was consternation as the baby's condition started to deteriorate. Elaine's condition also began to sink at this point and Les became very concerned, but the second baby somehow managed to emerge after a struggle, and it was another boy. Everyone's relief and joy that he had survived was immense, though he was in a collapsed state, responding feebly to resuscitation.

While attention was focused on the baby, Elaine felt herself becoming weaker and Les, with horror, noticed that she was haemorrhaging badly. Both babies were then hastily handed to him while the doctor and nurse turned their attention to Elaine. She survived the haemorrhage but the sudden massive loss of blood caused partial pituitary failure, resulting in a debilitating condition, Simmonds Disease, from which she never fully recovered.

Messages were sent to Fa who was very shocked to hear the news, and wanted arrangements to be made for Elaine to see a consultant endocrinologist in Nairobi as soon as she was able to travel. Another problem was that the second twin had suffered seizures due to oxygen deprivation during his birth and had some spasticity of his limbs, but he was feeding and putting on weight, so this was a good sign. The first twin was doing well and they were named Stuart and Murray. Stuart was the older one. During Elaine's pregnancy Les had said he hoped for a son this time and now he had two, so we felt this triumph, together with the survival of all three of them, mitigated some of the less successful aspects of the event.

We were all impatient to see Elaine and the twins, and as soon as consultations with a specialist in Nairobi had been completed, the family came to stay with us in Nakuru. Fa arrived from Kericho so all of us were together, except for Muz and Len who were tactfully secluded in Gooseberry Cottage. I expected Elaine to look limp and sickly but she was remarkably unchanged. The multiple medical problems associated with Simmonds Disease had been confirmed and explained by the Nairobi consultant, but she made light of them and I admired her resilience, while feeling frustrated that all this might have been avoided by a different approach to the birth.

'Don't you wish now that you'd listened to the rest of us and gone to Nairobi to have the twins safely in hospital?' I asked, feeling slightly exasperated by her complacency.

'No, not at all. Everything turned out all right as I said it would, with God looking after me.'

'But he wasn't. You nearly died, and Murray too. None of that should have happened. The doctor was incompetent. She failed to diagnose twins when it was obvious to the rest of us from an early stage. You were not in safe hands.'

'God saved us and that's all that matters.' Elaine was back on form, the grit that had carried her through so many previous traumas in her life was intact.

Fa meanwhile had the widest of proprietorial smiles as he circled his four grandchildren piled into one pram, his new camera recording the scene from every angle. Muz was less impressed with the small demanding tribe as Gooseberry Cottage became the most convenient place to drop them off while parents had a break. Ros, on a weekend home from Kaptagat School, said it was like a mad zoo full of wild infants screeching night and day. The twins were perpetually hungry, while nappies soaking in Milton occupied lines of buckets standing in the small bathroom, waiting to be washed by hand.

With Ros and Muz 'holding the fort' as Muz called it, Elaine was able to rest and sleep in between visits of friends arriving for lunch or dinner. The first night of this respite was blissfully quiet, but sometime before dawn on the next night we were woken by the dogs barking furiously, and when the night guard blew his whistle to indicate a problem, we were roused from our beds to go and investigate. Looking out from the veranda with torches, we could see a commotion some distance away at the end of the garden where it sloped towards a ravine forming a natural boundary.

'I do believe the dogs have bayed something down there,' Adam said, directing the beam of his torch towards the area of noise.

'*Ndiyo, Bwana,*' the night guard replied, pointing to a dark shape that loomed beyond the dogs standing in a tight pack barking furiously, Piglet's excited yaps piercing the thin night air as she joined in. '*Chui* (leopard), *Bwana,*' he said, sounding almost as excited as Piglet. A solitary leopard had a den in the ravine but it seldom appeared in the garden so Adam was puzzled. 'He's never attacked any of the dogs before. He does a bit of prowling at night occasionally, and the dogs are so rude to him he flicks his tail at them as a warning and that usually shuts them up. He knows, and they know, there are enough hyraxes in the *donga* (ravine) for him to have a feast every night if he wants. He isn't hungry, he isn't looking for dog meat, there must be something else getting them all worked up.'

A brief debate went on in Swahili with the guard, who then pointed at something else: another dark shape, shaking itself aggressively on the fringes of the melee.

'My God, it's a big old porcupine!' Adam shouted. 'See how it's got them all on standoff. 'They're having a rare good time tormenting it, knowing full well it's got the upper hand. None of them dares risk getting spiked.'

The dogs were already giving up, the sport of porcupine-baiting beginning to ebb as porcupines always won, and when Adam called them, they bounded up the dry slope that served as a lawn, panting with the exertion of so much barking and hysteria.

I turned to Elaine who had been watching, standing with us in her nightdress with a cardigan on top she looked frail and chilled in the pale light. 'Are you all right,' I asked, 'I'm sorry you've been dragged out by all this kerfuffle.' I wanted to put my arms around her, but our family didn't do hugs, so we smiled instead. She put a hand up to her head, touching her hair where it was twisted into a mass of tight curlers, fastened with a hairnet. 'I probably look a bit of a fright,' she said apologetically.

'Do you always go to bed in curlers?' I asked, astonished. 'Isn't it terribly uncomfortable having them sticking into your head all night?' She smiled again. 'It's worth a bit of discomfort to look nice during the day. You know what Muz says – women have to suffer for beauty.'

I wasn't convinced by this. Least of all by any advice on beauty from Muz. 'What about Les?' I persisted, 'doesn't he mind lying next to you like a hedgehog with all those pins sticking out.'

'He's used to it,' she laughed.

'What about on your honeymoon?' I persisted. 'You can't have worn curlers then, killing any chance of romance.'

'It's more romantic to have curly hair the next day, instead of dead straight,' she responded firmly. 'Les likes the way I look; he doesn't mind the curlers.'

I wasn't going to argue. Elaine was immoveable once her mind was made up on any subject as we all knew by now, and anyway what were we doing standing in the shivery gloom of the veranda with dew already falling, talking about hair curlers.

At the far end of the garden a series of short rasping growls from the leopard signalled that he was moving off, and a raised finger from Adam to the dogs was all that was needed to pre-empt any sound or reaction from them.

Since Elaine had become friendly with Jane, who was now married to John Fulcher, we invited her to visit with her three little girls who had been born one after the other very quickly. 'John is desperate for a son,' she told us. I already knew about that as one of the hospital sisters had described the scene when Jane was giving birth: John kneeling beside the bed praying that the baby would be a boy. 'I told him it was much too late for that,' the sister said, laughing at the memory. 'I suggested prayers during conception might be more effective. I felt sorry for his poor wife, doing her best.'

'Did he have his trusty pistol with him while he was praying?' I asked, imagining him on his knees with one hand on the pistol, adding emphasis.

'I think his wife is rather strict about the pistol and he has to keep it out of sight down the inside of his shorts these days.'

Oh, what a relief. But how uncomfortable, I thought.

John's mother had gone back to England and the family had moved into her house so that Jane was spared the challenge of raising babies in mud huts on the farm. On hearing that they were moving into Nakuru, Cen had offered to buy the farm as it had a common border with Glanjoro close to the cheese factory, and the extra land would be useful. John refused the offer on the grounds that Cen was not a believer and he would prefer to sell to someone who was a servant of the Lord.

'Bloody idiot,' Cen fumed. 'He'll get a God-botherer with no clue how to farm.' But the farm was bought by an African co-operative with money from the newly formed Settlement Board, a scheme that Cen very much approved of. Farms were changing hands rapidly in this way and we heard that Avondale, the Hemsteds' jewel of a farm which had been offered to Adam and me as a wedding present, had been sold for Settlement as well. Had we accepted the offer, though it would have been sad to give up the farm so soon, we would have become suddenly rather well off. Fa sympathised with my frustration at the missed opportunity; not from any financial consideration as he still pretended that money didn't matter, but the discourtesy of rejecting such a generous gift. The ingratitude in refusing it, he found most difficult to understand. Adam's reasoning about loyalty to his parents Fa saw as misplaced and immature.

He confided these misgivings to Muz when they met at his request to have a 'what next?' discussion since the arrival of Len in Muz's life had opened the possibility that she might reconsider a divorce. Fa was full of optimism for the future after taking up the post with Brooke Bond where he had been given a hero's welcome by his old friends and patients living on the tea estates at Kericho. I had not seen him look so happy for years, but with no hint of any future plan that included Babs, I was curious, and asked him about this.

'She will not come and join me until I am free, which means that your mother and I have to come to an agreement about divorcing. My hopes have been raised since seeing her back here making a new life for herself. The vivacious Fay I used to know has been restored, by Len, her new companion, much credit to him. She has become quite girlish again, which suits her. Our recent discussions have been much more positive and congenial on the subject of formalising things between us. Neither of us can properly move forward until that is done.'

'It would probably be easier to get a divorce here in Kenya where the courts are not so clogged up as in England. It seems to be treated almost as a trivial procedure here, organised by lawyers who take the papers to court, so you don't even have to appear in person.'

'We mustn't assume anything. Your mother and I have been married for over thirty years, it's not a trivial matter.'

It was left like that during Fa's visit on this occasion, but when Elaine heard about it during her visit she was mortified. She went to talk to Muz, to remind her about the immorality of divorce. 'You can't get divorced, it's against God's law,' she told Muz, 'and it's wrong for you to be getting so friendly with Len. You're still married to Fa. God wants you to get back together, it's the right thing to do. Marriage is sacred. You can't change what the Bible says.'

After Elaine had gone back to Ethiopia, Muz told me what had been said between them, and what she had decided to do. 'I still love your father with all my heart. There will never be anyone else. Len is a loving companion, in the sense of affectionate friendship, nothing more. The question for me is: do I love my husband enough to let him go? That surely must be the ultimate test of love in its purest sense. Not possession. Elaine did challenge me, but she sees married love in terms of Biblical law, instead of the love that conquers all things, as St Paul so sublimely puts it. So I have decided that my love for my Paul (her pet name for Fa) is strong enough to let him go. It's what I believe to be right, though I know Elaine will never see it that way.'

The eloquence and emotion of Muz's statement overcame any Craddock inhibition we might have felt about hugs, so we hugged and cried and laughed with the ecstasy of release from the struggles of what had seemed an insoluble problem, and the grief that it had to end this way. My admiration for her strength of character in finding this solution was immense. That Len had been a true friend in standing by her without making any demands as she found her way to this conclusion, swelled my estimation of him.

Elaine would have to be told, but she was already far away, and Ros, who was much closer, reacted to the news in the same way that I had. Muz wrote a letter to Fa with her blessing for what needed to be done, and so the future for him and Babs seemed now to be set fair.

Romance is infectious and the next focus, surprisingly, turned on Ros. The farm workers were full of gossip about her and Johnny, having observed them together and concluding that they were well matched. Since Adam and I had already produced healthy children, they reasoned it was obvious that Ros and Johnny should do likewise. It was a simple matter to them, just common sense.

Johnny made no secret of being in love with Ros and wanting to marry her, causing considerable alarm for Alison who felt compelled to speak to me about it.

'This is very tiresome,' she said. 'You must talk to your sister and make her see sense. She can't marry Johnny, it would be most unsuitable. Cen and I are very surprised that she would entertain such thoughts.'

I wanted to say: *unsuitable,* because she's my sister? But there was no need to make this point as Ros had already told me, although she liked Johnny very much and they were close friends, she was not in love with him, so she couldn't marry him.

I told Alison: 'You don't need to worry, Ros doesn't want to marry Johnny. He keeps asking her, but she will not accept.'

Alison was incredulous. 'You mean to say that she has *refused* him?'

'Yes,' I said, 'so your fears are at an end.'

With the marriage danger out of the way, Alison softened towards Ros and was happy to invite her and Johnny together for drinks or meals at their house. In return, and because she was generous-hearted, Ros gave Alison a portrait of Johnny that she had drawn, showing his fine features in a tender thoughtful pose. Alison had the portrait framed and it stood on a chest of drawers in her bedroom until years later it was eaten by white ants munching their way through the wooden frame and the paper inside, so that Johnny's noble face gradually disappeared in a multitude of tiny shreds carried off by the ants.

Johnny and Ros remained good friends despite her rejection of marriage, and the friendship brought him even closer into our family circle, so that all events included him and he became the organiser of Louise's birthday party.

The picnic site was mowed by Johnny and all traces of cow pats removed to Louise's satisfaction. His plan was for all the invited children to arrive at our house with their mothers and ayahs, where light refreshments would be served while gifts were presented and opened. Transport to the picnic would then be provided by tractor and trailer; the tractor driven by him while children sat on cushions in the trailer, mothers to follow in cars. All went to plan with a dozen or so children lifted into the trailer and the tailgate closed, all sitting comfortably as Johnny set off very gently with this cargo. The rest of us stood waving and taking photos as they went off down the drive, but within minutes loud wailing and distress was heard. Johnny stopped and we ran to see what had happened. We had failed to realise that children of that age have a deep fear of abandonment and when they saw us waving and disappearing from sight, they panicked. None of our explanations about joining them at the picnic site had registered, and now we had reappeared they were not going to let us go again, so all were rescued from the trailer and were taken to the picnic by car instead.

The picnic itself raised no further alarms as baskets of toys entertained those children who were happy to sit on the rugs playing, while others ran around in a game of tag organised by Johnny, and Ros sketched. Louise was impatient for the cake to be produced and candles lit, pointing out that it couldn't be a proper party until this was done and photos taken. 'Make sure you get a picture of me blowing out the candles,' she said, 'and don't let Simon get in the way.'

Simon was not the kind of child who merged into the background playing quietly by himself. He was never going to have a contemplative nature, observing others without getting involved. Even at this early age like many boys he was fascinated by fire, and candles were irresistible as we discovered on his first birthday when he grabbed the single candle on his cake as soon as it was lit, burning his hand.

If he was in his pram, he had to be strapped into a baby harness to stop him climbing out, but he still managed to find ways to open the buckle and dive over the side to escape. He would then crawl with surprising speed to find the dogs who were his best friends, and all would curl up together snoozing; a much more comfortable arrangement in Simon's opinion than the pram.

The ear infection that had caused such misery during the first year of his life was still a recurring problem and he found comfort in the dogs, who licked his ears when they were sore, as well as bruises when he toppled over or encountered head-on other hard surfaces. Once when he had been put for a nap in his pram on the veranda instead of outside under the fig tree (because it was raining), the brake somehow disengaged and the pram hurtled down the veranda steps, landing upside down on top of him, trapped in his harness. Elizabeth was distraught, thinking it must be her fault that the brake had come off, but it was probably the dogs jumping up when Simon called them. There were even more bruises this time, but no serious injury.

We were lucky that Fa was with us on one of his weekends off when something serious did happen. Simon's ear infection had entered the mastoid bone behind his ear, causing a large swelling on that side of his head which looked alarming, and was agonising for him. It was also dangerous because the infection could spread through the bone to his brain. Fa said the short courses of antibiotics that Bunny had been prescribing were never going to stamp out the infection for good, and Simon must be put on a course lasting several weeks, with an immediate injection of penicillin to stop the mastoiditis in its tracks. Fa always had his medical bag with him and gave Simon the injection as well as a sedative, then wrote a prescription for an extended supply of oral antibiotic syrup from the chemist, Howse & McGeorge in Nakuru. That was when Simon's ears began to mend, and all of us, for the first time since he was born, began to enjoy the luxury of a full night's sleep.

The Brooke Bond doctor's job was in many ways a perfect situation for Fa as there were enough interesting cases for him to feel sufficiently stretched, while the district of Kericho provided friends and stimulation as well as fine walks in grand scenery with trout rivers and forests full of birds and animals. It was wonderful to see him restored to his old beaming self: relaxed, thoughtful, entertaining, much loved and admired by all who knew him or came to know him. Andrena and Jon were delighted to have him living nearby and although they worked for a different company, all the 'tea people' mixed socially, meeting for parties at their clubs or the Tea Hotel. Added to these good things Andrena was expecting a baby, and often called to see us on the way to have check-ups with her obstetrician in Nairobi where she was booked to have the birth at the Mater Misericordiae Hospital.

In Africa daily surprises are a normal feature of life forming part of its charm as well as its challenge. We never knew how or where, but one day Piglet disappeared. She had gone with Adam in the Land Rover as usual, and jumped out with the other dogs whenever the car stopped at the dairy and other places where Adam was working. When he got home later that day and the dogs ran panting to their water bowls outside the kitchen, Piglet was not among them. Where was she? Adam went back over his route, stopping at each place, calling and searching, but there was no sign. Louise was very upset, and inclined to be morbid: 'Do you think we can go and see if there are any bits of fur or bones left, where Dad went with the dogs, in case something has eaten her?'

'He has already looked for traces,' I told her. 'She might have been stolen. Someone could probably get a good price for her in the market. A small dog with a sharp bark could be useful for guarding, and she doesn't need as much food as a big dog. They could breed from her too, and sell the puppies.'

'We'll have to go to the market and look for her then,' Louise said.

'We could offer a reward to anyone on the farm who finds her,' I suggested. We did, but the workers, who always seemed to know, said she was dead.

Eaten by a jackal or taken by a python down at the river where she would have gone to drink. It sounded plausible, but not very comforting. On a farm, animals die or are slaughtered almost routinely, and grief is overtaken by the inexorable march of new demands and things to do.

Adam was impatient for me to type papers needed for signing after Mr Gilani, one of the butchers in town, had bought beef animals from us. He was a very charming man, and whenever he came to inspect cattle, we would invite him in for tea. We enjoyed his company, discussing business and politics, since all foreigners like him, and us, were beginning to feel uneasy about the future for non-citizens in Kenya. Cen had applied for citizenship and so had a number of other Europeans, but many Asians were less confident about their prospects. There had been a massacre of non-European foreigners in Zanzibar after Independence, so it was not surprising that people like Mr Gilani felt insecure. Many were planning to move to England.

As we sat on the veranda drinking tea, I noticed that our dogs were sniffing at the turn-ups of Mr Gilani's trousers, and that he winced at the touch. Adam noticed too as each of us remembered that Mr Gilani was an Ismaili Muslim and dogs are unclean in that culture. We apologised profusely, and Mr Gilani said please not to bother ourselves, as he was a guest in our house there could be no offence.

The papers, however, were another matter as they were needed urgently to complete the sale, so I promised to have them ready by the next day. I had no typewriter of my own, and the one belonging to the farm was kept in a locked office at Glanjoro House. Whenever I needed to use it, I had to ask Alison for the key, which she was huffy about handing over, so I always felt awkward about it. This time, explaining the urgency, I was bewildered when she refused and became quite angry, telling me: 'We don't want you coming into the house office anymore, using the typewriter. It's not convenient.' I wondered if I had left its cover off the last time, or moved it, or done some other careless thing I wasn't aware of. Alison went on, 'We keep petty cash in that room so we can't have you coming in and out all the time. Our office is private.' With that she turned and went off, her keys in a bunch held tightly in her hand.

I stood there feeling startled and mortified at the implication that I could not be trusted on my own with the petty cash. This was absolutely the last straw. Alison had gone too far this time. Adam seemed incapable of standing up to her on my behalf so I would have to deal with it myself and put an end to this nonsense.

I had enough money saved from squeezing the weekly housekeeping allowance to be able to escape, I reminded myself. I would take the children and go first to the Hemsteds, who would understand completely and provide a breathing space for me to plan the next move, then to England where I could easily get a job to support myself and the children, however hard it was to leave Adam and my home. I had a friend from the Royal Free who was starting a private nursing agency and had written in a letter how much she wished I could join her. She thought we would make a great team, and there was also the offer to share her big rambling house with its twelve bedrooms should I ever be tempted, so there would be plenty of space for all of us.

I knew I had to act quickly, before anyone had a chance to stop me. The afternoon was the best time when servants were resting, and Adam would be out on the farm with the dogs. It was so easy once I had made the decision and pulled suitcases from under the bed to pack what was needed. I always travelled light. The children were having their afternoon nap and I carried them, still sleeping, to the Cortina. Anyone watching would have thought we were going on an outing as I put rugs over the suitcases, and with some extra items in a large bag including passports and cash, driving licence and nursing registration certificates, I was ready to go. The Cortina always started first time, which I was more than grateful for this time, and feeling the engine come alive I felt suddenly more alive myself, with the sense of freedom and escape from an intolerable situation. The children were still asleep on the back seat of the car; it was a hot day and the air was heavy at this time of the afternoon when people and animals were drowsy; even the flies were motionless, stuck like black dots in shady corners.

Turning into the drive, the road ahead was clear right up to the airstrip, and a mile further on would connect with the main road and freedom. For a moment I felt a pang at leaving my home and Adam, and Elizabeth too with no word to her or the other staff as I passed their group of huts. But caught up in the momentum of getting away and leaving the farm behind, I was determined that nothing could stop me now. Muz had gone to England to check on Spindle so there was no one at Gooseberry Cottage, and for once we had no visitors staying. The house had been empty and silent when the back door closed behind me; having the children with me was all that I needed.

A few hundred yards down the road when I was easing into second gear for the airstrip turn, a dust cloud appeared ahead, obscuring a vehicle that was approaching at speed. When it came closer I saw with annoyance that it was Adam's Land Rover. That's very strange I thought, too coincidental, and maddening that there was no way to avoid stopping. We both stopped. He leaned from his window, 'Where are you going?' he asked, sounding tense.

'I'm leaving. You can ask your mother why.'

'Milgo told me to come quickly. He said it was an emergency.'

'It is. How did he know?'

'Someone must have got wind.'

'Well, it's a pity you had to rush down here, because it's too late.'

'What do you mean?' He sounded alarmed and panicky. 'Are the children all right? Where are you taking them? What's happened?'

'Has your mother said anything to you about this morning, when I went to do the typing for you?'

'No, I'm completely in the dark. *Please* come back to the house and tell me what's going on, so we can talk about it. You can't leave. It would be a disaster for all of us.'

'Not for your mother.'

'Darling, sweetheart, she's out of her mind. This must not be allowed to happen. I'll shoot myself if you go. Come back. We'll make a cup of tea and talk about it. Mum has to be dealt with; she can't get away with it this time, I'm fully aware of that. If you go, she will say she always knew you were a bolter, and the victory will be hers. Don't let her do that. If we stand together she can't win. She will have to back down. I'm begging you, darling, don't give up. Don't go. Don't take the children away. This is their home. Your home.'

The colour drained from his face as, fearful that he was not getting through to me, and seeing no change in my expression, he fell silent. I had kept the Cortina engine running, ready to go as soon as he finished speaking, but the anguish and pallor in his face made him seem defenceless, and the plea about the children was a shot to the heart. They were his children too, and he was their dad. I didn't want to hurt any of them, but Alison's behaviour had gone beyond reason.

'I'm going to the Hemsteds anyway. I can't spend another day here enduring your mother's vile behaviour. It's no good making any more excuses for her, she's gone too far this time. You will have to decide what to do. It's up to you now.'

I knew that if I weakened it would only delay until later the time for taking action. The impetus of my fury drove me on, leaving Adam still stationary in the road, watching us go.

When we arrived unannounced at the Hemsteds it was almost as if they had been expecting us. 'You poor souls driven out by those scoundrels,' Joan sympathised. 'We knew it would happen. We did warn you. I suppose they are celebrating getting Adam on his own again, working like a slave for them, paying him monkey nuts. Anyway you're safe here now and we'll help you do whatever you decide.' She laughed suddenly, her attention distracted by squeals: 'Do look at the children and pugs on the floor, all roly-poly animals together.' Visits to the Hemsteds were popular events for the children playing boisterous games with the pugs who were their size, and just as daft and energetic when it came to mad scampering and romping around the place.

No one was celebrating at Glanjoro when Adam confronted Alison with the crisis and this roused Cen's annoyance. 'What the hell is going on? Where are the Gilani papers that Wendy was doing? Presumably you have done them yourself since you banned her from using the office and the typewriter. *Eh, Alison?*'

This outburst was reported by Adam when he phoned that evening and Joan answered the phone, in no mood to be placatory. 'So what did you say to them?' she demanded, 'I hope you gave them both barrels this time, instead of letting them walk all over you and Wendy. You're supposed to be married to her, not them.'

'I told them straight up that they have driven Wendy away with this idiotic feud against her, and it has to stop, or I will go too.'

'What did they say to that?'

'A lot of mumbling from Mum and harrumphing from Pa, but they did concede in the end.'

'What does that mean?'

'They agreed that the typewriter will live in the farm office from now on, and Wendy can use it whenever she wants. They have also agreed that nowhere on the farm is out of bounds, and Wendy can go wherever she likes.'

'Oh, that's very generous,' said Joan sarcastically. 'For God's sake, Adam, it's monstrous the way they have behaved. I'm surprised Wendy has put up with it for so long.'

'I think it's just that Mum hasn't known how to handle a daughter-in-law like Wendy, with a mind of her own.'

'Rubbish! Your parents are the most appalling couple of tight-arses and the sooner you cut the apron strings the better for all of you.'

Not wanting to pursue that line of discussion, Adam tried another tack. 'Mum said she would like to see more of the children and they could go and play in her garden when Wendy is busy in the office or clinic. Mum really loves the children and doesn't want any bad feeling. So we're hoping Wendy will come back very soon.'

Joan handed the phone to me and Adam repeated what he had said, sounding anxious and desperate for me to believe that things would be different, saying over and over how much he loved me and was miserable and desolate at home on his own. 'We're a family now, we need each other, we have to stick together.'

'Do you trust your parents to keep their word?'

Adam had an ace to play at this point: 'Mum has offered to have the children so you can come on safari with me when Eddie is here.'

This was certainly a golden offer. Eddie's family had a farm in Somerset near the Hills at Howleigh where Adam had spent school holidays when they often went shooting and hunting together. Adam had promised Eddie that, once he was in a position to do so, he would take him on safari to shoot buffalo and lion. This plan was now becoming a reality with dates being finalised. I had not expected to join them, but the carrot that Adam was flourishing to entice me back, was tempting.

There was another reason causing me to weaken and give in to the idea of returning. I had been ignoring the signs but now had to admit that I was pregnant again, and that possibly the effects had caused me to be more sensitive than usual, so that Alison's behaviour had tipped me over the edge.

CHAPTER 12

I could see that Alison genuinely loved the children but had been too closed up to express her feelings and reach out to them, or me. The shock of my sudden departure and the upset it caused had opened a crack in the edifice of her resentment, and when I returned she had calmed down. While not exactly welcoming, she was cordial and relaxed in conversation as she told me about plans for a play area in her garden, with a sand pit and small garden marked out for the children to plant seeds and watch them grow. This proved to be a big success and it was interesting to notice that when the children were with Alison, they seemed to have as much of a soothing effect on her as she had on them. With ayah Elizabeth in attendance they could stay in the guest wing while I joined the safari with Eddie.

Adam scorned any form of luxury on safari, believing this detracted from the raw experience of camping in the bush, so this safari was planned to be as basic as usual. Arrangements were in their final stages when a telegram came unexpectedly from Pam, telling us she was coming to stay and it would be a longer visit this time. We cabled back telling her that it wasn't convenient as we would be away on safari. A reply came by return:

GOOD NEWS ABOUT SAFARI STOP I CAN JOIN YOU

'No she can't. She can't come with us.' Adam was indignant at this sudden imposition. 'We can't have yet another extra passenger. It's supposed to be a hunting safari for Eddie and me, not a tourist jaunt.'

'Eddie might like some female company other than mine,' I suggested, 'he and Pam could get on quite well, both from county families, both unmarried.'

Eddie was the first to arrive: emerging from a taxi wearing a tweed jacket and carrying two leather suitcases, he dripped with perspiration and awkwardness. Introducing himself with a very bad stammer (which Adam had not warned me about), he tried to shake hands while his whole body jerked in the effort of speaking and I felt instant sympathy for the frustration of such a handicap. Especially on meeting strangers I thought, and was apprehensive about a serious clash when Pam arrived, bearing in mind how withering she could be in the company of guests if they failed to measure up. I had seen even the most eligible and charming of men wilt under her put-downs.

The contrast between the two of them when Pam made her entrance a day or so later was as stark as I had imagined. She loomed over Eddie who was slight of stature, so this made her appear even taller, more statuesque, poised, aloof and imperious, while Eddie's diffidence was emphasised by his speech difficulty, and all I could hope was that Pam would try to be polite to him and help to make the safari a success.

The original plan for minimal camp equipment had now to be changed for a second time. Sleeping under the stars was not an experience Adam expected Eddie to relish, so the luxury of a tent had been allowed this time, for them to share, but my inclusion required a second tent, for Adam and me, while Eddie had the other one. With the further addition of Pam to the party, the plan had to be further adapted so that she and I would now share a tent, with Adam and Eddie in the other. Adam's gun bearer Kofia, would find a space for himself as usual outside.

Pam, when she heard about the sleeping arrangements, was dismissive. 'I can't possibly share a tent with anyone else,' she said. 'I've never done that. I always have my own on safari. I wouldn't be able to sleep a wink if there was another person in it.'

Eddie, with admirable courtesy and gentlemanly forbearance, said that if Adam and I reverted to our previous plan, he could sleep in the Land Rover, and Pam could have the second tent to herself. She accepted this as no more than her due, and the rest of us sighed with relief that the matter was settled without rancour.

All the extra cargo meant that a long-wheelbase Land Rover with a trailer had to be borrowed from Tony, instead of taking our own smaller Land Rover which was the original plan. It was an eight-hour drive to the hunting area, with a lot of grumbling from Adam that we were overloaded with extra chairs and other comforts included for the accommodation of women, but he had been solicitous when I told him that I was pregnant, and though it was a bit soon for a third child he seemed quite pleased. I was feeling very well and exhilarated to be going on safari, but it was a long tiring drive and by the time we arrived at the camp site it was the usual scramble to get tents up and food organised before night closed in. I was in charge of collecting dry wood for the camp fire and getting a good blaze underway with food cooking and a basic kitchen organised.

Pam had found a camp chair and settled herself beside the fire with a damp flannel pressed to her head. Calling me over, she stretched out a hand, 'I'm gasping for a gin and tonic. The bottles are in a box over there,' she said, waving towards a stack of drink crates.

I decided it was easier to put a drink in her hand and leave her to sit by the fire where she was out of the way, rather than ask for help with supper. Everyone was hungry and tired, wanting an early night, ready to go off at first light.

We were grateful when Pam volunteered to stay in camp the next day, saying she had a good book to read, as camps left unattended were an open invitation for raids by anything with four legs or two legs passing by.

The first morning's plan was a recce of the area looking for tracks and finding out where the animals were. I went along, but stayed behind in the Land Rover at one point knowing I would not be able to keep up after fresh tracks were found and the men took off with their heavy rifles. There was a lot of tracking done that day, and the day after, but no kill.

Back at camp on the third evening we were surprised when black clouds rolled in and the weather looked as if it might change overnight, having been hot and dry before. There were ominous rumbles of thunder and occasional flashes of lightning, leading up to a sudden violent storm a few hours later when we were woken by torrential rain beating down on the tents. Kofia took refuge in the Land Rover with Eddie, and by morning as soon as there was a crack of light, we crawled out to find the whole site deep in mud, with rain still falling. There would be no hunting in those conditions with tracks washed away and animals sheltering out of sight.

The most urgent problem now was our own situation in this wilderness of wet, sticky, black cotton soil – we could be stuck for days or even longer, unable to move. If we packed up and made a dash for it, before things got worse and roads impassable, we stood a chance of getting out. Sadly it became obvious that this was our best hope, as disappointment at missing the rest of the safari turned into real fear at being stranded.

After emerging from her tent, Pam retreated to the front seat of the Land Rover, requesting that tea be handed to her through the window so she could keep out of the rain. The rest of us were too busy packing up dripping tents and equipment to do anything but try to keep her happy. Eddie, in particular, had become so nervous of being on the receiving end of her barbs that he became almost slavish in his desire to avoid aggravating her.

Land Rovers are the most robust and sporting of vehicles, and this one throbbed with horsepower as the tyres gripped and we crawled out of the flooded site and onto a track that we hoped would lead in due course to a definable road. We made very slow progress, frequently getting stuck when all hands were needed to dig and push, while Pam refused to move from the passenger seat for fear of getting her feet wet or muddy. By the end of the day as light was failing, we had only six miles to go before reaching tarmac and thought we'd made it, but then hit a bad patch where we got thoroughly bogged, and it was still raining.

'If we don't get out this time we'll have to spend the night here,' Adam said grimly. 'Pam has got to move so we don't have her extra weight in the front. She can't expect us to go on pushing with her stuck there like a sandbag, refusing to budge. She needs to help push instead. Go and tell her, Wendy,' he said, delegating the task to me. 'Make sure she gets the message this time.'

I went round to the window on Pam's side where she was sitting with her book held up in front of her face, reading in the dim light, and when I knocked on the glass she opened the window a few inches, wanting to avoid any splashes entering. I explained that it was going to be much worse for all of us if we were stuck there for the night, but she looked at me blankly, seeming to have no understanding of the urgency of our situation. 'You *have* to get out this time,' I said desperately. 'It's the one thing that can save us, reducing the load at the front, before it gets too dark to see anything.'

'But I need to finish my book before it gets dark,' she said plaintively, 'otherwise I won't know what happens at the end, and I'll be lying awake all night wondering.'

'You'll be lying in the mud outside wondering what happened to you instead, if you don't move.' I tried not to shout but couldn't help it as I was feeling totally fed up, exhausted and angry. It made no difference, she returned to her book as if I were just a silly annoyance.

I squelched my way back to where the others were taking a cigarette break, huddled under the back flap of the Land Rover.

'The only way we can get Pam out is by force,' I said. 'We'll have to drag her out. I've done my best, but she's welded to that seat, and her book.'

Eddie was the first to speak, always gallant. 'We can't force her; the last thing we need is any unpleasantness. We'll have to manage without her, and do our best, sharpish.'

We built a ramp for the Land Rover wheels as quickly as we could while the light held, collecting dead wood, stones and anything else solid lying about that we could find for one last mega-effort, hoping the wheels would grip and the ramp would hold. With heavy cloud and steady rain it was getting dark even earlier than usual and we got the last sections of ramp in place by the light of torches. With the Land Rover in low ratio on full revs and three of us pushing from behind, Adam in the driving seat operating the clutch and accelerator, the overloaded vehicle growled its way out with a gargantuan effort. We were motoring at last, and once we reached tarmac the sense of euphoria was overwhelming, despite the state we were in. All of us except Pam were plastered in mud and sweat, longing for nothing more than a hot bath, hot food, and a cold beer. When we reached Thomson's Falls we made straight for the Falls Hotel, where we were taken in and made to stand in front of a log fire to warm up and dry off with drinks in our hands before being shown to our rooms.

Pam's only complaint was that, having finished her book, she didn't have another one to keep her entertained until we got back to Glanjoro.

Alison was surprised to see us back so soon and seemed disappointed to miss having longer with the children. It was clear that they had established a bond and Louise was impatient to tell us about all the things they had been doing together. I noticed that Alison's 'Auntie Glum' expression dissolved when she was with the children, and her customary irritations vanished as she responded to their uncomplicated enthusiasm for simple things. She was able to communicate with them on their own level, which is a gift. I did not have that gift, and knew that I was not as attentive to the children as I could or should have been, so I was grateful to Alison for her kindness and involvement.

Muz was still in England, and Ros was due to go back at the end of her Kenya sabbatical to train as a medical artist in London. Fa continued in the best of spirits at Kericho, and Andrena's baby was about to be born. She had gone to Nairobi for the birth and, hearing no news after her due date had passed, I phoned the friend she was staying with. I was sure the baby must have arrived by now and was impatient to hear news, so the shock was immense when the friend said, 'Haven't you heard? The baby died.'

'What do you mean? It can't have died. How could that happen?' Such a catastrophe didn't seem possible.

'There were complications, the delivery was difficult. The baby was alive when he was born, but he died soon afterwards.'

I still couldn't believe what I was hearing. It was incomprehensible; too unbearable to understand or accept. I was glad that no one apart from Adam yet knew we had another baby on the way. It seemed unfair to say anything when this dreadful thing had happened to Andrena. But the extreme exertions on safari, battling floods and pushing the heavy Land Rover, had brought on signs of a threatened miscarriage. My previously stable pregnancy now felt uneasy.

Pam had left to continue her travels, and Eddie had gone to stay with Cen and Alison who would take him on flying trips in the Cessna to see more of Kenya, so we hoped this might compensate for the failures of the safari. Such a deluge was very unusual – six inches of rain in two days was almost unheard of in that part of the country. This setback, combined with Pam's unhelpful presence, was bad luck for Eddie on his first visit to Kenya. He never came back.

I was hoping that once we were free of visitors, Renny would come and stay with us for a few days, bringing Martin who was Louise's age, and Nettie who was soon starting school. Tony was seldom at home and Renny was often alone with the children on a farm that was isolated and challenging for a young wife and family.

Tony's absences became more frequent with increasing success in the world of professional hunting as his reputation attracted wealthy people who became regular clients. His expert knowledge of wild areas and animal behaviour, combined with an almost uncanny affinity for the bush, was remarkable in sensing where the animals were and guiding clients to them. In addition he was a consummate host on safari, a great raconteur and charming companion. Meanwhile, it was the fate of many hunters' wives to be left looking after the home and children, only seeing their husbands in between safaris and then expected to entertain clients brought back to enjoy legendary Kenya hospitality. Renny was a talented hostess, but the contrast in her life after Tony and the guests departed and the house was empty again, was often bleak in such a lonely place.

One of Tony's regular clients was a Hollywood film star, Stewart Granger, famous at the time for films such as *King Solomon's Mines*, *Scaramouche*, and *The Prisoner of Zenda*. When I met him at a dinner party with Renny and Tony, after we had been introduced he said, 'Call me Jimmy, all my friends do,' then, 'Is it true your children are left outside sleeping in the car while you are inside having dinner? It is illegal to do that in the States and you would be arrested.'

'Everyone does it here,' I told him, 'it's safer than leaving them at home. The night guard keeps an eye on them and will tell us if they wake up and need anything.'

'You're so darned blasé,' he said, laughing. 'You Kenya women are something else.' My apparent nonchalance seemed to intrigue him, and the next time we met, he asked a favour. 'It's like this,' he explained. 'A friend of mine came on safari with his son a while back. The son met a stunning girl in Nairobi who he's crazy about and wants to take her back to the States, but she's married.' He mentioned the name of a girl who was one of the Nairobi smart set. 'Do you know her?' I did, but not well. She moved in a circle far removed from upcountry farm wives like me.

'Why do you ask?'

'This idiot son of my friend has got himself a problem. You know what these rich kids are like. They think they can buy anything. His dad has contacts. The kind that will do anything for money. So this is the deal: a couple of hard guys fly from The States to Nairobi, all expenses paid. They take care of the husband, make sure he doesn't give any trouble, so the girl is free.'

'What do you mean?'

'No questions.'

'What do you want me to do?' I asked, feeling uneasy.

'I'm getting to that,' he said. 'After the money was given over and the guys had left for Nairobi, the dickhead son changes his mind and calls his dad saying he's met someone else and it's all off with the Nairobi girl. So he wants his dad to cancel the deal.'

'What happened?'

'That's what I need you to find out, for my friend,' he said, seeming to be genuinely troubled about it. 'Can you check it out?'

'I would have thought Tony is better placed to do that, with connections to the Nairobi circuit.'

'Tony says he's not in with that lot and doesn't know the guy. That's why I'm asking you.'

One person who was always plugged into the grapevine was the local hairdresser but enquiries through her revealed very little except that the husband was no longer in Nairobi and the couple had split. I relayed this rather unsatisfactory information to Jimmy and it seemed to reassure him that no bad news had been reported, but the mystery remained as to what had actually happened, or didn't happen.

The next time Jimmy came on safari he complained bitterly that his latest girlfriend, whom he was hoping to impress with his prowess in the bush, had instead been more impressed with Tony and spent the whole of the safari flirting outrageously with him, ignoring Jimmy. Immersed in the drama and tension of hunting, female clients were often drawn to professional hunters as heroic romantic figures who might be susceptible to seduction. 'I brought her along to shack up with me, not Tony,' he protested.

'You better put a ring on her finger then,' I said.

'I intend to.'

When Tony was at home in between safaris, he and Adam resumed their favourite sport of 'buffalo control', or, occasionally, 'hippo control'. At times when vegetation around the lake was sparse, the hippos left their wallowing pools to trek up-river where they could graze on ripening crops at farms like ours along the Njoro river. A hippo invasion was devastating, not only in the amount they consumed during their raids, but in the damage caused by the enormous bulk of their bodies rumbling through fields of crops like battle tanks. Having filled themselves they would then sink back into deep pools, lying submerged out of sight. Tony was summoned urgently one weekend to help Adam locate the latest raiding party of hippos, which could be persuaded to move back to the lake by the firing of shotguns overhead and strategically placed thunder flashes. It was illegal to shoot them, but they didn't know this, and the threat delivered by so much thunderous noise from guns and explosions was enough to scare them into lumbering off down-river, back to the safety of the lake.

This time we found no sign of hippos in the river after checking various locations, and concluded they must be further upstream where the river had been dammed to form a reservoir supplying water to neighbouring farms. The dam was an obvious place for hippos to conceal themselves, and Adam was certain he could see bubbles rising in a likely spot. We waited, watching for nostrils, ears, or a large head to follow the bubbles as one of them surfaced for air. They seemed to be taking their time, and Tony suggested opening the sluice gate sufficiently to expose a few broad backs. On inspecting the metal gate it was obvious that it had not been raised for several years and was firmly rusted into its supports, so a bit of persuasion from thunder flashes would be needed to loosen it.

'It just needs a short blast, enough to shift the rust,' Tony said confidently. It was a tricky manoeuvre getting the thunder flashes into position, but when they exploded against the corroded metal the effect was spectacular. With a muffled roar, instead of shifting slightly, the whole gate rose into the air in slow motion above a tsunami of water that burst through the gap, booming and rumbling as it swept down the river, collecting a bobbing tide of debris as it went. Adam and Tony stood by expectantly, waiting to see the hippos left stranded as the dam emptied. By this time a small crowd of Africans had gathered on the bank after hearing the noise and had come to see what was happening. When the last dregs of water and sludge had drained away, a vast mud bath was revealed, but no hippos. Several of the Africans remarked helpfully: 'We know where the hippos are. They were not in the dam. They are further up the river. We can show you the place.' But we'd all had enough excitement by then and climbed back into the Land Rover to go and report to Cen on the latest sightings, since he had wanted to be kept informed of the hippos whereabouts.

Back at Glanjoro House, we found Cen listening to the BBC News on the radio which could not be interrupted until he was satisfied that nothing momentous was escaping his attention. Meanwhile we were more than ready for a drink, but before there was time to lift a glass the phone rang and Cen went to answer it.

'That was the colonel on the phone,' Cen said, as he returned to his chair. 'At Molony's old place along the river, saying there's no water coming out of his taps, only mud. Do you happen to know anything about this?'

We left it to Tony to recount the drama, telling it in such a way that made it sound as if he and Adam had done everyone a favour by blowing up the dam, since it needed dredging he suggested. Cen listened attentively while lighting a cigarette then, leaning back in his chair, gave out great bellows of laughter in between wheezing through puffs of smoke: 'Colonel Blimp, crusty old bugger, won't get a bath now for at least a month, waiting for the dam to fill up. He can blame the hippos for the breech.'

Tony winked and smiled as he lifted his glass to all of us, disarming as ever.

Any lighter moments were welcome relief from those perplexing ones that had flown in lately. Andrena, and Renny too, my dearest friends, were going through difficult times and I worried about them greatly. Renny was becoming unhappy; too often alone with her small children on a farm surrounded by forest that could seem dark and forbidding, with its population of wild animals that included fierce ones like buffalo who recognised no boundaries and strayed into her garden. Kathleen had gone to live in Guernsey so there was no longer the neighbourliness of her mother-in-law living close by. To escape from her loneliness when Tony was away, Renny often went to stay with friends in Nairobi and gradually became absorbed into city society with its sophistications in an environment where possibly she felt more at home than trapped on a farm with few outlets. I felt I was losing her as I had no connections to that new scene at all.

Andrena, instead of stopping off to see us as she normally would on her way back to Kericho, had gone straight home which was entirely understandable after such a tragedy. I missed seeing her, and felt helpless, with nothing useful that I could do to make things any better. During this time, my own pregnancy was not proceeding at all well, and then Louise had an accident, so it seemed as if luck had taken a negative turn for all of us. When something bad happens, it seems to invite by some kind of baleful alchemy, a whole sequence of further unlucky events. Adam quipped: 'When sorrows come, they come not single spies, but in battalions.'

'Is that Shakespeare?' I asked, but neither of us could remember. We just knew that it was true, except that there was one piece of good fortune attending the day of Louise's accident – Fa was with us that weekend. He had gone for a walk and I was sitting at my sewing machine making nursery school uniforms. I made all Louise's dresses and most of my own, while some of my friends even made their husband's shirts. The school dresses were green gingham and I was pinning the seams ready to put through the machine, while Louise handed the pins to me, just as I used to do for Muz sitting beside her old Singer. The door to the veranda was open and a sudden gust of wind blew into the room, spilling the box of pins. 'Quick, Louise,' I said, 'go and shut the door, there's a draught coming in.'

She thought I said, 'There's a giraffe coming in, and ran to the door in a panic, pulling it shut so fast that one of her fingers was caught, and cut off at the top joint.

With all the blood and screaming it was difficult to see what could be done to save the finger, but it looked as if it might be possible to replace the severed part which was hanging by a thread, and keep it in place with a bandage while driving to hospital to have it sewn back on. Luckily Fa arrived back from his walk at this point, and after examining the injury said that suturing would cause further tissue damage, so it was better to stick the finger back together with antibiotic cream and immobilise it with a small splint. Having said this, he produced all that was required from his black bag and did an expert job on the finger. 'Leave the bandage in place for a week,' he said, 'keeping it dry. Then take it off and don't touch the wound except to apply more antibiotic cream, and bandage it up again. After another week you can take the bandage off and the finger should have healed up nicely with the joint intact.'

It was hard to believe this could be achieved without any stitches, but Fa's remedy worked perfectly, and the only residual sign of the injury to this day is a circular scar around the top joint of the finger.

A more serious injury to a child happened when one of the Fulcher girls got her hand mangled in a maize crusher. Jane and John were distraught and called Fa, who again luckily was available, and reassured them that the hand could be saved by some very fine work that he undertook using an operating microscope. Some weeks later, when I met Jane with the girls, she showed me the result of Fa's meticulous surgical repair which had restored a fully functioning hand with only minimal scarring. 'We are so grateful to God for the miracle of healing,' Jane said. She did not mention Fa's contribution.

I had always felt well during pregnancies but this time since the ill-fated safari I was convinced that something was wrong. Despite healthy signs of the baby growing and starting to move, I was feeling unusually tired and unsettled, with recurring cramps and sickness. When I went to see Bunny he was laconic in his advice, 'Just wait and see,' he said. 'If it decides to jump ship then get yourself into hospital and call me.'

When that moment arrived, as I had suspected for some time that it might, Fa was in Kericho and Adam was out on the farm somewhere. The miscarriage this time, instead of being a gradual process, turned into a sudden emergency with genuine cause for alarm. Shamefully, I was incapable of driving myself to hospital and with no telephone the only way to get help was to send the cook on his bicycle to find Adam. After a while the cook returned with a note in Adam's scrawl: 'Can't come just now. Try to hang on.'

'Go and get *mama mzee* (Alison),' I told the cook, 'or one of the drivers from the workshop. Anyone with a car.'

When the alarm was raised at the main house a message was sent to Adam to galvanise him, and when he saw the state I was in he relented, but said he first needed to pick up one of the night guards who wanted a lift to Nakuru. This meant driving to the workers' compound instead of straight to the main road and Adam's off-hand attitude struck me as odd since it was clear this was an emergency. I was beginning to see a pattern in his behaviour when faced with family situations that distracted him from work routine. He became rattled if anything interfered with his sense of duty to the farm, and the crisis which had brought me to the brink of leaving, had not changed this priority.

The detour to collect the night guard and then driving around Bondeni township in Nakuru looking for the place where he wanted to be dropped off, took so much time that when we finally arrived at the hospital I was too weak to stand up, and had to be wheeled in on a trolley. Adam went back to finish whatever it was that had been interrupted at the dairy, and Bunny arrived to look after me.

What followed was almost as prolonged and torturous as any birth, and when at last it was over, Bunny handed me, wrapped in a piece of gauze, a carefully washed miniature baby that looked like an ivory figurine, perfect in every detail. Its eyes were closed, and as I stared mesmerised at the little body, there was nothing that looked out of order. Even the tiny finger nails were perfectly shaped. I went on holding this small curled form, faced with the mystery of why it had died, and Bunny asked if I would like to look closer to see if it was a boy or a girl, but I was fearful that knowing would be too much to bear. 'There was nothing you could have done,' he said kindly, 'late miscarriages are sometimes the result of placental insufficiency, or a genetic fault, so this could be nature's way of avoiding problems later on.'

Bunny's reassurance was comforting, and within a couple of days I was able to go home, relieved that the ordeal was over. Fa had hurried down from Kericho to make sure all was well, and to see some of his old Nakuru patients who still valued his opinion on any subject that might be bothering them.

The pressing question that I wanted to ask him was about Babs and whether she might be coming to join him as soon as the divorce came through, since Len had gone over to England to see Muz and was optimistic this time that she might accept a proposal.

Muz however was surprisingly brusque with Len when he arrived at Forest Lodge where he was expecting to be welcomed and accommodated. 'It would be quite improper for Len to stay here under the same roof with me,' she wrote in her weekly letter. 'The neighbours would get entirely the wrong impression.'

'What were you doing, then, at Gooseberry cottage all that time with Len?' I wrote back. 'You seemed quite happy to be sharing a roof with him then, even if you were being platonic under it, you were encouraging his expectations.'

'Len isn't the right person for me,' she explained, after he had been banished back to Kenya, 'and,' she added mysteriously, 'there is someone else.'

This 'someone else', it turned out, was an old flame from her teenage years, the brother of her best friend, Mary. Muz had often entertained us as children with stories of this paragon, whose name was Andy, whom she described as an Adonis. 'He was the most beautiful man you've ever seen,' she would say, her face lighting up at the memory. 'Blond and muscular, like a Greek god.' She would pause at this point to give emphasis to the next observation, ignoring Ros and me looking at our hands trying not to smirk as the paean continued: 'And he was utterly devoted to his mother. At the age of eighteen he still liked to sit on her lap, with his arms around her. They would gaze adoringly at each other; it was very affecting and charming.' Whenever she said this, Ros and I exchanged glances with the same thought – that it wasn't charming at all, but extremely creepy.

'He was wonderfully affectionate to me as well,' Muz pressed on. The story never varied. 'I should have married my Adonis. We would have settled in a nice cosy home and put down roots. He wasn't a wanderer like your father. He rode a motorbike, you know.' (This *non sequitur* was almost the undoing of Ros and me each time, but we hung on.) 'He was very dashing.' She admitted, though, that he was not a very competent rider. 'One day he was riding along a perfectly straight road and there was a furniture van parked in front of a house, with its ramp down at the back. Andy hadn't noticed the van parked there and shot up the ramp, colliding with the back of the cab and knocking himself out.'

'Idiot,' Ros and I would mutter under our breath. We had never met this heroic clown and had a derisive mental image of him – what self-respecting adult man sat on his mother's lap like an enormous baby long after he should have crawled off and grown up?

Muz, taking no notice of our scepticism, would proceed at this point with a narrative of the family history: 'Andy's grandmother was travelling by train on a visit to her sister, when the baby she was expecting suddenly started to arrive. She was assisted to leave the train at Hereford Station and the baby, a girl, was born in the waiting room. The baby survived, but sadly the mother died, and when her sister was given the news she offered to take the child and look after it herself, to spare the father in his grief.'

The next part of the story was as good as any told by the Brontes or Jane Austen, so Ros and I would sit up and pay attention, as Muz continued: 'The sister had a good position as housekeeper to a wealthy family living in a large country house. They took pity on this motherless child and took her into the nursery with their own children where she was brought up as one of their own, cared for by nannies and nursemaids. This was a happy situation for all concerned, but later when the girl became of age there was a problem as her lowly birth meant she could not have suitors among those chosen by the family for their own daughters. Eventually a solution was found, and she was married off to a local farmer with a small dowry to seal the match.'

We liked this story however many times it was told, and listened intently as Muz continued with the next bit: 'This gentrified girl, you have to remember, had been brought up as a lady with airs and graces. She had never cooked, washed a dish, or touched a broom. Her husband, grateful for the dowry and somewhat in awe of her elevated upbringing, indulged her, and waited on her so she never did learn to do anything for herself, or for him, but she managed to produce two children. These were Andy and his sister Mary.'

I had met Mary who was a lively, busy and capable person, with no grandiose illusions, while Andy it appeared from Muz's account had been brought up in the manner of a country gentleman, a dandy, with a motorbike.

Hearing from Mary that Muz was getting a divorce, Andy, who had recently become a widower, homed in on her and started an elaborate courtship. This had been reciprocated by Muz with such enthusiasm that poor Len was summarily replaced and booted out of view with barely a second glance. Muz wrote glowing letters about Andy, and his kindness in accompanying her on visits to Spindle, and how good it was for the 'poor lad' as she called him (though he was an adult aged twenty-five now), to have a man in his life since Fa was conspicuously absent. With Andy so attentive, any prospect of her coming to visit us in Kenya seemed unlikely. I missed her, and Ros too, while news from Elaine was patchy as few letters survived the wilderness of Ethiopia's postal system.

MAF sent out periodic newsletters which the Nairobi office mailed to us and this filled in some of the gaps, but statements supplied by Elaine for the newsletter could be irritating, written in 'mission-speak'. Describing a visit to us when I had lent them my car, leaving me stuck at home while they went out visiting friends every day, Elaine wrote in the newsletter that they gave thanks to God for a very enjoyable holiday, adding: 'God even provided us with a car.' I wanted to say: It wasn't God. It was Me. Marooned at home without transport for a whole week.

Any communication with Elaine had to skirt around the minefield of divorce or any mention of new relationships, while she was still confident that it was God's will for Muz and Fa to be reunited. Mary, who was a practising Christian herself, was doubtful, but equally dismissive of any bond between Andy and Muz. 'You two are entirely unsuited,' she said to Muz. 'I know my brother, he's putting on an act, polishing himself up to impress you, while all he's looking for is a new housekeeper after boring the last one to death.' Mary was surprisingly forthright in her views on Andy, anxious to save Muz from further heartbreak: 'You deserve better than a nonentity like my brother. He's so lazy it's a wonder he remembers to breathe. He exists in a state of chronic inertia and will be nothing but a big lump permanently slouched in your best armchair if you ever let him into your life.'

'You're too hard on him,' Muz responded (as she told me later). 'It's all because your mother doted on him while you were expected to wait on them both like a skivvy.'

Despite her excitement at the thought of new prospects with Andy, Muz was still experiencing periods of intense grief. Fa's absence sometimes affected her as an actual physical pain, cramping her chest so acutely that the doctor thought she might have angina, while another explanation could be simple heartbreak. When Ros went home for weekends she often found Muz in bed, too depressed to get up and face the day. 'What's the point?' she would say.

Fa was the love of her life, but her love of music finally roused her. She had always been passionate about ballet and when the Bush Davies Ballet School, in premises a short distance from Forest Lodge, advertised for a pianist to accompany lessons, this was an ideal opportunity. Musical improvisation was one of her special talents and she could adapt melodies or compose original music to fit any dance rhythm or step sequence. This was so much appreciated by Miss Bush that she very soon promoted Muz to Musical Director at the School. Muz was once again in her element.

CHAPTER 13

Adam's sister, Elizabeth, wanted to keep a foothold in Kenya when she left with husband Peter to go and live in Ireland, and when a house came up for sale at Malindi on the coast, Cen and Alison offered to go halves on the purchase and share the house with them. Adam and I were surprised to hear this as all of them hated the coast and never went anywhere near the sea normally. Cen despised deep-sea fishing which he described as: 'Buggering about in a stinking boat for hours getting roasted by the sun, all in aid of catching something big enough to boast about, but can't be eaten because it's inedible. The whole exercise is a fool's errand, and worst of all there's nothing else to do at the coast except get pickled on gin and blasted by sand in every orifice.'

Even less of a seaside lover was Peter, whose face swelled like a pumpkin when exposed to sunlight, but Alison and Elizabeth thought it would be nice for Mikey to have beach holidays in Kenya, escaping the long dark days of Irish winter. When they said that Adam and I were welcome to use the house for our own holidays, it was a big thrill for us, imagining the luxury of breaks at the coast reliving the indulgence of our honeymoon, and taking Louise and Simon to paddle on Malindi's wide beach.

The house was bought and we were shown photos of an impressive double-storey whitewashed Moorish style building, a short walk from the beach down a lane behind the Sindbad Hotel. After an initial foray by Cen and Alison to try it out, very few subsequent visits followed, which left the house empty most of the time and we were allowed to use it whenever we liked. The six-hundred mile drive from Nakuru, instead of being onerous, was one of the highlights of each holiday as we stopped overnight at friendly places like the Mtito Andei roadside inn. Well rested, we would then leave the busy Mombasa road to detour through Tsavo national park. Here there were rhinos and elephants and every sort of game to keep the children occupied spotting them on the way to one of Tsavo's thatched lodges for the night.

The next day, on the long gradual descent to Mombasa, there was always a feeling of intense anticipation as the road approached sea level and the last hundred miles announced itself in an abrupt change of air and scene. Palm trees replaced baobabs and there were hints of humid saltiness as we waited for the first glimpse of blue in the distance. This was Mombasa with its busy port and traffic, best avoided by skirting the city and heading north along the coast where there were two river crossings served by ancient ferry boats. The first of these ferries, at Mtwapa creek, was pulled across by a team of ferrymen hauling on ropes, singing as they gripped and heaved. The lyrics were improvised, describing the passengers, often with bawdy observations but good humoured. These singing ferrymen became part of a legendary experience everyone looked forward to, but sadly and inevitably the service succumbed in due course to the demands of modernisation, and the friendly Mtwapa ferry was replaced by a bridge. The next big river on the way to Malindi was at Kilifi with a motorised ferry that had none of the romance of the hand-hauled one, but could take more passengers and vehicles. The Kilifi ferry liked to wait until it was fully loaded before it crossed and this could mean a long wait, but after Kilifi it was only another fifty miles to Malindi, and we were soon there.

The house had a resident caretaker, Jairo, who lived on site and ran to open the gate as soon as he heard our car, welcoming us as enthusiastically as if we were his own family arriving. He was alerted to this by one of the Malindi residents, Dodo Allen, who supervised the care of several holiday homes in the district, keeping in contact with upcountry owners by phone or telegram. This supervision did not extend to the more refined elements of coastal housekeeping I noticed during our first visit.

The water supply that I had assumed came from a borehole as it did at home, had a very different source at Malindi where the small town lay at the mouth of a big river, the Galana, which discharged into the sea at one end of the beach. The town's water supply was piped from this river after it had flowed through hundreds of miles of hinterland picking up silt, so that it was the colour and consistency of thin brown soup by the time it met the sea. There seemed to be salty elements added to the mix as the house plumbing was regularly jammed with rust as well as mud. Arriving after a long dusty drive the first essential was a cool shower, and in our case with a baby, a load of nappies to be washed, but these would have to wait until the next day. Disposable nappies were a distant prospect, but even had they been available, they would have been thought expensive and wasteful.

In the case of the showers, Jairo was inventive and had a way of getting them to work by banging on the pipes with a block of wood, while the same method employed in the kitchen produced enough of a dribbling stream to wash dishes. A large ceramic urn fitted with an internal filtering system produced drinking water, and once the mud had been removed in this way, its colour improved, but it still needed to be boiled.

Another discovery was waiting in the bedrooms when we went upstairs to unpack. Jairo bounded up in front with our suitcases, eager to show us our rooms. The beds were covered in old newspapers which were littered with something that looked like animal droppings, and Jairo explained: 'It is because of the bats,' pointing to where a small colony of them hung from battens that were holding up the ceiling. 'It will be quite fine for you later,' he continued. 'When night comes they will go out for hunting, and I will take the papers away, so you will see underneath everything is terribly clean.'

Unsure about relying on this advice, I enquired about mosquito nets, thinking these might shield us from being dive-bombed by the bats as well as mosquitoes.

Jairo laughed so much at this suggestion, I thought I must have missed some obvious point. 'These bats,' he said (using the Swahili name *popo*), 'they eat all the mosquitoes and *dudus* (insects) so you will not be disturbed at all. You will be sleeping like dogs in these good beds, not even waking up.' He was so keen to please, and we were so spent and weary from the journey, I was ready to accept almost anything that allowed us to lie down later and drift off to the sound of distant waves on the shore.

Once we had settled the children into their beds that first evening, in a room identical to ours, and explained about the bats which they thought was like having exotic new pets actually living in their room, we were glad to subside into wicker chairs on the veranda with cool beers brought by Jairo. We could hear cheerful noises coming from the kitchen where Jairo's wife was helping him, and when we were called to dinner he served an accomplished dish of prawn pilau, with fresh slices of mango to follow. Electric light from a single overhead bulb flickered feebly and Jairo suggested it might be sensible to turn in before the lights failed altogether. We needed no encouragement, and he was right about the doubtful electricity as we had to use torches to check the beds before we got in. We were too tired to care very much as bats circled overhead in the dark with little squeaks, while some of the ones that had overslept on their ceiling perches carelessly plopped onto the thin sheet covering us, where they did vigorous wing exercises before recovering enough to dart off into the night.

The next day on this first visit, a priority was to retrieve the bucket of nappies from the car so they could be washed and hung out to dry before we ran out of clean ones for Simon. I needed to locate a washing line but the garden was a jungle with no line in sight. Jairo explained that it had been set up in a far corner where it could not be seen, as the Memsahibs (Alison and Elizabeth) said it was not polite to have *dhobi* (laundry) hanging anywhere near the house. I went to look for the polite line. Any path that might once have been trodden through the tangle, had since been reclaimed by bush and thorn. I had to force a way through, ducking under branches while my feet in flip flops stirred up dry leaves covering the ground. After a few yards of slow progress, a dark scaly head reared up from the leaves in front, spreading its hood menacingly.

Good grief, a cobra, I thought, backing away, resisting the temptation to run. At a safe distance, not wanting to be defeated in my search for the washing line, I decided to try another route to the corner of the garden indicated by Jairo, and make enough noise this time to scare off any more snakes or unfriendly creatures that had taken up residence in this derelict garden. Pressing on, puffing a bit with exertion in the muggy heat, at last I spotted a sagging line not too far away and was busy stamping a path to it when, no doubt infuriated by the disturbance, another beady head rose from the camouflage of dry leaves to stare at me with hooded warning. But this one was bigger, and that was enough. I turned and ran for the kitchen and Jairo.

'You didn't tell me about the cobras,' I said accusingly as he came to the door, alerted by my panic. It's very dangerous for the children if they go out in the garden. And how can I get to the washing line when these *kali* snakes are everywhere? What did the other Memsahibs do about it when they were here?'

'Bwana Hill, he shot them,' Jairo said, 'but their relatives came back after he and the Memsahibs went home.'

Adam, overhearing snatches of this conversation, came into the kitchen. 'Did you say cobras?' He sounded thrilled. He loved snakes.

'Yes. The garden is swarming with them,' I said, with deliberate exaggeration. He looked jubilant. 'They could be Egyptian cobras. What a find. Dad did say something about them. The children must see this.'

'*Please* don't take them out there, and don't try to catch one.' I was wary of his enthusiasm for handling snakes.

'I'm not an idiot. No one messes with cobras. But you can't miss a chance to see one in its natural habitat.'

'The garden is not a natural habitat for cobras when there are children around. Your dad was right to shoot them. And what about the washing line? Where am I going to hang the washing if the garden is allowed to be a snake park?'

'Oh, for Christ sake, stop fussing. Hang the washing on the fence out at the front. Who cares what anyone thinks?'

We need not have worried about the sensitivities of neighbours as there was just one neighbour, his name, MASON, carved in large letters on the trunk of a baobab where his gate stood opposite ours across the lane. On the second night, having sunk into sleep after resigning ourselves to bats landing on the bed or swooping overhead, we were woken by piercing screams that sounded like someone being butchered out in the lane. 'Bloody hell,' Adam yelled, sitting up in bed. 'What now?' He went to investigate with a torch and found our neighbour staggering around in the lane howling like a wounded animal. His African servants were trying to get him back into the house, fending off blows as he raged, fighting them like someone possessed. When Adam offered assistance (the Mason family were friends of the Hills, and anyone in this kind of trouble could not be left to be trussed up and dragged along the ground as was about to happen), the African staff said, 'Let us do it this way, we know how to do it. Bwana Mason will be quiet when he is back in his bed with *dawa* the doctor has given for him.'

When we asked Jairo about this, he explained that Bwana Mason was regularly attacked in his brain by a demon called Dees-Tees. We wondered if we should go across and visit him in a good-neighbourly way once he had recovered, but the house remained shuttered each day. It had looked deserted in this same closed way when we arrived, leading us to assume that no one was there. 'Even his relatives do not come,' Jairo said, 'in case he attacks them. But he is not a bad man. It is the demon that is bad.'

Another neighbour, of an entirely different kind, was an elderly Swiss doctor who had been a pupil of Jung during his student days and enjoyed reminiscing and discussing the concepts of Jungian psychology. This was a happy discovery for me as Dr Rossinger was an interesting and intriguing man who was also very welcoming, viewing us as a couple whose relationship excited his attention as a subject for study. 'You have a *frisson*,' he said. 'I like to examine that, to decipher its elements.' He said this with a twinkle. Despite his considerable age he was sharp and sparky, and I was attracted to this and the way he liked sparring with words and ideas. His house became one of the first calls I made after arriving at Malindi each time, always slightly anxious whether he would still be there, but he was physically and mentally robust, still seeing patients and making calls at Malindi hospital.

The layout of the town was random with narrow streets full of tiny bright shops selling spices alongside *kikois* and *kangas* which are the traditional dress of coastal men and women. It was a Muslim town where the beach was not a place for people to strip off and go swimming, but was more of a thoroughfare, bypassing traffic on the road. All this coming and going made it less than ideal for children to paddle and play as busy people hurried past on bicycles or on foot, carrying fish to and from a market that traded noisily at one end of the beach where the town with its

Vasco da Gama pillar met the sea. The pillar had been built by the great Portuguese explorer in 1498 as a monument to the welcome he received from the Sultan of Malindi when he landed there during his voyages. This coastal strip is rich in history and artefacts from thousands of years of trading, evidenced by the settlements of lost people who thrived for a time, and then were swallowed up by the ever encroaching tendrils of forest and swamp.

Just now in 1968, development had surged again with the arrival of tourists from Europe and the popularity of holidays and honeymoons among European residents. New hotels and beach clubs were appearing, scattered among the palms and Casuarina trees along the hundred mile sandy shore between Malindi and Mombasa. One of these was the Driftwood Club at Silversands Point, south of Malindi town, where a flamboyant bachelor, Dick Soames, had built a friendly low-key beach retreat of thatched guest rooms with a restaurant and swimming pool. This was where we spent most days, avoiding deficiencies back at the house with its eccentric water supply and feeble electricity. At the Driftwood Club we could laze beside the pool with the children, or play with them on the beach, which was quiet with few footprints on the fine white sand. Louise and Simon were not instinctive playmates if left with only each other for company, but when 'Daddy' was there engaging them in joint activities, the dynamic changed. Simon at this time was beginning to look more and more like Adam which amused everyone, especially Ian Parker whose comment that Simon was 'painfully legitimate' became a joke in the family.

Louise, like me when Elaine was born, had resented Simon's arrival and was very edgy with him from the start, continuing into their teenage years. Simon, conversely, looked up to her with constant but sadly unrequited longing for her approval and friendship. Apart from the intervention of his birth, what really aggravated her was his boisterous nature for he had only to enter a room for it to become disorderly simply by his presence. As soon as he could crawl he exhibited an insatiable curiosity about everything around him, often with unwelcome results such as causing an explosion when he inserted one of my knitting needles into an electric socket. Anything that presented an opportunity for investigation attracted his interest. The proximity of dogs at ground level fed a fascination for exploring their anatomical features, so that tails would be lifted up, ears peered into, lips peeled back for teeth to be inspected, claws tested, and fur searched for ticks and fleas that, in their turn, would be closely examined. This kind of behaviour drew indignation from Louise, but didn't bother the dogs at all.

The buzz and clicking of my electric sewing machine at home, whenever it was in action, held a particular fascination for Simon. He would be underneath watching my foot going up and down on the pedal, waiting for pins to drop so he could collect them and stick them back in the pincushion. Absorbed in what I was doing one day, I didn't notice that he had picked up my dressmaking scissors and was busy experimenting with their cutting blades on the machine's electric cable, until there was a mighty bang, flash, and smell of burning. At my feet a bemused Simon sat with blackened hands and singed hair, while wisps of smoke curled from the scissors lying twisted on the floor. Surprisingly, no damage was done to him but all the fuses blew, and my machine was dead until a new cable connection could be supplied from Nairobi. The scissors had to be replaced as well – contact with the live cable had damaged them and blown a nick out of each blade. How Simon escaped being electrocuted was a mystery.

Adam was more tolerant of the noise and disruption caused by small children when he was not feeling exhausted by long hours of dairy work, and I was grateful for his help during the Malindi holidays as ayah Elizabeth seldom came with us. She felt uncomfortable among the Swahili and Giriama people who lived along the coast with cultures that were foreign to her, and even worse she strongly disapproved of the food on these holidays. Lobsters and crabs she insisted were insects, not fit for humans to eat, and she refused to go into the kitchen if Jairo was preparing anything with more than four legs.

For the rest of us, these holidays at Malindi were the happiest of times when normal life was suspended and any problems seemed far away. We could ignore doubts about our future in Kenya with changes brought by Independence that were causing many Europeans to feel insecure. Despite the boom in property development, some farming families were packing up and leaving since the Settlement Board needed their land for redistribution to Africans.

The famous 'Winds of Change' speech made by Harold Macmillan a few years before was now seen as prophetic, in particular among those with school-age children. Government schools had been opened to all races, both for pupils and teachers, and the rush to get these intakes in place caused some to worry about standards and culture. Louise would be starting at Lugard Primary School in Nakuru when she turned five the following year, and rumours were already circulating about new relaxed attitudes in the school which alarmed some parents. Freedom from colonial rule extended beyond politics to society in general, and boundaries started to be tested to see what personal advantages might be gained from these new liberties.

Some of the changes were seen as quite shocking by those who expected certain norms to continue as before. Renny, while staying at Lawfords (one of the beach hotels in Malindi) with a German friend, Marianne, had a rude encounter. During dinner the waiter heard them speaking German, and later when Renny had gone to her room, she was surprised to receive a visit from the waiter. He said that if she or her friend required his services during the night he could return at any time. Renny was furious and gave him a blast in Swahili, which very much surprised him. He backed off, apologising, saying he had thought they were German tourists. 'How dare you take this attitude to German people,' Renny stormed at him, and next day reported the incident to the hotel manager. He said he was very sorry this had happened to her, but some of the guests expected and even requested this kind of service, so the waiter could not be reprimanded for trying to oblige and adding to his wages in this way.

'Isn't it shocking that young waiters are being corrupted like this?' Renny said when telling me this story. It was not just waiters; policemen were often to be found standing by the side of the road, waving at cars to stop. They would ask for a driving licence and then inspect the car for faults. A scratch on the paintwork, or splash of mud on a brake light, prompted another look at the licence accompanied by finger tapping on an open page, indicating that a bank note was required to be slipped inside before being allowed to proceed. It was annoying, but serious issues of crime were still low, and we could live with minor irritations. There was a further and more practical reason for staying on as it was not long before we had another baby on the way, so it was not a good time to be packing up and moving.

The end of one decade and beginning of another always feels like a new dawn with unimagined possibilities. The free-wheeling sixties had arrived as a burst of stardust on a drab world, energising everyone with a kaleidoscope of opportunities, and now the sixties were coming to an end, but for us there was no slowing down in the pace of our lives. Economic progress on the farm was leaping ahead as cattle and crop sales prospered and the cheese factory was a magnet for customers.

Johnny had a new girlfriend, Margaret, a petite nurse recently arrived from England. She soon booted him out of the Rift Valley Club bar and onto the temperance wagon, where he languished for a while looking woebegone, but Margaret was one of those no-nonsense nurses and kept him on it. This was the first girlfriend Alison had approved of and she didn't even object when Margaret started spending weekends with Johnny at his house. 'Johnny has a perfectly good guest room,' she pointed out as proof against any suggestion of impropriety. Quickly changing the subject to avoid discussion on how it was that Johnny had coincidentally bought a double bed after Margaret's arrival, she drew my attention to another issue.

'You know poor old Edna Graham is having a hard time of it since John died and she had to leave the farm. Everyone thought she would be safer in one of those horrid flats in Nakuru, but the old servants who came with her have all run away since she exists in a state of perpetual fury with them, cooped up in what she calls an egg box. She can't bear the ignominy of living in such a confined space, and of course she has never boiled a kettle or made a bed in her life, so she needs someone to go in each day and do what they can to help. We thought, with your nursing experience, you could do the bed thing, and make sure she's eating.'

Edna had spent most of her adult life in India as the wife of an Indian Army officer, attended by fleets of servants, and when she and John retired to Kenya their lifestyle continued with very little change. Like many other ex-Indian Army retirees they embodied a type of feisty privileged Britishness that was fast fading in the post-colonial era, while those stylish elements that had seen them through wars and campaigns in harsh environments seemed merely incongruous now. I liked Edna, and was glad to call on her and see what I could do.

'I suppose Alison has sent you, poking her nose in, making out I'm a helpless wreck,' Edna said irritably when I called, 'but since you're here you can make tea and listen to my complaints about 2LO.'

2LO was Edna's favourite adversary. Her real name was Val North, but she was called 2LO by all who knew her. She was large, loud and domineering, with a booming voice that was said to replace the need for a telephone since she could be heard broadcasting her views from her farm at Elburgon as resoundingly as the BBC Marconi House radio station in London – known by the number of its Post Office broadcasting licence: 2LO.

'Whenever Val comes to Nakuru to do her shopping, she comes in here to take a list for me, and that's very kind,' Edna said, 'but while she's here, she prowls around looking at all my possessions, noting down which ones she thinks I should leave her in my will.'

Edna was surrounded in the small space of her flat by a remarkable collection of treasures that had filtered down from wealthy forebears in England. Ornamental objects crowded every mahogany surface, jumbled together with photos of long dead relatives in glowing silver frames. Among the objects scattered around were a collection of silver despatch boxes that I was sure held a story, and asked Edna about them. She explained that they had carried messages, attached to the belts of mounted cavalry during military campaigns, but she didn't want to talk about those while she was telling me about 2LO.

'Last time she came,' Edna went on, referring to 2LO, 'she stalked around doing her usual inspection of my things, and seized on that big china hen you see over there.' She pointed to a life-size china hen painted in buff colours flecked with gold, sitting on a china nest.

'The hen lifts up so eggs can be stored underneath.' Edna said, 'It's supposed to live in the kitchen, but you've seen the size of my kitchen, and anyway the hen is too valuable to get smashed in that cubby hole. Of course, 2LO knows what it's worth, and is determined to make off with it.'

Her indignation rose. 'Can you beat it, 2LO then said: "Edna, you know I'm very fond of this hen, and I know you've left it to me in your will. But if it goes on sitting here it will get broken by some idiotic servant, or stolen, so I'll take it now."

'No, you bloody well won't,' I told her. 'you can wait till I'm dead.'

We both laughed, but that wasn't all, as Edna hadn't finished. She pointed to a small portrait hanging on the wall. 'As well as nagging me about the hen, 2LO wants me to have that portrait valued by an expert in London, in case it's priceless.'

'What makes her think that?' I asked, puzzled, as the painting was unremarkable and appeared to have been painted in a hurry, resulting in the dull image of a man's head and shoulders on a smudged background.'

'It's a Van Gogh,' Edna said dismissively. Before he became famous. He was struggling to make a living and did cheap portraits for anyone who came along wanting one. Some distant relative of John's, pottering around France, met this shabby young man and, feeling sorry for him, got his portrait painted. So there it is. No one has ever taken the slightest bit of notice of it until 2LO came along and peered at the signature.'

'Why don't you just leave it where it is and keep quiet about it?'

'That's what I think, but 2LO says it needs to be insured, and that means getting it valued. I suppose I can just let her organise whatever needs to be done. At least it will distract her from ogling my hen all the time if she can take charge of the picture, thinking she's doing a good deed.'

Val duly contacted a London expert on Edna's behalf and a carefully organised plan was put in place. The painting was wrapped up and taken to Nairobi by a trusted friend where it was handed in person to the pilot of a plane going to London. The package was kept safely in the cockpit and, on arrival at Heathrow, it was handed over personally by the pilot to a courier. A short time later, another courier arrived with identical authorisation. This one it turned out was genuine, so the first one must have been fake. Some kind of skulduggery appeared to have taken place and the portrait was never seen again, according to Edna.

But had it all been a ruse to fool 2LO and put her off the scent? Edna would only say, once the dust had settled, that 2LO had asked her plaintively, 'You'll still let me have the hen, won't you?'

Increased prosperity on the farm put Cen in a buoyant mood so that, despite political uncertainty, he was planning further expansion of Glanjoro Farms Ltd, looking to buy Ronda Estate with its 8000 acres on the other side of the river that marked our southern boundary. Ronda's land extended almost to the lake and had a common border with the Nakuru Municipality African township where there was an urgent need for more housing. This had inspired Cen to think about acquiring Ronda and offering plots for sale.

Ronda was owned by our neighbours Richard and Beryl Christmas, who were ready to retire but highly distracted at that moment by a family drama. Beryl's sister who lived in Nakuru, wanted to fulfil a long ambition to visit another sister who lived in California. The Nakuru sister was nervous of travelling and needed a great deal of encouragement to embark on such an epic trip, involving several connecting flights, but the Nakuru Travel Agency assured her that they would arrange and take care of every stage. All was booked meticulously by the agency and in due course she set off for Nairobi Airport with her tickets, a typed itinerary, and phial of smelling salts in her handbag should she feel faint and need reviving.

Assistance had been organised at every airport connection, with an escort to look after her as she changed planes on the legs from Nairobi to London, London to New York, and New York to Los Angeles. Feeling tired but relieved when she was nearly on the last leg, she fell asleep in her seat, and when she woke up the pilot was announcing that they were about to arrive at … *Heathrow*. Her return ticket had somehow been substituted for the onward one, or there was some kind of mix-up that was never explained. Arriving back in London, she was so panicked and disorientated that she refused to take any more planes and retreated to a hotel, from where Richard and Beryl were trying to extricate her.

'Bloody stupid New York people putting her on the wrong plane,' Cen fumed, 'and now she's gone to ground and we're held up while the Christmases are in a dither.'

Apart from selling plots, the other plan for Ronda was a grazing scheme to raise beef which would be part of Adam's cattle management job. He was excited about this, thinking he might focus on beef production while Milgo ran the dairy. 'I like the idea of being a rancher,' he said. 'It's a gentleman's life, unlike dairy where you're stuck forever at the back end of a cow. Talking of which,' he went on, 'Dad wants me to go and look at new milking machines and bail equipment at Hosiers in England. I told him I would only go if you came too, with the farm paying both our fares.' I had never known Adam take such a bold line, and could imagine Cen scoffing at the suggestion.

'What did he say?'

'Surprisingly he agreed, and what's more, Mum said she would have the children so we can make it a holiday, before the new baby comes and we're more tied.'

This sudden turn of events was particularly welcome news as it meant I could see Muz and Ros in England, as well as visiting Howleigh and being introduced to Adam's aunts and Granny Hill for the first time. It would also be the first time I had been back to England in six years. Looking at Hosier bails and milking equipment in the company of my husband was, for me, the most exciting prospect of all. I had become an all-round farmer's wife, never happier than when feeling and smelling the warm flank of a cow at close quarters, helping Adam with a calving or sick animal, or just walking among cattle in a field as they grazed. The soft sounds and movements they made as they browsed the grass blended with my own sense of contentment. Dairy cows spend most of their lives in various stages of pregnancy so that milk production is not interrupted, except for a 'holiday' period of three months each year when they are dried off and given a rest before delivering the next calf. I began to feel like one of the herd with my repeated pregnancies but, unlike them, I was not much good at milk production.

The welcome at Howleigh was ecstatic. Aunts Katharine and Diana, unmarried with no children of their own, had taken Adam to themselves with such devotion during the school holidays he spent with them, it was as if a lost child had returned and the reception prepared for him, and me, was royal in its proportions. Touchingly, my status as the mother of a male heir to the family was celebrated here in these modest surroundings as if there might be a grand estate with a castle and deer park to inherit. These considerations extended to protocol at meals, so that if Cen was visiting he would take the head of the table, while in his absence Adam sat at the head. Later, if neither of them was present, Simon was given that place even when his feet didn't reach the floor, while all other males regardless of age sat along the sides.

Granny Hill was a martinet who took her place regally at the other end of the table on the precise hour of each mealtime, waiting to be served by her daughters who scurried about with trays and dishes. These needed to be held securely while running from the kitchen, negotiating backwards the green baize door that hid any proximity of domestic services. Katharine was always late, for everything, and this led to frantic scenes at mealtimes while Granny sat stiffly at her place, hands poised above knife and fork ready to start. Any female relatives who happened to be staying were drafted in to help serve the food, while male relatives sat waiting with Granny. During this first visit of ours, unfamiliar with the way things were done and thoroughly flustered along with the aunts racing around, I put a cook pot on the tray, thinking it could double as a serving dish. Katharine was horrified. 'You can't take that into the dining room. Mother would have a fit. Quick, transfer it, and run.'

Subjects for discussion at table also came under Granny rules, though certain exceptions were allowed such as politics as Katharine was a Conservative agent, and all of them were ardent supporters of Edward du Cann, the MP for their part of Somerset. Any talk of sex of course was forbidden, even to the extent that pregnancy, whoever it related to, could not be mentioned since it was unlikely to have resulted from an immaculate conception. Once the child had been born, then somehow, magically, sex was not involved any more, and the subject of Hill children from any branch of the family became of particular interest. In the meantime it was preferred that any expected addition remain tactfully camouflaged. Suitable clothes such as a smock or tent dress were standard for pregnant women even in the liberated sixties, and fashions that came later with tight clothes flaunting pregnancy would have been thought 'common' and vulgar.

Religion was allowed to be discussed if it related to the parish church at Angersleigh where the whole family gathered every Sunday for Matins and always sat in the same pew. After the service, Granny visited her husband Percy's grave in the churchyard to brush fallen leaves off the cover stone, bending down with difficulty to do this. 'It's all I can do for him now,' she said gently. 'It's like making his bed, making him more comfortable.' With that small gesture her usual rigidity fell away, revealing an unexpected tenderness.

A young girl from the village arrived at the house each morning to make beds and do chores. 'She's a bit simple,' Granny explained, as if that accounted for her permanently dazed expression, muddling around with a bucket and duster, 'but she will clean your shoes if you put them in the boot room.' The poor mystified girl never remembered, and when I went to retrieve Adam's shoes from the boot room I found myself in a maze of dark mouldy rooms behind the kitchen, leading to an enclosed space outside where washing was hung. This was on the north side of the house where no rays of sun could penetrate but, more importantly, no untoward glimpses of laundry could be seen from the driveway either.

The south side, as in all similar English houses, delivered a blaze of colour in a front garden that was alive with sunlight. A local man who lived in one of the gardeners' cottages down the lane, came each day to look after the lawns and flower borders, vegetable patch and orchard. There was a stable block now used as garages on one side of the gravelled drive, while beyond lay nothing but the great wide green rolling fields and hills of Somerset. The joy of Howleigh was in all this – the glory of its situation. But also in the aunts themselves, who were spirited and fun, devising every kind of entertainment and outing to make our visit enjoyable.

They did this within the limitations of an Edwardian household with a kitchen so primitive it was only their resourcefulness and ingenuity that resulted in any edible food appearing, but it was far more than just edible, it was inspirational. Their repertoire revolved around the favourite dishes of traditional English cooking: roasts rich in juices that had dripped from the meat while it sizzled slowly in their ancient solid-fuel Aga; steak and kidney pies with golden pastry; buttery kedgeree for supper, and the most soul-satisfying puddings that included Katharine's speciality – Apple Cheese with clotted cream. This was made with windfall apples from their own trees, simmered for hours with a prodigious amount of sugar until the puree turned thick, amber-coloured and luscious. Because I liked it so much, Katharine always made it whenever we visited. They were darling aunts, their sense of family deep and committed, so that no effort was spared for any of us during visits.

Sherry parties were a favourite event when neighbours and friends were invited; all crowded into the tiny drawing room from which Diana's mad spaniels had been banished. Untrained and undisciplined, they were hooligan dogs who charged around the house in a frenzy for lack of adequate outdoor exercise. None of the sedate sherry guests would enjoy having their cocktail outfits clawed at or glasses knocked out of their hands if the spaniels were let loose. Sherry parties had long since died out in most social circles but Howleigh remained crystalized in its own inimitable time warp. This was represented most poignantly by the spinster sisters living at home with their matriarchal mother, preserving all the old conventions and rituals as if the clock had stopped when Percy died.

We had to remind ourselves that the main purpose of our visit was to view dairy equipment at Hosier's headquarters deep in farming country near Avebury in Wiltshire. All around this area on the edge of Salisbury plain, traces of prehistoric culture could be seen in stone monuments and earthworks that still possessed a powerful aura, so that our visit included the fascination of this discovery as well as its more practical purpose. Once the dairy purchases had been made, we were free to resume family visits, this time to Muz, but Diana was jealous of any time spent with her. 'I don't want your mother monopolising you,' she said, 'Adam needs to be here with his own family. I know your mother wants to see you both, but you don't need to spend more than one weekend with her, surely?'

We did a dash across country to Forest Lodge where both Ros and Spindle had joined Muz, all of them keyed up with anticipation of this rare time together, but instead of rapture as at Howleigh, the atmosphere was strained. Fa's departure and absence still hung in the air like a deadweight and I was shocked at the sight of Spindle, hunched and shuffling with the stoop of an old man though he was only twenty five. He kept his hands grasped together to disguise the tremor that was a side effect of years of treatment with anti-psychotic drugs. His blue eyes, still clear and alert, had sunk in their sockets, but they lit up when he saw us at the front door. 'I knew you would come,' he said. 'I've been waiting such a long time for you to come. My whole life is all just full of waiting. Is Fa coming too?'

'You know he's gone,' Muz said, unnecessarily blunt I thought. 'He's left us, you know that.'

'We've got something for you,' I said quickly. 'Something we brought from Kenya,' and took from my bag a small carved elephant wrapped in tissue paper. 'We thought you could keep it on the locker beside your bed at the hospital, to remind you of Africa. A little bit of Africa.'

Muz interrupted: 'It would be stolen immediately by one of the other patients, or smashed, or thrown in the rubbish. Nothing is safe from those maniacs,' she said, and I knew it was true. 'But he can keep it here at home in his room,' she added more gently, 'with his collection of stones and fossils and pieces of meteorite.'

'Thank you for bringing the elephant all the way from Africa,' Spindle said with the shy smile that was so tentative when he wasn't quite sure what to say. 'It will be safe in my bedroom here; then I'll have it when I come home.'

However ill or drugged he was, he was always polite and appreciative, though as time went on his sweet smile was replaced by a haunted look that settled on his face like an ashen mask.

The subdued atmosphere at Forest Lodge was too much for Ros who escaped back to London the next day, and Spindle, despite the horrors of hospital life, was impatient to return to his ward. Losing Fa had left Muz feeling so crushed and empty, she was still subject to recurring intervals of despair, so that even the luminous arrival of Andy in her life had failed to dispel these persisting moods. I didn't like leaving her in that situation, but she was not in a state of mind to enjoy having extra people in the house, and was busy at the ballet school on weekdays, so we were free to return to Howleigh where yet more jolly times had been planned.

Summer with the aunts was all about beach picnics, agricultural shows and long country rambles with the dogs. These were enlivened by hysteria when the spaniels ran off chasing sheep as happened each time Diana let them off their leads, leaving the rest of us to lope across fields after them, shouting their names inanely. Eventually we would catch up with them where they lay panting, waiting for us. All our excursions involved the dogs, and car journeys accompanied by these frantic animals were an ordeal as they scrambled between the seats, slobbering with excitement at the prospect that they would soon be let out to cause joyful mayhem in a public space. Even without this distraction the aunts were eccentric drivers with odd misconceptions. They insisted on having one of the indicator lights permanently switched on, clicking away annoyingly, and when Adam objected to this, they said it saved having to switch on each time they turned either left or right.

'What if it's indicating the wrong way when you want to turn?' he asked.

'We just switch it over,' Katharine replied, as if that was obvious.

'What about other drivers getting stuck behind you, thinking you are about to turn? Or the police?

'No one has ever complained,' Katharine said 'And anyway, why should they, it's not against the law.'

Failing to notice the petrol gauge hovering on empty was another foible, but the solution again was obvious as Katharine explained: 'If we start running out of petrol we just drive faster so we can get to the next service station before it runs out. Anyway, we're very economical with petrol. We never use the engine going downhill.' This particular practice caused many terrifying moments on car journeys when the ignition was turned off at the top of a hill, allowing the car to coast down gathering speed and loss of control before arriving at the bottom in a flurry of braking and swerving. Adam, sitting in the back with me and the dogs, would be cursing and swearing in between protests: 'If your brother was sitting here instead of me, he would never put up with these dangerous manoeuvres.'

'Oh, he never lets us drive,' they laughed. 'He insists on doing the driving himself.'

'I'm not surprised,' Adam said. 'Another time, if we bring the children, it might be safer if I do the driving.'

'Yes, of course' they replied eagerly, next time you come, you must bring the children. Then we'll try and get Monica over at the same time.'

Monica was the middle sister: the only one who had married. She and her husband Tom Savage lived in South Africa where he was Bishop of Swaziland and Zululand. Tom and Monica were fierce opponents of apartheid which put them in conflict with the governing party and ultimately led to them having to leave, but later, after Mandela was released, they returned to a great welcome.

Arriving home after a whole month away when we had missed the children very much and were anxious to see them again, we found them quite settled into life with Grandma and Grandpa, all having gone well except for an incident involving Louise and Cen's plane. On a polo weekend at Kinyatta they had flown there in the Cessna, and later, arriving back at Glanjoro, Louise was helping to push the plane into its hangar along with other helpers when her foot got run over by one of the wheels. She screamed so loudly and for so long that Alison lost patience and told her to stop, no harm to the foot being observed. 'But it did hurt very very much,' Louise was impatient to tell us, 'and Grandma was cross instead of putting a bandage on it.' This had been the most important thing to tell us as soon as we arrived so she could get some sympathy at last.

Elizabeth the ayah had been helping, staying each night at the guest cottage where she slept in the same room with the children. She had their suitcases packed ready to put in the car when we left, and Louise asked, 'Where are we going next?' as if she had forgotten that her home was just down the road.

CHAPTER 14

A break away from home is good for providing perspective and the trip to England had added certainty that our decision to remain in Kenya, whatever happened, was the right one. Each time I came back to Kenya, flying the familiar route across thousands of miles of desert that after several hours changed to mountains and then the wonder of Mount Kenya's icy peaks, there was the same sense of exhilaration and completeness that I was coming home and there was nowhere else I wanted to be. Adam, like me, gazing down on the red earth and burnt colours of rock and bush passing below as the plane approached Nairobi, remarked, 'The trouble with England is it's too green. All that green is unhealthy. There's too much rain in England, and all anyone ever talks about is the weather.'

'The rainfall is the same amount that we get here – thirty inches,' I reminded him. 'But you're right, because instead of raining properly in great big dollops twice a year as it does here, it drizzles down like endless pee in England, so there's never anything cheerful to talk about because they're huddled together under a cloud the whole time, being peed on.'

After collecting the children and dogs from Glanjoro House and driving the short way home, there was a rush as doors were opened and all of us ran through the rooms happy to see our own things again. I was impatient to get the household reorganised, as well as the clinic and calves that had struggled under Alison's ministrations. She complained: 'I can't tell you how tiresome it's been with you away. All the malingerers hanging about outside expecting me to do the clinic, and Kamau is hopeless with the calves, encouraging them to die so he has fewer of them to look after. As soon as you're up to it you can have them all back and good luck to you,' she said, her face creased with the burden of all these cares. Added to this was frustration that negotiations on the Ronda project were stalled until the Christmases returned from London, where Beryl's sister was still holed up in her hotel room, resisting attempts to retrieve her.

Louise was due to start nursery school and wanted to try on her uniform dresses in case they had got smaller in her absence. She was convinced that some of her clothes had shrunk while she wasn't looking. 'Why are all my clothes getting smaller?' she asked, puzzled, unaware that she was growing all the time. We had been preparing her for nursery school for months, telling her what fun it was going to be, and she was excited. She kept checking the gingham dresses hanging in a cupboard, and the drawstring bag I had made with her name embroidered on it, containing a pencil box, crayons and spare handkerchief.

On the first day of school, after arriving and putting her bag on the hook labelled with her name, she was told to sit on a bench where at first she was the only one – sitting bolt upright with her feet dangling in their new Bata shoes. From this perch she observed solemnly some of the other children sobbing and clinging to their mothers, while some of the mothers clung onto their children, close to tears themselves. Louise sat primly like Miss Muffet, hands in her lap, looking disapprovingly at these emotional displays. 'You can go now if you like,' she said to me.

I was feeling very well, hardly noticing being pregnant this time except for unusual cravings, in particular for chalk, blackboard chalk, and had to ask the school to let me have some. The chalk was gritty and crunchy, a not altogether unpleasant sensation, but it was damaging my teeth. There was no reliable dentist in Nakuru so I went to Nairobi and was told that my teeth were in a bad state and needed a number of fillings. The dentist said chalk contains calcium, which could explain the cravings, while several pregnancies during the last six years may have sucked calcium from my bones and teeth.

He was keen to involve me in an experiment after reading that pregnant women develop increased resistance to pain in anticipation of labour, and, if I agreed, he would do the fillings without local anaesthetic to test the theory. Some of the fillings were big ones he warned, and I must tell him if the pain became too intense. I didn't mind obliging in my present state of good spirits, so I agreed, and he was so pleased he said there would be no charge for the treatment, even if anaesthetic had to be resorted to.

The worst part was having to sit immobile in the chair for what seemed like hours, holding a steady position with my mouth open and large stomach like a beach ball stuck in front. I couldn't say that the all the drilling was painless but it was bearable, and the dentist was gratified. Not having to pay for so many fillings was the best part and that pleased Adam too, so everyone was happy. When I told Fa about it, he said it was an interesting theory, but required more evidence to establish any reliable conclusion.

Since going to work for Brooke Bond at Kericho, Fa was a new man, and when he came for Christmas he had big news to tell us: Babs had at last agreed to join him. Up to now she had insisted she would not come to Kenya until he was divorced and they could be married, but the divorce was taking too long and they had reached a point where they could wait no longer. Fa wanted my approval and support for Babs, to help smooth her arrival in a strange country where she knew no one and risked hostility from Muz's many friends, as well as perhaps some of his.

With her arrival imminent, I thought the best thing I could do was write her a welcoming letter. She wrote back appreciatively and asked what kind of wardrobe she should bring, and whether to include cocktail and evening dresses. This was a big change from Muz who had no taste in clothes and took little care with her appearance, so it was intriguing to think of Fa acquiring such a different style of companion, not just in the way she dressed but in her whole personality and character. Babs was all the things that Muz wasn't: feisty and assertive, confident, strong-willed; Babs was the female equivalent of Fa in all these. They were two bubbling egos waiting to converge in what could be quite an explosive mix, I thought, and wondered how Fa would cope with the other side of Babs – the muddle that attended her wherever she went. Her flightiness and disorganisation must surely drive him to distraction after a lifetime relying on Muz's calm, orderly back-up service, which had previously and almost invisibly smoothed his path.

Ros and I were mystified as to how Babs ever managed to run a hospital ward in her senior position as ward sister, or even function as an efficient nurse in any capacity. Was it simply force of character, dragooning hospital consultants into compliance as they trailed in her wake, staff nurses wheeling the trolley of patients' notes, providing practical assistance while keeping things under control. We knew from reports that she had a fearsome reputation, ruling her ward along highly authoritarian lines, but this was not unusual among ward sisters at the time and certainly she was respected. Her saving graces were a sharp mind and ready wit. She had a gift for disarming people and making them laugh, which, in Fa's case, was especially valuable as by nature he was edgy and tense. In Babs' company he relaxed, allowing her to tease him and dismantle his defences. The change in him from years of being frustrated and morose, to the new unburdened genial Fa, made it impossible to be anything but happy for him, despite my misgivings for Muz.

The next time Joan Hemsted called during one of her Nakuru shopping trips to see how we were getting on, bringing as always baskets and buckets of vegetables and flowers from her river garden, I asked what she thought about Babs coming to live, unmarried, with Fa.

'He deserves someone lively and fun in his life,' she said, 'someone who will stand up to him and refuse to let him be so serious all the time. Your mother was a doormat, thinking that was the way to please him. Putting him on a pedestal.' I knew that Joan had a low opinion of her and it embarrassed me that Muz made so little effort to stir herself in their company, or even to offer normal hospitality in return for their boundless generosity over the years. 'It puts me all in a flutter if Joan arrives booming into our household,' Muz used to say. 'Nothing that I could offer would ever match her extravagant expectations, so it's better just to lie low and avoid disappointment.' Lying low, I thought, being a doormat, yes, sadly that's true.

Joan had strong opinions on every type of subject and the Hills didn't escape her censure either. 'Your in-laws live like poor whites despite having bags of money stashed away,' she said. 'Alison brought a handsome dowry with her when she married Cen. The Black family made a fortune in publishing, and Cen has done very well for himself, buying up all the neighbouring farms like Monopoly. But look at the suit he wears, it's worn to a thread. The worst thing is,' she continued now she was hot on the theme, 'they are expecting you and Adam to live like poor whites too. How are you going to afford a third child on Adam's pittance of a wage? That's why I bring these food parcels – to keep you alive!' We laughed, and she went on, 'The least the farm could do is pipe irrigation from the borehole so you could have a proper veggie garden for yourselves. Alison has irrigation for her roses and lemons and you can't even eat those.'

'The one thing that would help more than anything else is a telephone, and that would cost much less than irrigation pipes,' I suggested. With a baby on the way I was fearful of another emergency like the last one.

Emergencies and other unexpected events seemed to be a recurring feature of life just then as Elizabeth came to me one morning in a state of distress. She was friendly with the Fulchers' ayah who had sent a message that Jane had died suddenly the previous evening. This was a profound shock as I had seen her quite recently looking a picture of health and radiance after at last producing a son. My first thought was to go over and see if there was anything I could do. Poor John I thought, left with four small children. And poor Jane. All the rejoicing and relief at the birth of this longed-for little boy – what could have happened? Was it an accident? A sudden stroke or heart attack, or a delayed complication of childbirth? It was hard to believe that she could be gone, just like that. Maybe there was a mistake. Elizabeth said there was no point going over as John had already left with the children, and Jane's body had been taken away soon after she died. 'Still wearing her apron,' the ayah had told Elizabeth. Such are the odd small details remembered at times like this.

A story emerged later (as told to Elizabeth) that everything had been normal on the day that Jane died, and the family sat down to supper that evening at the usual time. During this meal, with no warning Jane had fallen from her chair onto the floor, showing no signs of life. John prayed, but there was nothing anyone could do. It was a sudden unexplained death.

I knew that Elaine, who was in Nairobi to see a specialist about her continuing illness, would want to go to the funeral as she had been very friendly with Jane. I didn't know what funeral arrangements had been made and when I phoned the vicarage to find out, I was told that Jane had already been buried as John didn't want any fuss. There had been no post-mortem that we were aware of and we were left with a sense of emptiness and unease about Jane and what had caused her sudden death. I asked Fa about this and he said, in these circumstances, there would normally be a post-mortem before burial or cremation, but it appeared not to have happened in this case.

Standard procedures like this were no longer as standard as they had been before Independence. We were in a post-colonial transition with new ways of doing, or not doing, things that had previously been expected. But while these uncertainties still threatened to undermine our resolve to stay and join Kenyatta's call to 'Harambee' (pull together), we genuinely wanted to adapt and make things work for everyone.

We had many friends who were upbeat and increasing their stake in the country. Among these were Ian and Chris Parker who had bought a rundown house on ten acres in Langata, one of the growing suburbs in Nairobi. Ian had started a wildlife management company to advise on animal populations in national parks, and provide services such as culling where numbers were getting out of hand and destroying the habitat. In Tsavo, elephant numbers had prospered under the care of outstanding wardens such as Bill Woodley and David Sheldrick, but this could have perverse consequences when an increasing elephant population outstripped the food sources available.

Ian often called to see us on trips around the country and more frequently when he was advising national parks in Uganda, flying to and fro. While we were having lunch one Sunday there was a sudden very loud clattering noise overhead and when we went outside to see what it was, we found Ian trying to land his helicopter on the lawn. It refused to settle in one spot and abandoning the attempt, Ian flew off to land on the airstrip where we met him with the car. The flat airstrip he explained, was better for landing a helicopter than the sloping surface of our lawn.

We asked if he would agree to be godfather to the baby when it arrived, which looked like being quite soon. He said he was happy to oblige, but not to expect him to undertake any duties connected with the role at any time during the child's life. This was typical of Ian, always ready to contribute in any way if he happened to be around, but never likely to be around at any precise moment. These idiosyncrasies, however, were part of his charm and he was a truly good friend and first choice as godparent, while Tony was already godfather to Simon.

'Are you sure it isn't twins?' he said teasingly, as I looked suspiciously large. Other people had been asking the same question, and next time Mary Rooken Smith called, I persuaded her to use her dowsing skills on the bulge. Mary could predict the sex of babies by this method, and it was claimed, had never been wrong. I hoped she could detect more than one occupant if that was the case, as well as the sex.

Louise insisted it must be a girl this time, or girls. 'We don't want any more boys,' she said firmly, meaning that she didn't want any more like Simon. Overhearing this remark, Simon spoke up: 'We need a boy so he can play guns with me.' Ignoring this and pressing on, Louise came up with several suggestions for girls' names, and I told Simon he could choose boys' names. Adam was sure we were having a girl and said he liked, 'Suzanne Lucinda', though his first choice was 'Pippa' as a tribute to his first love, Pippa Howden, Lucinda's sister. I was not having any of that, just as Adam would never have agreed to a son being called Lanner. A consensus was then reached by all of us, except Simon, agreeing on the mellifluous combination of the two names chosen by Adam.

So it was settled, and we waited for Mary to do her dowsing. She used my wedding ring suspended on a strand of hair, poised over the beach ball stomach. The ring hung motionless at first, seeming to orientate itself while Mary held the fine ends of hair lightly between her fingers. With all of us watching intently, after several moments the ring began to stir, very slowly at first as if moved by a whisper of air, getting its bearings. Next, it started to rotate in a deliberate rhythm that became quite animated, though Mary's fingers did not move at all. It was obvious very quickly that something fairly decisive was being indicated.

'What does it say, Mary?' We were agog.

'No twins. Only one baby, and it's a boy.'

'How can you tell it isn't twins?'

'It's just the way the pointer behaves, once you get used to it.'

'How clever. Have you tried it on yourself?' Mary herself was expecting a third baby which was due, coincidentally, on the same day as ours.

'Yes, but I'm not going to tell you what it said.'

'Oh, shame, Mary, we're hoping it said a boy.' Mary had two girls and we assumed that Don, her uber-male polo-playing husband, would be looking for a team of boys to train up. They might just as easily have had a polo team of girls, but it seemed a general assumption that men wanted sons. Adam said this was a myth. John Fulcher was the only man I knew who displayed his preference for sons ostentatiously, with success at last, only to lose the wondrous Jane. We heard quite soon that he had married a close friend who was a school teacher within a short time of Jane's death and I was glad for him, and for the children; long periods of mourning only adding to grief in my view. But Jane's death was still unexplained and the mystery surrounding this remained.

Another surprising event, but a good one this time, was news that one of Adam's long-standing bachelor friends Charlie Moore, had married. Of all the bachelors we knew, he seemed the one least likely to find a girl attracted to his dishevelled looks and lifestyle while prepared to endure a frugal existence in a shack somewhere out in the bush. Aside from these drawbacks he had personal charm and generosity of spirit that, we imagined, could be disarming enough to draw someone to share his Robinson Crusoe existence.

It wasn't long before Charlie brought his new wife to meet us, and where we had expected her to be a Bohemian earth-loving type like him, even more surprising was the discovery that she was a talented musician who was also a Nightingale nurse from St Thomas' Hospital in London. A girl straight off crowded streets, more used to city lights than stars at night, but they were clearly in a dotty state, moonstruck, barely able to detach themselves from each other long enough to acknowledge the presence of anyone else who was there. Conversations with them were interrupted by urgent kissing that continued even during mealtimes. The children watched this with bug-eyed fascination, and Adam, who normally would applaud and encourage such displays, was embarrassed for the servants waiting at table, and tried to distract Charlie with questions about his new job on the Galana river.

This was a conservation initiative well suited to Charlie's experience with National Parks, a perfect job for him. His new wife, another Jane, was in that state of mind where all she wanted was to be wherever he was, and, filled with enthusiasm, invited us to go and visit them at the Galana Project headquarters. They were living in a makeshift house on the north bank of the river where there was no bridge connecting their camp to the south bank road, so the only way to get across was by boat. The boat, Charlie explained, was an inflatable that had recently been washed away on a strong current, so they now had to wade or swim. 'It sorts out who our real friends are, if the only way they can come and see us is by swimming across the Galana,' he said. ' You should try it. No one has drowned yet.'

Adam was all for including a visit on our next trip to the coast as there was a good road heading west from Malindi following the course of the river on its south side. If we took this road, after a couple of hours we would come within sight of Charlie's camp on the other side, and could leave the car parked on the bank while we swam across. 'Let's go for a quick holiday to Malindi before the baby comes,' Adam suggested, 'and drive over to see the Moores. It will be interesting to see that project, and see how Jane is coping.'

Cen allowed Adam time off in that New Year of 1969 as he always worked over Christmas. We took a bit of a risk with the baby due so soon, but we needed a break. David and Margaret Kingsford had built a palatial house with numerous guest rooms at Silversands, near Malindi, and were hosting a horde that included Andy Hill and his current girlfriend, whose nickname was Ackers. We met each day at the Driftwood Club and had swimming races in the pool which, despite my handicap, I almost won a couple of times and felt triumphant, teasing Andy that he was only barely able to keep up with a pregnant woman. He and I had a rapport based on joshing and trading insults in an affectionate way like brother and sister. We teased Ackers as well, for her Englishness. Like all unwary Poms on their first visit to the Kenya coast, she embraced the burning sun with plump offerings of white skin that turned flaming red within hours. This required liberal applications of calamine lotion which was a standard rescue in the absence of sun-screen products, that were still waiting to be invented.

'You must cover yourself with a *kanga*, (sarong-style dress worn by coastal women), and stay in the shade,' we told her, sending her off with Andy to buy *kangas* in one of Malindi's dusty shops where these, with bags of spices, bicycle tyres and cooking pots, crowded every inch of hot interior space.

'How do you tie *kangas* so they stay on?' Ackers asked when she and Andy got back to the club, where Andrena, who was also staying at the Kingsford's beach mansion, had joined us. We showed her how to do it, wrapping it round under the armpits. For some reason, curiously in Ackers' case, it didn't stay in place and as she twirled to show it off, the whole thing came undone and fell around her feet to loud jeers from the open-air bar. She hitched it up, ignoring the cat-calls, but however many attempts were made to fix it, the thing still refused to stay up.

'You've got the wrong shaped tits,' Andy suggested helpfully. 'Instead of sticking out, they're hanging down, so the thing slides off.'

'Spaniel's ears!' Adam shouted, prompting more rude laughter and remarks, while Ackers stood with her *kanga* bunched at the front, doing a shimmy to show how little she cared whether her chest was the right shape or not. Andy may have been attracted by her liveliness and lack of inhibition, but he was beginning to find her a handful. They were on a short stop-over at Silversands before continuing on a trip that included a visit to Jane and Charlie at Galana. 'These Pommie girls arrive with a bikini and pair of shorts but no money, thinking they are entitled to free holidays because people like us are enchanted to have them sponging off us,' he complained, and I thought of Pam.

'You're lucky you didn't get latched onto by Pam,' I told him. 'She would have chewed you up as well as fleecing you.'

Our neighbour at Malindi, Dr Rossinger, walked the short distance to visit us each morning before we went out, to check how I was, becoming convinced that the baby was imminent and he should be on hand to do the delivery. He explained, earnestly, that it was a long time since he had done any maternity work and it would be useful for him, as well as a privilege, to conduct the birth should labour commence while we were there. This prospect spooked me so much that I persuaded Adam we should do the Galana trip without delay and then go home. He agreed, not wanting to risk any messy complications at Malindi, so we packed up early, much to Jairo's disappointment, and set off on the visit to Charlie's camp. The only concern at this stage was what sort of state the river would be in, as rain had been intermittent, and both the flow and volume of water were key factors in the safety or otherwise of swimming across.

Arriving at the spot where a clearing had been made to park vehicles on the river bank, we gave a blast on the car's horn to signal our arrival. Charlie and Jane ran out waving and indicating that the river was safe to cross, which was a relief. It was about thirty yards wide at this point, muddy and flowing sluggishly. We suspected there might be crocs but Charlie assured us they hadn't seen any. We put a change of clothes into bags to hold above our heads, locked the car, and waded in – Louise on Adam's shoulders and Simon on mine. I was soon out of my depth and started swimming, with Simon in charge of the clothes bag balanced on top of my head. I was making good progress, hampered only by the weight of my stomach dragging in the current, and could see that I was going to land some way downstream. This amused onlookers who ran along the bank waiting to pull me out. The children thought the whole exercise was a thrilling adventure and were congratulated on keeping the bags dry as they held them clear of the water. Towels were produced, clothes were changed, and drinks handed round while waiting for lunch to appear from a smoke-filled kitchen out at the back.

With a long drive ahead it was a short visit, but worth the diversion for us to see how happy Jane and Charlie were, and still behaving like honeymooners. We were given an escort on the return crossing to help carry the bags and children, for which I was grateful, now feeling slightly weary after the previous swim with so much baggage. Arriving back at the car we stood there dripping as Adam felt in his shorts' pocket for the car keys. Nothing. He searched both pockets and after a great deal of swearing, concluded that the keys must have dropped out while we were swimming across. 'I know the effing keys were in my pocket when we started out,' he stormed 'They shouldn't have bloody well fallen out. Damned keys. Now we'll have to break a window to get in, and wire the ignition.' We didn't have any spare keys. We would have to drive to Mombasa to find a Ford Cortina agent and get new ones.

By the time we got to Mombasa we were all in a state of exhaustion from heat and bumpy roads, as well as the frustration of finding ourselves in this exasperating situation. All I wanted was somewhere to have a wash and cold drink with the children. Adam dropped us off at Mombasa Club where we were grateful to find a cool veranda overlooking the old harbour with its timeless traffic of ocean-going dhows and all sizes of lateen craft. These carried cargoes of people, coconuts, animals, sacks of maize-meal or rice, and anything else that could be crammed on board. Watching this scene and soothed by it I was able to rest and feed the children while Adam trawled Mombasa to find an agent who might have spare keys. This took some time and we were a bedraggled little family returning in darkness to Malindi to spend the night there, say another goodbye to Jairo, and continue next day on the long slog home.

Waiting for us at Glanjoro was an urgent message from Fa. He had to go at short notice to Mufindi in Tanzania where Brooke Bond had estates and needed him to do a locum for the Mufindi doctor for a whole month. Meanwhile Babs was arriving the following week, so it would be helpful if I could meet her at the airport, Fa suggested, and bring her to Glanjoro to stay with us until he returned. Another long drive was not appealing, but there was no alternative and whatever qualms I might still have on Muz's behalf, it seemed the only decent thing to do. I didn't want Babs arriving on her own without a welcome, and braced myself for a whole day spent wedged behind the steering wheel in a hot car, hoping the baby didn't decide to arrive on that day, as well as Babs. I was slightly anxious as the bump had suddenly gone very quiet and was hardly moving at all, unlike Simon who had been trying to kick his way out at this stage. I went to see Bunny for reassurance. He did a bit of tapping, like sounding a drum, and said the baby was fine and floating around in a rather large water bath which accounted for my discomfort and size, but it would not be for much longer and there was every reason this time that all would be well. 'Third time lucky,' he said with a wink.

Babs arrived off an early flight in a fluster of bags and assorted suitcases that had lost their labels, so she was not sure if all of them were hers, but we gathered them up and I put into action my plan to take her straight from the airport to the National Park a few miles away for a picnic breakfast. The wide plains of the park were turning golden as we stopped for thermos tea and bacon sandwiches at Mzima Springs, where vervet monkeys cavorted on branches overhead in the fever trees, and other animals came to drink at the springs. It may not have been an ideal plan to confront her with so many overwhelming impressions after a long flight, but it helped to ease what might otherwise have been an awkward encounter in the absence of Fa, who should have been doing the honours instead of me. He was impatient to know that she had arrived safely, and telegrams flew between them until, after a couple of weeks shielding Adam from Babs' twittering and fluttering, Fa returned from Mufindi and swept her off to Kericho.

Andrena thought it a bold step to move a mistress into his house under the noses of the highly conservative local directors of Brooke Bond.

'What do you think will happen?' I asked her.

'He's so popular, nothing will be said at first unless someone complains, but they need to hurry up and get married before it turns into an issue that can't be ignored,' she said.

Muz was holding out for an agreement to put Forest Lodge into her name so that she had the security of a home that was fully hers, and Fa at last agreed to this, so the divorce could go ahead. As the remains of her legacy from Grandad had helped to buy the house, Fa should have had little claim on it, but he persisted in a proprietorial attitude to marital assets. Babs will never let him get away with that when they are married, I thought: he's met his match there.

Andrena had been hoping by now to have another baby on the way but it hadn't happened so far and there was no explanation for the delay, except that sometimes too much longing and focus on conceiving has the opposite effect. Fa was very sympathetic and suggested plenty of contact with small babies and children, believing that this stimulated a physiological response, having observed it in others experiencing the same predicament.

'People won't let me have their babies to look after, even just to stay the night,' Andrena complained. 'They think it's cruel to give me theirs when I can't have my own.'

There was a new maternity regime in place at Nakuru hospital since midwife nuns had arrived. Each time a woman in labour was admitted, the nun assigned to her stayed until the baby was born, however long it took. When my turn came, my nun arrived on a scooter looking nothing like any nun that I had previously met. Wearing shorts and tennis shoes, she hopped off the scooter and introduced herself as Sister Mary Francis in a business-like way, showing me into a general ward instead of the usual private room. There was one empty bed and I heaved myself onto it as she pulled curtains around the cubicle.

'You say your pains have been coming since four o'clock this morning, and now it's eight o'clock, but you're not very far on,' she said, as if I was not trying hard enough. 'I'm going to let you get on with it for now and see if you speed up. If you go on being slow, I'll have to give you a booster injection to get things going,' she explained, then added, 'This baby needs to be out by lunchtime,' and left as abruptly as she had arrived.

The curtains remained drawn for which I was grateful as breakfast was being served to other patients and I didn't want to put them off by looking tortured with stifled groans. I wished Adam was there, but he didn't want to hang around, thinking that I must be familiar with the procedure by now and there were not predicted to be any problems. Sister Mary Francis looked in to check on progress from time to time, and when I was still labouring away at ten o'clock, she produced a syringe and injected something so powerful it produced instant contortions, shaking my whole body with monumental stomach cramps. She watched appreciatively, 'You're coming on grand now,' she said, and every fifteen minutes gave me another injection, increasing the paroxysms until she was satisfied that the baby was ready to drop. I thought a trolley or wheelchair might appear at this stage to carry me to a delivery room, but Mary Francis said I better walk and do it fast because there wasn't time to call for transport. It was a grotesque walk, clutching the descending bulge with both hands as other patients stared at me curiously, and Mary Francis said, 'Come on now, not far to go.'

The comfortable friendly maternity wing where Louise and Simon had been born, had closed as fewer private patients used the hospital, and deliveries now took place in one of the old operating theatres. I was beginning to feel wobbly and Mary Francis gave me a leg up onto the table. 'Dr Griffiths will be here soon,' she said reassuringly. I could hear Adam's voice outside in the corridor asking if there was any news and I called out to him, hoping he might be allowed in, but Mary Francis went to the door and told him that nothing had happened yet, so he could go home.

'Please tell him to wait,' I pleaded. 'Don't let him go. Tell him the baby is almost here. Please.' But Mary Francis was adamant, 'Husbands are not required at these times. Dr Griffiths will be here any moment.' On cue Bunny appeared, pulling on a gown as he rolled up his sleeves just in time to do the delivery himself and hand me a healthy seven and a half pound boy. As soon as the baby was put into my arms he smiled. It can't be wind, I thought, he looks genuinely happy, unlike most babies with their bewildered crumpled faces. His eyes were wide open and even Mary Francis noticed the smile. 'This one will always be a smiler,' she said.

The next day Adam came with Elizabeth, Louise and Simon, who all sat in a row on a bench in the hospital lobby waiting to take turns holding the baby as he was passed from lap to lap. Elizabeth was beaming, 'Another one for me,' she said, and Simon protested: 'No, he's for me.'

Louise was not so impressed. 'Did God decide about us having a boy?'

'Yes,' said Elizabeth. 'It's *shauri ya mungu* (God's business).'

'We could have asked for a girl,' Louise suggested.

'It's a bit late now.' Adam reached over and tickled her cheek to make her laugh. 'Anyway, we need some boys' names, and you can help with that.'

Meanwhile in the absence of a name he went on being called 'the baby', and Sister Mary Francis was right about his temperament as he continued smiling, demonstrating that not all boys were noisy and turbulent like Simon. This one lay placidly in his cot, and smiled so much at Louise she decided that she quite liked him after all.

The transition from two children to three surprised me with its impact. I had thought one more would not make much difference, but the family unit which had previously felt balanced with one parent per child, now seemed unwieldy and more demanding of time and energy. I wanted to focus on feeding this one myself after failing dismally with the others, and was happy to let Alison fill in for me at the clinic and calf sheds until I was ready to go back.

'It will take you longer this time, now you've got three squeakers to look after,' she said. She always referred to the children as squeakers. 'Anyway, I've got the calves and clinic skivers so well under control you don't really need to come back at all,' she added with such an air of finality, it made me feel as if my world had shifted even further from its normal territory.

'Don't worry, she'll come round by the time you're ready,' Adam said. 'Anyway we all need get back to normal again, being social and having a lark. We've been invited to a party in Nakuru on Saturday. New people. Army. It should be fun. We haven't been out in ages. I think we should go.'

'Who are these new people?' I asked suspiciously, not yet feeling ready for socialising. 'Why are they inviting us if we've never met them?'

'The wife works for Hugh Cran (the vet) as his receptionist at the surgery. She's lovely, blonde and bubbly, very friendly. Every time I go in there, she says we must make a date so she can meet you, since you don't go into the surgery very often. Now they're giving this party she has invited us, and I've accepted.'

'For pity's sake, it's only three weeks since having the baby. I'm not up to coping with parties yet. I would have to feed the baby half way through, sitting in a room all by myself. I might as well stay at home. Why don't you go by yourself? '

'It would look very odd, don't you think? Everyone would be asking if you were all right, as you usually love parties. You weren't put off with the other two. What's the problem this time?'

'It seems to be taking longer to get back to normal. None of my clothes fit with all this blubber. I feel a freak. These new people will be giving more parties. If they're army, they will be doing little else.'

'I've accepted, so we can't get out of it now. Anyway, you look wonderful, darling, you always do. You don't look fat, or out of shape, you're gorgeous. Come here. I'll show you what I think.' He was so disarming, I relented, not wanting to spoil an evening out for him and thinking that I needed to make more of an effort to be a fun wife instead of a dreary one, I roused myself and we went to the party that Saturday.

The army couple were called David and Angela, with two small children, recently arrived from England. David had been posted to Kenya with BATT, the British Army Training Team, and had a smart new Land Rover with an array of high-tech gadgets that impressed Adam almost as much as

Angela herself with her many shining attributes. She had an effervescent personality and David was dashing; the two of them a stylish pair. They were accomplished party hosts, equipped with the latest dance records: Herb Alpert and the Tijuana Brass, James Last, Bert Kampfert – the mood at their party was irresistible, even though I didn't know any of the other people there. Several were British Army couples, the wives very groomed, wearing the latest fashions, which made me feel a complete frump, but as soon as I had a drink in my hand I was anyone's equal.

Adam had a few dances with me before it was time to feed the baby who was safely stowed away in his carry cot in a spare room, while Louise and Simon slept on a mattress in the car. This new little boy was a slow feeder, falling asleep all the time when he needed to concentrate on getting the job done, so that I could go back to the party. When at last after about an hour I was able to join the others, the lights had been dimmed and couples were slow-dancing, draped around each other. I thought I could just about see Adam, or the shape of him, pressed against Angela, shuffling together on the parquet floor.

Suddenly feeling tired and not bothering to get another drink, I found a space to sit down, glad to be anonymous in the semi-darkness. A man detached himself from the clump dancing and came to sit beside me. It was David.

'Have you had something to eat?' he asked kindly.

'Yes, thanks. I took a plate with me when I went to feed the baby.'

'I'm glad you came. I didn't think you would, so soon after having him.'

'It was for Adam's sake really. He's been a bit starved of parties lately and I didn't want to spoil things. It can be frustrating for husbands when a wife is taken up with all the baby fuss. They need an escape.'

'He's certainly making the most of escaping. Look at him. He hasn't danced with anyone except Angela for the past couple of hours.'

'He can be a terrible flirt. I've never wanted him to turn into a tame husband. Don't you think it's a compliment to me if other women are attracted to him?'

'Up to a point. You know of course that Angela is crazy about him, ever since meeting him the first time at the surgery, but don't worry, it doesn't mean anything. She gets mesmerised when someone like Adam comes along, paying that amount of attention to her. Then, when he falls into her Venus fly trap, she loses interest.'

I laughed at the absurdity of it. 'She hasn't done that to you so far,' I pointed out.

'I'm her safety net. I provide the arena,' he said, indicating with a wave of his hand the soft glow of the room with its expensive furnishings and décor.

On the way home I asked Adam what he thought about the evening, surprised that he wasn't chatting away, full of exclamations and comments as usual after a successful party. I thought he might be tired, or trying to concentrate on the road after too many whiskies, but it turned out that he was grumpy at having to leave the party before it was finished. I had insisted on leaving soon after midnight, when at other times I might have indulged his inclination to stay well into the early hours. We were almost always the last couple to leave any social gathering and this embarrassed me, feeling it was discourteous when hosts were waiting to clear up, but Adam was a habitual lingerer. 'They can sweep me out with the crumbs,' he would say as he stayed smoking and telling jokes when everyone else had said goodnight and gone home. Like Aunt Katharine, oblivious to such constraints, he was also late for everything and this was another embarrassment, for me, but not for him. He liked to make an entrance and to be noticed as he arrived, but he could also be very disorganised, leaving everything to the last minute, faffing about instead of getting ready. Aunt Katharine was just too scatty to be on time for anything, but I didn't want to think that Adam could have inherited the same tendency.

The next day when I had been forgiven for making him leave early, he perked up and became eloquent with praise for the evening and its glittery setting, presided over by such capable hosts. 'It's very good for us to meet new people,' he said. 'I've invited Angela to come and see round the farm and have lunch next Sunday. David is away on exercises. She gets lonely and it will be nice for her to have a day out with the children so they can meet ours and enjoy playing together.' It was good to see Adam happy again, and I wanted to make Angela welcome and get to know her better.

She arrived with flowers for me and sweets for the children and was captivating company. It was impossible not to like her. After lunch Adam took her to meet his parents and Cen almost choked on his cigarette in haste to shake her hand and offer her a spin in his plane.

'I'm coming too,' Adam said quickly before Cen had a chance to snaffle such a treasure from under his nose. Off they went – up into the cloudless afternoon sky, skimming the lake and climbing to circuit Menengai's wide crater as the rest of us watched from the veranda at home. Angela's children stood rather in awe and possibly some trepidation as the tiny plane with their mother disappeared over the crater peak, and were visibly relieved when they saw it reappear on its descent coming back to the farm.

We seem to have made some very unexpected new friends, I thought later, so much more sophisticated than we are. They've opened a door into a world we didn't even know existed, and we're opening a door for them into our Kenya world. Adam's right, we need to spread our wings. Next year a new decade will open, and all kinds of new things could happen.

CHAPTER 15

The new baby was a happy little boy who went on smiling all the time and hardly ever cried. Louise was charmed by him and so was Simon, the two of them taking it in turns to hold him without any of the contentiousness that usually arose between them. Fa and Babs were our first visitors, hurrying down from Kericho, Fa in a state of unabashed elation for the combined joys of a sixth grandchild and Babs with him sharing these good times. 'Life is one long honeymoon,' he declared. I didn't doubt it from the look of him, and was glad that any honeymooning activity was taking place at the other end of the house in the guest room, and that Muz was safely oblivious, far away in England.

'You must come and visit as soon as you can,' Babs said warmly. 'We can't wait to show you our house and such a wonderful garden, with lots of new friends for you to meet.' I promised we would, explaining that weekends off for Adam were rare events, but we were just as impatient to see their new home as they were to show it to us, and a trip to Kericho was always a treat. There had been no mention of wedding plans I noticed, and in case it was a sensitive subject, I didn't ask.

Choosing names for the baby was our own sensitive subject; the same arguments taking place as before when choosing names for Simon.

'Angela likes "Ivan", Adam said, 'but it would be vetoed by Mum.'

'We shouldn't be taking any notice of what she thinks,' I said. 'She's had her turn choosing names for her own children. It's our turn now.'

I was still trying to persuade Adam to think more imaginatively about names, without much success, when an unlikely arbiter turned up in the shape of Father Patrick Prunty, who arrived in his battered pick-up, bounding into the house, excited after hearing we had a new baby. 'What's the grand little fella's name then?' was his first question.

'We're not doing very well with names for him,' I admitted, feeling a bit foolish.

'I'll tell you then,' he said, 'you have Simon already, so this one is Peter. Just as it says in the Good Book.'

Adam seized on this enthusiastically. 'That's it then,' he said happily. 'Let's drink to it before anyone has time to object,' looking at me.

Offering Father Prunty a cigarette, which he accepted gratefully, Adam went on, 'Irish coffee to go with our smokes, that's what we need at a moment like this. Thank you, Patrick, for divine intervention on settling the boy's name. It saves us a lot of strife.'

When we told Alison that 'Peter' was finally decided on, she sniffed, and pointed out that we already had one Peter in the family.

'Father Prunty suggested it,' Adam told her, 'to go with Simon.' He knew his mother could not object since Father Prunty had become a good friend of the family, after Elizabeth had converted to Catholicism in support of her husband Peter,

Now that we had a name for the baby, we could register his birth and get a birth certificate. 'Angela wants a lift with us when we go to Nairobi to get the birth registered,' Adam said. 'She has shopping to do. New clothes. Everything in her wardrobe is out of date she says, and with her wages from Hugh she is raring to re-equip from the latest imports.'

'Do I have to come?' I grumbled, hoping to avoid a long hot day in Nairobi, hiding in café corners feeding Peter.

'No, as long as you don't mind me going off with Angela.'

'You could take her to lunch at Muthaiga,' I suggested. 'She'd like that. British Army people all congregate at boring old Nairobi Club, so Muthaiga would be a new experience. She'll make an impression, you can bet. All our friends at Muthaiga will sit up so suddenly they'll crick their necks looking to see who this stunning girl is, that you've brought in.'

'Do you really want me to start a scandal?'

'No one seems to be producing scandals any more,' I complained. The riotous ones are getting too old and running out of steam. No one is galloping horses down city streets at midnight, shooting out the lights with pistols. There's hardly any gossip worth reporting, people are skittery and losing their panache.'

'Not altogether,' Adam brightened, 'you could reverse that. David is a spit for Michael Caine, and charming as hell, you could give him a run and see if that lets Angela off the hook for me.'

'Don't be mad. David is a Pom.'

'Lanner was a Pom. That didn't seem to put you off.'

A few days later Angela came to show me her new clothes and indulge in comic descriptions of the day spent with Adam, brazenly flirting in front of friends they met. 'They will be racing to tell you, hot news straight off the street,' she giggled, 'and then you can pretend to be horrified, or say it's all terribly boring, whichever is more fun. But you could do with a new wardrobe yourself. Why don't you come with me next time? I can show you the best places.'

'I haven't got any money for clothes. We're even more broke than usual since the baby came.'

'Sell something,' Angela said. 'What can you sell? What about jewellery, anything with gold in it, old brooches and that sort of thing.'

'I've only got my engagement and wedding rings, and a pearl necklace that Adam gave me. I'd never sell those.'

'I'll wheedle Adam next time I see him. Persuade him you need new clothes. Especially after having a baby,' Angela said. 'He just needs telling.'

'Best of luck with that. He's more likely to think new tack for the ponies is a more pressing need.'

New clothes were nowhere on my radar just now. What I wore was irrelevant when all I wanted was to get all three children settled into a routine so I could go back to work. Louise was happy at nursery school, but dismayed to find that learning to read and write was a gradual process instead of something that was instantly implanted by the teacher on the first day, as she had imagined. Drawing and painting came more easily and pictures were brought home to show us, with plaintive comments from her on how much better they would be if I would get 'proper' crayons for her, like the ones all the other children had, instead of cheap wax ones that were 'only for babies'. Her pencil box was kept closely guarded from Simon's investigative fingers, and she was as meticulous about its contents as she had been with the objects she organised so precisely during early years in her pram.

The same big beautiful Swan pram that Renny had given us for Simon (after Martin no longer needed it), was now occupied by Peter each day after feeds, parked under the fig tree that grew from a tumble of rocks halfway down the garden. Usually Elizabeth was in charge of Peter and the pram, keeping an eye on it, and him. On her days off, I was the one in charge, easily distracted at times with all the other things demanding attention: visitors arriving; staff disputes; the school run; Simon to be rescued from increasingly perilous explorations that now extended beyond the garden; dogs getting caught in snares and, most bizarrely of all, any snakes needing to be shot. I had acquired a totally irrational reputation for deadly accuracy in this particular art, since being called by the gardener one day to shoot a snake sunning itself on some steps rather too close to the house for comfort. I took an air rifle and approached cautiously. Taking aim from a few yards away, astonishingly my shot went right through its eye. This was a complete fluke as Adam kept reminding me, but the gardener had taken the dead snake, with the hole drilled through its eye, to show everyone at the workers' compound. This resulted in a quite unmerited but legendary fame, so that I was called whenever a snake was spotted, wherever it was. My initial finesse never quite managed to be repeated, but the anticipation among onlookers that it might be, and the sight of the actual rifle that had achieved this celebrated triumph, in some curious way created awe.

A rather less glorious reputational achievement occurred on one of Elizabeth's days off when I was in charge of the children. I had given Peter his afternoon feed as usual and put him in the pram for his nap under the fig tree. All went well and he slept peacefully as the afternoon proceeded with normal activities. Tea was taken on the veranda as always at four o'clock, and then a walk with the dogs before the older children's bath time at half past six. Peter always had his bath in the morning. Children's supper came after their baths and by then it was dark outside as Louise and Simon sat at the table, and Louise asked, 'Where is Peter?' I looked blankly at her, unable to recall where he might be.

'Ring the bell so you can ask Juma,' Louise suggested, and then, 'I'll ring it for you.' She climbed down to press the electric bell, visible as a small lump under the carpet by my feet. I always sat at the same place at table and this discreetly hidden device regularly surprised visitors when Juma appeared as if by magic to clear plates or top up glasses, summoned by the invisible bell.

This time when he came in, Louise asked, 'Do you know where Peter is?'

'*Labda gari* (maybe in the pram),' Juma said.

'Where is the pram?' Louise persisted, and I remembered it must be still under the fig tree where I had put it after lunch, completely forgetting to retrieve it and Peter during all the other comings and goings that had happened since.

'You stay here,' I said sternly to the others, not wanting them running around in the dark outside, causing even more problems. Fetching a torch I went out, feeling mortified and panicked about forgetting Peter. Shining the beam towards the tree I could see the pram was still there, and when I got closer, inside, with his eyes wide open staring at the stars, was Peter, looking quite unperturbed. He smiled when he saw me and I snatched him up in a sweat of guilt, needing to reassure myself that he was all right. When I got back indoors with him, Louise looked up very reprovingly, 'He could have got eaten by the leopard.'

'Well, he didn't, and he's not even making a fuss about what happened.'

'Can we see if there are any leopard tracks around where the pram was?' Simon asked eagerly.

'We can look tomorrow, I said.

Simon came over and put his face close to Peter's. 'Did you see the leopard?' he enquired earnestly. 'You could have seen him prowling around. You need to remember, so you can tell me about it when you can talk.'

Juma, of course, lost no time in telling Elizabeth about the drama, and when she arrived for work the next morning I was roundly scolded by her in Kipsigis, Swahili and English. 'How can I leave my children with you if you don't look after them? My baby outside in the dark, no one hearing him cry.'

'He wasn't crying, he was quite calm, waiting to come back in. And look at him, no harm done, smiling just like always.'

'That is because *Mungu* (God) was looking after him. Not you. I'm cross with you.'

'I'll make you some tea and a sandwich, with jam, to say sorry.' We both laughed then, and hugged each other with relief that nothing bad had happened.

When Angela offered to organise Peter's christening we were glad to hand the arrangements over to her, with suggested budget restraints and limits on the guest list. She ignored these, but did help with expenses, and her party skills turned the event into a much more jolly occasion than would have been achieved by us on our own. Her own parties at the house on Menengai continued each weekend, with Adam providing a star turn, popular with all her friends and often recruited on errands such as ferrying milk, cream, butter and cheese to the house during party preparations. I wondered about him taking so much time off when normally he was extremely reluctant to leave work for any reason at all, and began to sense that he was becoming fixated on Angela, and flattered by her admiration. I also wondered what David thought about it, and asked him one day when we had taken the children to play with theirs.

Angela had decided on a whim that she wanted Adam to drive her to the top of Menengai where Protea plants were flowering at the edge of the crater so he could help her bring some back for the house. When they had left I asked David if he thought there was anything going on between them.

'I did warn you,' he said, 'but it's never serious with Angela. It's just a game, seeing how far she can go before things start to get complicated; then she gets bored.'

'That's all very well, but what she sees as a game is, in reality, playing with other people's marriages, and that's dangerous.'

'It's the danger that is so irresistible to her. Like big game hunting, in her case other women's husbands. Once she has set her sights, she never misses. Adam has allowed himself to be fair game.'

I felt a jolt but didn't want to show it. 'What about you? Don't you mind?'

'What I mind about is the children, making sure someone is looking after them. That's why I'm here, standing at the window with you, keeping half an eye on them while Angela goes off up the mountain with her latest sensation, to pick flowers.'

'Do you think it's more than picking flowers?'

'What do you think?'

I must have looked stricken because he moved to give me a hug and I felt grateful for it. He was wearing an old army shirt that felt rough and smelt musky like warm nutmeg, which somehow was comforting and I wanted to stay like that, pressed against it, shutting out whatever might be going on further up the mountain. I had danced with David lots of times, and been just as close to him, feeling his warmth and nearness, which was never disagreeable. But was David part of the game? Angela traps the husband and then David consoles the wife? This thought broke the spell and I stepped back. 'I don't want to be part of the game,' I said.

Adam and Angela had enough Proteas to fill the house when they got back, though it was hardly necessary to have harvested so many as the house was already filled with flowers, expertly arranged in a variety of vases.

'Anne (the florist) delivers a weekly order and then I do my own arrangements,' Angela had said when I admired them at the party on our first visit. Some days later, meeting Anne while shopping, I remarked on the displays that Angela had done so expertly. Anne made a face. 'I take Angela's order to her house every Friday and do all the arrangements for her. She would never have time to do them herself, and of course she's not at home anyway as she's working at the vet's.' Anne looked at me quizzically, 'How well do you know her? The question hung in the air while I hesitated, not sure what to say, sensing that something was implied by the inflection in her voice. Something that I was failing to take in.

Later, telling Adam about my conversation with Anne, I wanted to see what he thought about such extravagance. 'How can Angela need to have all those bouquets and flowers everywhere?' I asked him, 'costing a fortune, especially the roses.'

'She's a working wife, with her own money,' he said, rather pointedly I thought.

'I used to be a working wife, and I need to be a working wife again, even if it's unpaid. Please tell Mum I'm ready to come back, and clear it with her. '

'I'll see what I can do,' he said, smiling, and with a kiss, added: 'This is going to be a phenomenal year for us. The farm is doing extraordinarily well, with good rains for a change. All we need is the Christmases to do a deal on Ronda and then we'll have even more to celebrate.'

The year was 1969, and on 20th July there was an event genuinely so phenomenal it shook the world, when the American Apollo space craft landed on the moon and this was broadcast, live, from the NASA space station. I sat with my ear pressed to the radio, listening to the countdown, hardly able to believe this could really be happening, as people around the world listened at the same time to the astonishing beeps and commentary. When the first astronaut emerged and spoke the few simple words that so encapsulated the spirit of that momentous event, there was almost a feeling of spirituality about the whole experience, something other-worldly, beyond normal comprehension.

Waiting until the moon was shining that evening, I went to the farm workers' compound to share my exhilaration with them, and discuss the news. People gathered round, and I pointed to the moon: 'This is a very important day for the world, and I want to look at the moon with you, for all of us to see where two very brave American men are walking around up there tonight. The first people ever to get there, with a radio so they could tell us about it. I heard their voices on the radio today as they stepped out of the space craft and walked on the moon.' There was silence as everyone looked at me pityingly. 'No, Mama, that is not possible. God would never allow it.' No one believed me, and that might not have been too surprising as I could barely believe it myself.

Louise and Simon were much easier to convince as we gazed upwards, and were full of questions: 'What happens when the space men walk on the upside-down part; will they fall off? And how can they eat with those bowls on their heads?'

I was impatient to get back to work on the farm now the urge had taken hold. Angela was full of advice on how to win round Alison, and full of attentions paid to Adam as she flitted between Nakuru and the farm so frequently that I wondered how she ever got any work done at Hugh's surgery. And how Adam was managing so many absences from the farm during working hours, not even coming home for lunch sometimes. We had friends coming for lunch on a day I asked him to make sure he didn't forget and would not be late. He said Angela was delivering some inoculation doses from the vet's during her lunch hour so she could come too.

After lunch, when I went to feed Peter in the bedroom, Angela came to keep me company, which I appreciated because it was boring sitting alone on the bed while others had interesting conversations next door. She chatted for a while in her usual animated way, and then shifted her position to lean closer as if to tell me something especially confiding. 'I can't keep this to myself any longer. I have to tell you though you must have guessed. I didn't know how you would take it, but anyway it has to come out. I have fallen completely madly in love with your husband, and he feels the same, we're off our heads with it. You must have noticed?' She stopped, waiting for me to say something, but I couldn't speak, and she went on, 'I thought you must have guessed.'

I hadn't guessed. I hadn't wanted to guess. What was I supposed to say? I felt dazed and held Peter even closer as if that somehow protected each of us from whatever it was she was trying to do. After a few moments of blank silence, she slipped off the bed and left the room, followed by the sound of a car driving off. I put Peter in his cot and went to rescue the guests, hoping that I didn't look as shaken as I felt.

Adam stood up and said, 'Angela had to shoot off, and I must too,' leaving me to look after the lunch guests and remember to collect Louise from nursery school.

My car was in the workshop having an oil change and Alison had let me borrow hers. This was a clapped out Deux Chevaux, a cheap and cheerful French car that had become weirdly popular despite possessing no observable technical or design merits of any kind. I was late for picking up Louise and bundled Simon into the back with Alison's dogs who all leapt in, thinking that I was taking them somewhere for a run.

The car had a complicated gearstick which habitually got stuck when needing to change up or down, but this time thankfully we started off smoothly enough before cruising along in top gear on the long straight run into town. When I needed to slow down for the first roundabout, the stick malfunctioned and nothing happened, so I stamped on the brake and we hurtled around the circle much too fast. The car tilted violently and the flimsy lift-up door at the back flew open with the weight of the dogs sliding against it, jumbled up with Simon. There was a thump as they all rolled out onto the road together, but I couldn't look back while struggling with the controls. At that moment, luckily, the car stalled, so I was able to jump out and retrieve them all before other traffic came along. None of them, remarkably, seemed any the worse for being pitched onto the hard tarmac, and there was not even a whimper from Simon as he scrambled up from the road, calling to the dogs. He probably thought, by now, that accidents were a way of adding variety to life. The idiotic door would not close again, so we continued the journey with it flapping overhead like a demented sail. Louise was very disgruntled to find dogs occupying the seats while the open back area sucked in clouds of choking dust as we rattled home. I was not as fussed by all this as I might have been, since Angela's words continued running through my brain like a hot wire.

Alison was not best pleased to have her little car retuned with the back door stuck skywards, and a graphic description by Simon of how he and the dogs got thrown out at the roundabout. 'We were all rolling over and over in the road,' Simon told her gleefully. 'We could have got run over, and the dogs tried to run away, but Mummy caught them.'

'Thank God for that,' Alison remarked with a sniff. 'So tiresome and tedious, dust getting into the gears so they keep sticking, and that ruddy door forever springing up since it twisted itself somehow and doesn't fit properly any more. She had failed to notice signs of damage after backing into something solid that had also escaped her notice when she was reversing.

All I wanted now was to get home and get through the rest of the day, so that I could clear things with Adam later when the children were in bed and hear what he had to say about Angela's declaration. Waiting until after dinner when the servants had left and we were alone with our coffee,

I told him what she had said and demanded to know what was going on. 'Angela made it pretty clear there's more to it than just being good friends.'

'Well, she's a liar if she's pretending anything else,' he said. 'You know what she's like, and you know me. I don't need anyone else, I've got you, and you're enough of a handful to look after, keeping me out of mischief. Angela's good for a laugh, a good-time girl, someone to have fun with. She's a ball of fire, that's for sure, but not the kind of fire I need to play with.'

'If you really mean that, you'll have to prove it. How are you going to disentangle yourself? You can't keep running around with her, giving the impression you're up for it. There's David to consider as well, and the children, while you're sweeping her off her feet.'

'I think David's given up trying to nail her feet to the ground. He told me there are times when he's come back from exercises and found the children at a neighbour's house because there was no food at home, and no sign of Angela. She is wilful, and has enough money to do what she likes. She complains Nakuru is too tame, too mediocre. She hankers for the Nairobi fast lane, the smart set, much more in her line.'

'We could introduce her to some of those characters.'

'Good idea. Once she's on that circuit she'll lock on to all the dilettantes like a magnet.'

'Poor Renny. She's been swallowed up by city life and we've lost her. I can't reach her anymore. Losing her friendship was like a bereavement, I missed her dreadfully, and Tony had become maudlin and distracted, in despair that he was losing her too. What's happening to us, I wondered; it's like a virus infecting some of the least likely people, and now Adam is caught up in it too, captivated by Angela.

Nettie and Martin often came to stay with us when Renny was away and Tony on safari. They were the easiest children to look after, sweet-natured, polite and quiet. Too quiet maybe, I thought, and this worried me, but they were soon to start school as boarders at Greensteds School near Gilgil and this was a kind, happy school. They were staying with us when term started and I took them with their two small suitcases on the first day, unpacking their clothes and possessions into lockers in each dormitory and taking them to find other children they already knew. It was heart breaking leaving them there but I reminded myself that they were among friends so that was consoling, and next time I saw them they were smiling and settled so the school evidently provided a haven for them. Louise needed to start primary school later that year and a group of Nakuru parents were organising a school run to Greensteds, so their children didn't have to board. This was an obvious solution for Louise, but Greensteds was a private school and the fees were beyond what we could afford, unless the farm helped out.

'I'll talk to the parents,' Adam said. 'Lots of farms help with school fees. It's an accepted perk on family farms. They can't reasonably refuse.'

But they did. 'Why can't Louise go to Lugard (a government school) where the fees are much less?' Alison suggested. 'The farm can't be expected to pay these kind of expenses, otherwise where would it end?'

'Lugard has gone so far downhill, we're not happy about sending Louise there,' Adam told her.

'There must be alternatives. And while we are on the subject of family matters, now that Wendy has three children to look after, she needs to be at home with them. We don't want her coming back to do the calves and the clinic. I've got those under control now. Please explain that to her.'

When Adam reported what had been said, I felt both furious and fearful, as if all the certainties that I had been able to rely on, were being pulled from under my feet. Too many changes were happening all at once. I had lost Renny; Joe and Liz had gone back to England; Charles and Rosie Harris had moved to the other side of Nairobi; Don and Mary Rooken Smith were leaving for Rhodesia; and other friends were going to Australia or New Zealand. Even the Hemsteds had succumbed and were considering surprising options: 'It's either South Africa, Switzerland or the Isle of Wight,' Joan declared.

'Sounds a bit random,' I remarked, 'I can't imagine you fitting into life on the Isle of Wight. Whatever would you do there?'

Each of those places, Joan explained, had connections with dogs that they had imported, so it was a kind of homing instinct. Everyone needed a thread of connection to attract them to a new place, some more tenuous than others.

'Let me get this straight,' I said, turning back to Adam. 'The farm won't help with Louise's education. That's been decided. I am banned, yet again, from working on the farm. That's been decided. What options do we have now?

'I'll have another go talking to the parents. They usually come round in the end.'

I felt entirely unconvinced by this, and riled enough by recent events to take a stand.

'We have to start making up our own minds at this stage, doing what's best for us as a family in our own right, not simply an appendage of your parents. And what about Angela? What are you going to do about her?'

'We can't drop out of her birthday bash on Saturday, just like that, we'll have to go, otherwise there'll be a hell of a stink. After the party, I promise, that will be the end of it.'

'The end of the affair?' I added sarcastically.

'It isn't an affair. You could call it slightly more than a flirtation,' he said.

'Isn't that the same thing?'

'Not in this case,' he added firmly, closing the subject.

The birthday party was lavish enough to have been set in the Hollywood Hills, with a DJ hired for the dance floor and fairy lights in the garden overlooking a wide panorama with the flamingo lake luminous in moonlight below. Waiters hired for the occasion, dressed in white, circulated with trays of champagne while a buffet occupied the whole of one room and flowers filled every other space. As soon as we arrived, Angela commandeered Adam, steering him among guests from the Gilgil garrison whom she wanted him to meet, giving every impression that he was her escort for the evening. I watched the two of them drift away, Angela drawing admiring glances for her new ball gown, floor-length and figure-hugging in silvery satin, while most of the women were wearing similar finery. I had one good party dress and was wearing it, too tight, but not unflattering, in midnight blue taffeta. It was second-hand from a friend and I had altered the high neckline, scooping it out carelessly, so it ended up looking, as Adam observed, rather more vulgar than elegant. But David said the dress was stunning and he wanted a dance before anyone else got their hands on me.

I was glad to be rescued and, after Angela's announcement, thought: Why not seize the moment and break some rules for a change. It was easy to feel drawn to David and become entwined as the dancing went on and we fell into a rhythm of our own, interrupted only by the occasional duties expected of a host when he had to go and attend to something else. In between these interruptions and circuits of the dance floor, we sat and talked as he told me about his life before the army and school at Wellington. He was barely out of Sandhurst when he met Angela and they married impulsively after an intense courtship of only two weeks. 'I got carried away,' David laughed, 'rather literally you might say. Another victim of her undeniable charms.'

I told him about her confession and how it had startled me. He fell silent for a while, but didn't seem surprised. 'Don't take it too seriously,' he said, and told me more about her, what lay behind the flightiness. 'Her mother is a rackety sort of person, completely unreliable, flitting around, a bit of a parvenu and butterfly. After Angela and I got married she went to visit my parents who are quite ordinary unsuspecting people, and incredibly she set her sights on my dad. She seduced him and took him off to her lair on one of the Greek islands, leaving my mother devastated, and destitute as well since she relied on Dad's pension for support.

'Where are they now?'

'The lovers? Still holed up in a love nest somewhere.'

'What about your mother?'

'On her own, grieving.'

'Angela has never said anything about it to me.'

'She's embarrassed by her mother, and it's sent her a bit off the rails, as you can see.'

'Yes, but it should not be a licence to destabilise other people's lives. Sooner or later there will be a reckoning if she carries on like this, and you could be one of the casualties next time.'

'When that happens I might need to call on you for nursing and other comforts,' he said, laughing, and turning to hold my face between his hands he gave me a quick kiss of such warmth that I began to wonder about my own grip on fidelity.

Later, on the way home, Adam was impatient to tell me about a conversation he'd had with someone at the party, eager to pass on information about bright prospects for young families in Rhodesia. Despite UDI (Unilateral Declaration of Independence) from Britain, or perhaps because of it, he was told that the country was prosperous and stable with full employment among all races and excellent, inexpensive schools and healthcare. 'I think we should go and look at it,' he said. 'It would solve the education problem; take you away from the miseries of Glanjoro since Mum is back on the warpath; give us something to build on for the future in a new country and, best of all,' he added, turning in his seat to give me a dig, 'stop you getting involved with David.'

'Don't start on me. You're the one needing to get out of a hole.'

'We're both in a hole. We both need to get out.'

This new idea was a surprising outcome from the evening, and even more surprising was how quickly Adam moved on a plan to go and explore prospects in Rhodesia. Flights to Salisbury were booked, and Louise and Simon were packed off to stay with Alison who had taken the news of our sudden departure with one of her droopy sighs: 'I suppose it's for the best,' she said. 'Johnny can move into your house. He'll need more room if he ever decides to get married.'

Finding somewhere to park Peter was more difficult. Alison didn't like babies and Cen was emphatic on the subject. 'Until children start learning civilised behaviour they should be kept out of sight as well as sound.'

There was one person I thought might help out: Andrena. Friends entirely disapproved of the idea, saying it was tactless. But Andrena was never one to refuse a challenge and said she would be glad to help. Fa very much encouraged the plan, being convinced that conception could be assisted by fostering or adopting a baby. He was not alone in this view: women of the Masai tribe also claimed that handing a baby to a childless woman meant she would soon have one of her own. So a visit to Kericho was organised to put the plan into action, at the same time spending a weekend with Fa and Babs as had been promised ever since Babs arrived.

They had by this time married secretly in a civil ceremony conducted by a magistrate in Kericho, with Andrena and Jon as witnesses. The occasion was described afterwards by Andrena as having turned farcical when Elaine arrived unexpectedly in the middle of the small reception they were having with friends at their house. We had all been careful to shield her from the impropriety of Fa and Babs living in sin together, and it was the weirdest of coincidences that she happened to turn up abruptly on their wedding day. No one seemed to know how she had got there, and her sudden appearance caused such consternation (as described by Andrena), that elements of celebration were hastily suspended, champagne corks arrested in mid-opening and pretences made that just a few friends had dropped in while Babs was visiting. Elaine appeared not to notice any signs of disarray and everyone played their part deadpan, keeping up appearances.

Fa himself was in such a state of euphoria that nothing was going to impinge on his joy at being married, at last, to Babs. There she was with him sharing the splendour of Kericho's lush lifestyle. He had found his Shangri La at last, after all these years of searching, and Babs was absorbed into the tea-planting community with enthusiasm. The change in him was extraordinary. One of its manifestations was a sudden ending of the migraines that had plagued him all his life. These could be seriously debilitating and I had often seen him come back from an operating day at the hospital, his face white and gaunt after hours spent under the intense brilliance of theatre lights. He never allowed himself any relief until he had finished his list, and then would go home to lie down in a darkened room until the migraine passed. Now, with Babs by his side, the migraines had mysteriously ceased.

The only snag to this harmonious situation was Babs' attachment to her elderly parents who relied on her, their only child, to rescue them whenever crisis loomed, which was often. Fa had no objection to these trips back to England and told me with some satisfaction that Babs had her own money for fares, so did not require any help from him, a factor that appealed greatly to his stingy instincts. She hasn't managed to convert him from Scrooge to Santa yet, I observed.

So engrossed was Fa with his new life that the news of our imminent departure for Rhodesia, to look at possibilities for moving there, barely entered his consciousness. I was relieved about this after worrying that he might feel we were deserting him and Babs, but he gave us his blessing and said he would look forward to visiting us in Rhodesia, a country he had not yet explored and would be glad to have that opportunity.

Several friends had already moved there, blazing a trail for others to follow, and we had a number of good contacts, including Mike and Anne Rowbotham (christened the Paddlebums by Tony), who had bought a small farm near Salisbury and had nothing but praise for the country and its government under Prime Minister Ian Smith. Basing ourselves at a central point with friends who could advise and show us around seemed a good idea, and the Paddlebums were welcoming, and full of useful information for us.

Sanctions had been imposed by Britain in retaliation for UDI and these had resulted in a spectacular national effort, with corresponding rapid increase in GNP instead of the intended negative effect that was supposed to bring Rhodesia to its knees. Alongside this growing prosperity, the country offered a quality of life enhanced by an environment of surpassing beauty and diversity. The rich colours, shapes and textures of bold landscapes under wide skies were glorious to the eye and heart.

Mike advised Adam to switch from dairy farming to tobacco, which was a principle export crop. Young men who went to work as tobacco assistants on established farms could make enough money from their annual bonuses to set up on their own within a few years. This sounded very appealing and I was certain that Adam would accept one of several offers from tobacco farmers that were made to him there and then, but he was firm on wanting to stick to dairy. 'That's what I know, and what I like,' he said.

I argued with him. 'Dairy managers are so badly paid, whether it's Kenya, Rhodesia or wherever. We need to break out of that bracket and start moving up in the farming world.' But he was insistent that tobacco-growing was a new process he would have to learn, and he didn't want to change horses at this stage of his life. He was thirty three.

A dairy manager's job was advertised at Gwelo, a large farming area some distance south of Salisbury, and after speaking to the owner of the farm on the phone, Adam was offered the job, which he accepted on the spot.

We flew back to Kenya with a letter of appointment to start as soon as we could pack up and move to Rhodesia, not having seen either the farm or Gwelo, but excited to have made the decision and to be starting a new life.

When we went to retrieve Peter from Andrena and Jon, they were more than glad to return him to us, as none of them had slept a full night during the entire time we had been away and they were all in a state of nervous exhaustion. Andrena concluded that Peter, suddenly finding his parents and devoted ayah had vanished, was too anxious and fretful to sleep. Fa had been consulted and prescribed a sedative that provided some relief, but the whole experience was so fraught that Andrena said it had put them right off having children. Now they could get back to normal and enjoy being just themselves again, they were going on holiday to recover and catch up on sleep. By the end of this holiday, when they got back, Andrena was pregnant, which gave Fa much satisfaction since he had predicted the encounter with Peter would produce this outcome. We were on the cusp of a new decade as Andrena's baby would be born in July the following year, 1970, and this return of good fortune confirmed my belief that each new decade opens a door to new and auspicious prospects. I was on my way to Rhodesia as the seventies beckoned, just as I had set out for a new life in Kenya at the start of the sixties.

Printed in June 2021
by Rotomail Italia S.p.A., Vignate (MI) - Italy